D0759694

Technology, Television, and Competition

In the late 1980s and 1990s, the advanced industrial countries considered replacing the existing analog television infrastructure with a new digital one. A key common feature to the debates over digital TV (DTV) in the United States, Western Europe, and Japan was the eventual victory of the ideas of digitalism (the superiority of everything digital over everything analog) and of digital convergence (the merging of computing, telecommunications, and broadcasting infrastructures made possible by digitalization) in public debates over standards. Jeffrey Hart's book shows how nationalism and regionalism combined with digitalism to produce three different and incompatible DTV standards in the three regions, an outcome which has led to missed opportunities in developing the new technologies. Hart's book contributes to our understanding of relations between business and government, and of competition between the world's great economic powers.

JEFFREY HART is Professor of Political Science at Indiana University, Bloomington. His publications include *The New International Economic Order* (1983), *Rival Capitalists* (1992), *Globalization and Governance* (1999), *Managing New Industry Creation* (2001), and *The Politics of International Economic Relations* (2003).

Technology, Television, and Competition

The Politics of Digital TV

Jeffrey A. Hart

CAMBRIDGE
UNIVERSITY PRESS

PUBLISHED BY THE PRESS SYNDICATE OF THE UNIVERSITY OF CAMBRIDGE
The Pitt Building, Trumpington Street, Cambridge, United Kingdom

CAMBRIDGE UNIVERSITY PRESS
The Edinburgh Building, Cambridge, CB2 2RU, UK
40 West 20th Street, New York, NY 10011-4211, USA
477 Williamstown Road, Port Melbourne, VIC 3207, Australia
Ruiz de Alarcón 13, 28014 Madrid, Spain
Dock House, The Waterfront, Cape Town 8001, South Africa

http://www.cambridge.org

© Jeffrey A. Hart 2004

This book is in copyright. Subject to statutory exception and
to the provisions of relevant collective licensing agreements,
no reproduction of any part may take place without
the written permission of Cambridge University Press.

First published 2004

Printed in the United Kingdom at the University Press, Cambridge

Typeface Plantin 10/12 pt   *System* LaTeX 2$_\varepsilon$ [TB]

A catalogue record for this book is available from the British Library

Library of Congress Cataloguing in Publication data

Hart, Jeffrey A.
Technology, television, and competition : HDTV and digital TV in the United
States, Western Europe, and Japan / by Jeffrey A. Hart.
    p.   cm.
Includes bibliographical references and index.
ISBN 0 521 82624 1
1. High definition television – United States.   2. High definition television –
Government policy – United States.   3. High definition television – Europe.
4. High definition television – Government policy – Europe.   5. High
definition television – Japan.   6. High definition television – Government
policy – Japan.   7. Competition, International.   I. Title
HE8700.74.U6H37   2003
384.55–dc21   2003053194

ISBN 0 521 82624 1 hardback

The publisher has used its best endeavours to ensure that the URLs for external
websites referred to in this book are correct and active at the time of going
to press. However, the publisher has no responsibility for the websites and
can make no guarantee that a site will remain live or that the content is or will
remain appropriate.

To my wife Joan

Contents

Preface

High definition television (HDTV) became a contentious issue in American politics after the European Community rejected a bid in 1986 by the Japanese national broadcasting company, Nippon Hoso Kyokai (NHK), to have its HDTV production method adopted as an international standard. The US government supported the Japanese effort initially, but after the European rejection many people in the United States began to question that support. For some, the Japanese HDTV initiative raised concerns about the relative decline in US competitiveness, even in high technology industries, and the need to respond more effectively to the increased competition from Japan and Western Europe. For others, HDTV was important because it might affect a wide range of industries – broadcasting, film, video, consumer electronics, computers, and telecommunications – and therefore needed to be considered more carefully before buying into the Japanese approach. As a result, the United States began a process to choose a standard for advanced TV that took until April 1997 to reach its conclusion. The US choice of a digital television (DTV) standard forced both Japan and Europe to reexamine their earlier decisions on HDTV. This book is about the forces behind these events.

Acknowledgments

The research for this book was supported by grants and contracts from the Office of Technology Assessment of the US Congress, Motorola, Inc.; the Berkeley Roundtable on the International Economy; the Electronic Industries Association; the National Center for Manufacturing Sciences; the Advanced Research Projects Administration of the Department of Defense; the Technology Transfer Institute; the College of Arts and Sciences of Indiana University; the West European Studies Department of Indiana University; the Alfred Sloan Foundation; and Stanford Resources, Inc.

I would like to thank the following individuals for their help and encouragement: François Bar, Michael Borrus, Joel Brinkley, Joseph Castellano, Alan Cawson, Stephen Cohen, Dale Cripps, Warren Davis, Joseph Donahue, Hernan Galperin, Darcy Gerbarg, Larry Irving, Greg Kasza, Hans Kleinsteuber, Ellis Krauss, Stefanie Lenway, Junji Matsuzaki, David Mentley, Jörg Meyer-Stamer, Ed Miller, Tom Murtha, Russ Neuman, Elie Noam, Greg Noble, Jerry Pearlman, Aseem Prakash, Harmeet Sawhney, William Schreiber, Pete Seel, Gary Shapiro, Marko Slusarczuk, Alvy Ray Smith, Sid Topol, Laura Tyson, Adam Watson-Brown, and John Zysman. Thanks also to the anonymous readers of the manuscript for their suggestions and advice.

Research assistance for this book was provided by the following current and former students at Indiana University: George Candler, Youngmin Jo, Sangbae Kim, Mark Marone, Craig Ortsey, Khalil Osman, Aseem Prakash, and Robert Reed. John Thomas co-authored an earlier version of chapter 6.

Acronyms

ABC	American Broadcasting Corporation
ACATS	Advisory Committee on Advanced Television Services
ACTV	Advanced Compatible Television
AEA	American Electronics Association
ALTV	Association for Low-Power Television
AMST	Association of Maximum Service Telecasters
ANSI	American National Standards Institute
ARD	Arbeitsgemeinschaft der Rundfunkanstalten Deutschlands
ARPA	Advanced Research Projects Agency (see also DARPA)
ATM	asynchronous transfer mode
ATRC	Advanced Television Research Consortium
ATSC	Advanced Television Standards Committee
AT&T	American Telephone and Telegraph
ATTC	Advanced Television Testing Center
ATV	advanced television
BBC	British Broadcasting Corporation
BCG	Boston Consulting Group
BDB	British Digital Broadcasting
BIB	British Interactive Broadcasting
BRITE	Basic Research in Industrial Technologies for Europe
BSB	British Satellite Broadcasting
BSkyB	British Sky Broadcasting
BSS	broadcast satellite services
BTA	Broadcasting Technology Association
CATV	community antenna television
CBS	Columbia Broadcasting System
CCD	charge-coupled device
CCIA	Computer and Communications Industry Association
CCIR	Comité Consultatif International de Radio-Diffusion
CECC	Consumer Electronics Capital Corporation
CEMA	Consumer Electronics Manufacturers Association

CENELEC	European Committee for Electrotechnical Standardization
CEO	chief executive officer
CICATS	Computer Industry Committee on Advanced Television Standards
CIF	common image format
CLT	Compagnie Luxembourgeoise de Télévision
CNCL	Commission Nationale de la Communication et des Libertés
COFDM	coded orthogonal frequency division multiplex
CompTIA	Computer Technology Industry Association
COO	chief operating officer
CRT	cathode ray tube
DARPA	Defense Advanced Research Projects Agency (see also ARPA)
DBS	direct broadcast satellite
DG	Directorate General (European Union)
DIVINE	digital video narrowband emission
DM	deutsche mark
DSS	digital satellite service
DTH	direct to home
DTN	Digital Television Network
DTV	digital television
DTVJ	DirecTV Japan
DVB	Digital Video Broadcasting
DVD	digital versatile disk
EBU	European Broadcasting Union
EDTV	enhanced definition television
EIA	Electronic Industries Association
EIAJ	Electronic Industries Association of Japan
EPG	electronic program guide
ESPRIT	European Strategic Program for Research and Development in Information Technology
ETSI	European Telecommunications Standards Institute
EU	European Union
Eureka	European Research Coordinating Agency
FCC	Federal Communications Commission
FSF	Free Software Foundation
FSS	fixed satellite services
GA	Grand Alliance
GDL	Grand Duchy of Luxembourg
GI	General Instrument

GNU	Gnu's Not Unix
GPL	General Public License
HBO	Home Box Office
HD-MAC	high definition multiplexed analog components
HDTV	high definition television
HTML	hypertext markup language
IBA	Independent Broadcasting Authority (UK)
IDTV	improved definition television
IEEE	Institute of Electrical and Electronics Engineers
INTV	Association of Independent Television Stations
ISDB	integrated services digital broadcasting
ISDN	integrated services digital network
ITC	Independent Television Commission
ITU	International Telegraphic Union
JESSI	Joint European Semiconductor Silicon Initiative
JSAT	Japan Satellite Broadcasting
JSB	Japan Satellite Broadcasting
LPTV	low power television
MAC	multiplexed analog components
MHz	megahertz
MIT	Massachusetts Institute of Technology
MITI	Ministry of International Trade and Industry
MMBG	Multimedia Betriebsgesellschaft
MOU	memorandum of understanding
MPAA	Motion Picture Association of America
MPEG	Motion Picture Experts Group
MPT	Ministry of Posts and Telecommunications
MST	Association of Maximum Service Telecasters
MSTV	Association for Maximum Service Television
MTV	Music Television
MUSE	multiple sub-Nyquist sampling encoding
NAB	National Association of Broadcasters
NACB	National Association of Commercial Broadcasters
NACS	National Advisory Committee on Semiconductors
NBC	National Broadcasting Company
NCSA	National Center for Supercomputing Applications
NCTA	National Cable Television Association
NHK	Nipon Hoso Kyokai (Japan National Broadcasting)
NII	National Information Infrastructure
NPRM	Notice of Proposed Rule Making
NTIA	National Telecommunications and Information Administration

NTL	National Telecommunications Limited
NTN	Nippon Television Network
NTSC	National Television Standards Committee
Oftel	Office of Telecommunications (UK)
OMB	Office of Management and Budget
ORTF	Office de Radiodiffusion Télévision Française
OSI	Open Source Initiative
OSS/FS	open source software / free software
PAL	phased alternation by line
PBS	Public Broadcasting System
PITAC	President's Information Technology Advisory Committee
PTT	postal, telegraphic, and telecommunications agency
QAM	quadrature amplitude modulation
RACE	Research and Development for Advanced Communications Technology in Europe
RAI	Radio Audironi Italiane, later Radiotelevisione Italiane
RCA	Radio Corporation of America
RTL	Radiodiffusion-Télévision Luxembourgeoise
SC	spectrum compatible
SDTV	standard definition television
SECAM	séquential couleur à mémoire
Sematech	Semiconductor Manufacturing Technology
SES	Société Européenne des Satellites
SMATV	satellite master antenna television
SMPTE	Society of Motion Picture and Television Engineers
TCP/IP	Transmission Control Protocol / Interconnection Protocol
TDF	Télédiffusion de France
UHF	ultra high frequency
VCR	videocassette recorder
VHF	very high frequency
VHSIC	very high-speed integrated circuits
VSB	vestigial sideband
WARC	World Administrative Radio Conference
WAZ	Westfälisch Algemeine Zeitung
WWW	World Wide Web

1 Introduction

We live in the midst of a transition to an age of digital technologies. As in previous large technological transitions, many established interests are threatened and many new ones have arisen. The semiconductor, computer, telecommunications, and software industries (the core information technology industries) have become the political voice of these new interests. Just as innovators like Andrew Carnegie came to symbolize the iron and steel industry in the nineteenth century, and Henry Ford the automobile industry in the early twentieth century, industry figures like Steve Jobs of Apple, Andy Grove of Intel, and Bill Gates of Microsoft represented the spirit of the information age. These new icons of innovation lobbied for policies that were sometimes inconsistent with those favored by older industries, such as textiles, steel, chemicals, and motor vehicles.

Joseph Schumpeter called this displacement resulting from technological change of old interests by new ones "creative destruction."[1] Older industries, according to Schumpeter, would organize politically to block the institutional changes that accompanied the introduction of new technologies. If these changes were delayed, then a shift in the distribution of political power could also be delayed. But eventually, competitive pressures would overcome the resistance to institutional change and a new distribution of power would emerge to force the old interests to come to terms with the new.

Something of this sort occurred in the debates over high definition television (HDTV) and digital television (DTV) that began in the early 1980s. The established interests connected with broadcasting, program production, and consumer electronics resisted the changes that advances in digital technologies made possible. However, some within this group of established interests transformed themselves into advocates for change. Representatives of the information technology industries advocated more

---

[1] Joseph Schumpeter, *Capitalism, Socialism and Democracy* (New York: Harper, 1975), pp. 82–5.

1

radical change than those pushing for change in the established industries were willing to embrace. What emerged was a compromise that did
not satisfy anyone and confusion on the part of both consumers and
producers.

The uncertainty associated with technological transitions results in a
search for new ways of conceptualizing problems and formulating solutions. Sometimes this search for new ideas is purely opportunistic: new
ideas are used to justify actions taken for reasons of expediency. Sometimes the search for new ideas is motivated by a genuine puzzlement and
a sincere desire to do the right thing. During periods of transition, different political and social actors may adopt divergent policies with respect
to change that have long-lasting consequences.

In *The Second Industrial Divide*, Charles Sabel and Michael Piore argued
that:

relatively short periods of technological diversification punctuate longer periods
of uniformity. The technical knowledge that is accumulated during interludes
of diversity creates the possibility of divergent breakthroughs: circumstances in
different regional or national economies move technology down correspondingly
different paths.[2]

One of the key questions raised by Sabel and Piore was the extent to which
divergent policies would converge after the dust settled and a "period of
uniformity" was reestablished.

I will be arguing below that one of the more important ideas that influenced the decisions of the major industrialized countries with respect to
HDTV and DTV was the idea of *digital convergence*. Digital convergence
is the blurring of boundaries between previously separate industries made
possible by the transition to digital technologies. My argument about the
impact of the idea of digital convergence will be defended in greater detail
below.

The debates over HDTV and DTV are an important window into
the transition from analog to digital electronic technologies – what some
people call *digitalization*. This book focuses on HDTV and DTV because
of what they might tell us about that broader transition, even though
television broadcasting is an important subject itself.

This book focuses on the debates over television standards that occurred between 1984 and 1997 in the United States, Western Europe,

---

[2] Charles Sabel and Michael Piore, *The Second Industrial Divide* (New York: Basic Books,
1984), p. 39.

and Japan – often referred to as the "triad." The economies of the triad are the largest and strongest of the capitalist world. Because of the overwhelming economic power of the triad countries, it is always helpful to try to understand how their domestic decisions affect their relations with one another and the rest of the world. HDTV was one of many issues that divided rather than united these countries during the 1980s and 1990s, but that does not necessarily mean that it will continue to do so, especially if a consensus on collective interests emerges. Such a consensus cannot emerge, however, unless everyone has an accurate perception of what the others are doing and why. It will become evident by the end of this book that such accurate perceptions were distinctly lacking in the 1980s and 1990s.

The selected period is particularly interesting because it coincides with a time of questioning of the ability of the United States to lead the capitalist world as it had done since the end of World War Two. Concerns about US global competitiveness grew steadily through the 1980s as the "twin deficits" (spending and trade) mounted. Public worries about US competitiveness had a lot to do with the outcome of the 1992 presidential elections. Bill Clinton scored many points against George Bush with the electorate in 1992 by criticizing his administration for ignoring the decline in US international competitiveness. When Clinton took office, he put into place an economic team that would be considerably more aggressive than the Bush Administration in the area of trade and competitiveness.

During the period studied here, the US Congress frequently disagreed with the Executive Branch on what should be done to promote US competitiveness. During the Bush Administration, the Democrat-controlled Congress frequently introduced proposals to promote specific industries in response to perceived weaknesses in the US position. The Bush Administration consistently blocked these initiatives only to see them reinstated later on. In the mid-to-late 1980s, Congress targeted HDTV for special assistance from the Department of Defense (DoD). When a Republican-controlled Congress was elected in 1994, Congress continued to support these programs for HDTV even while opposing initiatives by the Clinton Administration to assist related industries, including the flat panel display industry.

Similar debates occurred within Western Europe and Japan, although there was generally less controversy over the need for governments to help new industries in both regions. Instead, the Europeans and the Japanese responded to the challenges posed to established industries – especially public broadcasters and consumer electronics manufacturers – by the growing importance of digitalization and US policies promoting digital television broadcasting.

The methods used in this book to describe these debates include the usual documentary sources combined with field research with a heavy emphasis on elite interviews. I was fortunate to receive small amounts of funding over a span of about ten years that enabled me to visit and interview key officials and business representatives who participated directly in the HDTV and DTV debates. In addition, I compiled some statistical information about the consumer electronics and related industries (see chapter 3).

The role of TV broadcasting in advanced industrial societies

Television broadcasting is a particularly sensitive area for policy-making in advanced industrial countries. Television is particularly important because it is the only visual medium (with the possible exception of print media) that commands large enough audiences to create and maintain a sense of national community and purpose. The leisure time available to the citizens of advanced industrial countries and their increased reliance on television for entertainment and news makes television particularly important to national policy-makers.

In most wealthy nations, over 95 percent of households own at least one television receiver. In the United States, the average household views over seven hours of television programming per day. Watching television has partially displaced both reading and attendance of cinemas as a leisure-time activity in the United States. Some scholars have argued recently that this shift has undermined important community-building activities that traditionally helped to build "social capital." Instead of engaging in social activities outside the home, people are spending more of their time at home in front of a video screen.

Robert Putnam, in an article entitled "Bowling Alone," makes the following observations:

There is a reason to believe that deep-seated technological trends are radically "privatizing" or "individualizing" our use of leisure time and thus disrupting many opportunities for social-capital formation. The most obvious and probably the most powerful instrument of this revolution is television. Time-budget studies in the 1960s showed that the growth in time spent watching television dwarfed all other changes in the way Americans passed their days and nights. Television has made our communities (or, rather, what we experience as our communities) wider and shallower. In the language of economics, electronic technology enables individual tastes to be satisfied more fully, but at the costs of positive social externalities associated with more primitive forms of entertainment. The same logic applies to the replacement of vaudeville by the movies and now of movies by the VCR.[3]

It should be noted that the introduction of television was but one of the hypothesized causes of the decline in social capital formation in Putnam's argument. Putnam's thesis was by no means universally accepted by students of American politics and society. In a debate on this subject published by *The American Prospect*, several noted social scientists criticized Putnam for overemphasizing the decline in civic participation and giving too much weight to television in changing patterns of behavior in the American public.[4] However, there was little dispute about the changes in the importance of television in leisure-time activities and of increased reliance on television news for information about political candidates and elections.

What is HDTV?

In CCIR Report 801, high definition television (HDTV) was defined as follows:

A high-definition television system is a system designed to allow viewing at about three times picture height such that the transmission system is virtually or nearly transparent to the level of detail that would have been perceived in the original scene by a viewer with average visual acuity.[5]

The dream of an electronic window on the world has been around since the beginning of television. One of the major differences between film and TV is that TV is a real-time medium, producing pictures immediately without photographic processing. This means that any full-motion coverage of immediately unfolding events has to be on video rather than film. Of course, the two media coexist even in the realm of news coverage, as most TV news broadcasts combine filmed and videotaped material with live broadcasts to provide the variety of images that appeal to viewers. The actual performance of current video systems is less than perfectly window-like, as anyone with a big-screen TV knows quite well. The difference in resolution between video and film is quite noticeable,

---

[3] Robert Putnam, "Bowling Alone: America's Declining Social Capital," *Journal of Democracy*, 6 (January 1995), pp. 65–78. Also available at http://muse.jhu.edu/demo/journal_of_democracy.

[4] See Michael Schudson, "What if Civic Life Didn't Die?" *The American Prospect*, 25 (March–April 1996), pp. 17–20; Theda Skocpol, "Unravelling from Above," *ibid.*, pp. 20–5; and Richard M. Valelly, "Couch-Potato Democracy?" *ibid.*, pp. 25–6.

[5] Appendix II of CCIR Report 801.

especially when comparing projected video and film on a theatre-sized screen. So one aspect of the dream of producing an electronic window is to reduce the gap in resolution, contrast, color quality, etc., between film and video.

Current TV systems are more window-like than the earliest TVs. The first TVs were not capable of displaying real-time motion, only a series of static frames. The first cathode ray tubes (CRTs) produced distorted and unrealistic pictures because of the technical difficulty of constructing accurate magnetic yokes for directing the flow of electrons from cathode to screen and of getting flat rectangular surfaces for the imaging end of the tube. It is for this reason that the post-World War Two generation of monochrome TV technology was initially billed as "high definition television" when it was first introduced.

A perfect electronic window on the world is an ideal that is not likely to be realized. Even if the HDTV picture is much sharper than current TV, it will still fall short in some respects. It will be lacking in contrast, color accuracy, depth of field, three-dimensionality, and other qualities enjoyed by reality. It will continue to be of lower quality than the images produced by film because film technology is continually improving. While better images can be obtained by the application of advanced technologies, the cost increases dramatically as one pushes out the technical envelope. A more practical definition of HDTV arose out of series of investigations conducted by a variety of television research laboratories about what viewers were likely to want in a next-generation TV system. These scientific and technical investigations led to negotiations among television programming producers, broadcasters, and other actors to come up with a working definition (more on this below).

HDTV, in practical terms,

is defined as having twice the vertical and twice the horizontal resolution of conventional television, a picture aspect ratio of 16:9, a frame rate of 24 Hertz or higher, and at least two channels of CD-quality sound.[6]

The higher resolution and wider aspect ratio are designed to make the viewing of HDTV more like the viewing of wide-screen cinema images. When the picture is sharper, the viewer can sit closer to it without seeing visual "artifacts." When the aspect ratio is wider and the viewer is closer to the image, there is more viewer involvement in the action portrayed. This is why the modern wide-screen cinema displaced the earlier narrower screen.

[6] Charles Poynton, *A Technical Introduction to Digital Video* (New York: Wiley, 1996), p. 29.

The widening of cinema screens has created something of a problem for the producers of films:

As widescreen films moved "down" through each successive tier of exhibition, the participatory experience of the original theatrical presentation of these works diminished. They played on smaller and smaller screens; they were cropped to fit the much narrower TV screen; and they were edited to meet community standards.[7]

With the increasing viewing of films in VHS format on videocassette recorders (VCRs), many film viewers were seeing movies only on the smaller TV screens despite the fact that they were made to be seen on the wider screens in movie theatres. A famous example of this is a scene in *The Graduate*. The graduate (played by Dustin Hoffman) is speaking with Mrs. Robinson (played by Anne Bancroft), and in the wide-screen version you can see both of them on opposite sides of the screen, but in the VHS version you can see only one of them. There is also a scene in a Fred Astaire movie where the VHS version has Fred jumping from off-screen onto a table, whereas in the wide-screen version he is quite visible prior to the jump.

Reformatting wide-screen films for video formats often involves a technique called "panning and scanning." In this technique, the reformatter moves the window that is available for video viewing according to where the main action is. In order to reduce the expense connected with panning and scanning, contemporary directors often try to keep the main action relatively centered in the film. Doing so, of course, reduces the artistic room for maneuver created by the wide-screen format. Thus directors, film producers, and Hollywood producers especially, have a reason to support wider aspect ratios for television. They will still have to crop the pictures produced for cinemas to reformat them for television viewing, but the process will be simpler, less expensive, and less of a sacrifice in image quality than is currently required.

Viewers tend to perceive an interrelationship between the quality of images and the quality of sound. A TV picture with higher quality sound has been perceived by subjects in laboratory tests to be sharper than a TV picture of equivalent resolution but with lower quality sound. In any case, the addition of CD-quality sound to the specifications for HDTV is driven by the importance of increasing both picture resolution and audio quality to achieve higher levels of viewer satisfaction and involvement, similar to those achieved in wide-screen cinemas.

---

[7] John Belton, *Widescreen Cinema* (Cambridge, MA: Harvard University Press, 1992), p. 211.

The basic intention behind the development of HDTV, at least for mass consumer applications, is to create a viewing experience in the home that is similar to that in a movie theatre. One of the key questions behind the development of HDTV technology, therefore, was how costly and difficult it would be for HDTV to approximate the brightness, resolution, and contrast ratios of contemporary film technology. Since film technology was a moving target, there was always the risk that HDTV would fall short of the mark. The various HDTV systems already deployed and still under development were designed to produce images more like the highly involving images seen in contemporary movie theatres than those on TVs in contemporary living rooms. It remains to be seen whether consumers will be willing to pay the premium required to purchase these new systems.

In a survey of the literature on consumer acceptance of HDTV, Michel Dupagne and Peter Seel concluded that viewers would prefer HDTV to conventional television but that most of them would be unwilling initially to pay the price premium that would be associated with HDTV receivers.[8] Thus, the diffusion of HDTV would depend on the ability of set manufacturers to quickly realize static and dynamic economies of scale. This, in turn, would depend on the ability and willingness of content producers to make HDTV programs and of broadcasters to broadcast them.

The development and deployment of HDTV technologies would involve major shifts all along the well-developed chain of production of video images. Video producers would have to convert their equipment and techniques to the new HDTV formats. Signal deliverers – the network and local over-the-air broadcasters, cable operators, satellite operators, and video rental stores – would have to do the same. Consumers would have to buy new televisions, VCRs, video cameras, etc., to take advantage of the new format. In short, the television production, transmission, and reception systems would have to be transformed to deal with the new TV images. Thus, there were three principal areas of uncertainty in connection with the transition to HDTV:

- Would producers of video materials convert to HDTV formats?
- Would video signal deliverers modify their existing delivery systems to accommodate HDTV signal delivery?
- Would consumers buy HDTV equipment?

Before any of these questions could be answered even approximately, uncertainties about the HDTV system itself, with its requisite underlying

[8] Michel Dupagne and Peter B. Seel, *High-Definition Television: A Global Perspective* (Ames, IA: Iowa State University Press, 1997), ch. 8, pp. 284–9.

technologies, had to be reduced so that producers, broadcasters, and consumers could make the necessary calculations about potential profitability and value. This was where technical standards played a central role. Much of this book deals with the politics of HDTV standards. Understanding the politics of HDTV standards requires a bit of background in related technologies, which will be provided in the remainder of this chapter. But first I would like to develop the theme of digital convergence.

Digital convergence or digital divergence?

It can be argued that HDTV is a technology that is inherently too expensive for most consumers and that therefore it is likely to remain a relatively small "niche" in the market for video images. This may indeed be true – only time will tell. But HDTV is part of a larger process of the digitalization of information and the creation of a new infrastructure for delivering that information. So by studying HDTV we can learn quite a bit about that larger process.

One of the ideas associated with the larger process is *digital convergence*. With the rapid increases in the capacity of computers to process digital information and of telecommunications infrastructures to deliver that information, many new opportunities for realizing synergies in information-related businesses have arisen. This was already occurring to some extent in the creation of multi-media firms, such as AOL Time-Warner, Disney Corporation, Bertelsmann, Rupert Murdoch's News Corporation, and Hachette, where the ability to cross-merchandize films, magazines, books, and other types of intellectual property was the basic incentive behind the mergers of book and magazine publishers with film studios, record producers, broadcasting networks, etc. Because consumers often purchased book versions of movies they had seen, were more likely to buy a record if they saw a music video, and so forth, the competitive advantages of being able to repackage and resell more or less the same content in different formats was evident to the owners of large media firms.

The delivery of that content is still a major expense for media firms. For example, film studios must produce multiple prints of a film for showing in a network of theatres, book publishers must print out multiple copies of books for delivery to bookstores, magazine publishers must print copies of magazines for delivery to newsstands, etc. They spend enormous sums advertising their latest products.

The possibility of supplementing the existing delivery systems with digital ones, either through computers or (possibly in the near future) advanced television systems, is attractive to media firms because it may reduce their production, delivery, and advertising costs and open up new markets. With the very rapid proliferation of personal computers, the rapid growth of the Internet, the (rather slower) conversion of the public telephone networks into high-speed digital telecommunications networks (the so-called Information Superhighway), and the increasing rates of subscription to digitized cable and satellite television systems, the opportunities for accessing mass audiences via digital delivery of text, audio, and video materials are fueling mergers, new investments, and cross-industry partnerships that bridge the electronics and media industries.

One example of this is the partnership between NBC and Microsoft Corporation called MSNBC. NBC agreed to produce television news programming for digital delivery over the Microsoft Network (MSN). NBC is a broadcasting company; Microsoft is a computer software firm; MSNBC broadcasts news and other content in a multimedia format over the cable networks and the Internet.

Similarly, the Cable News Network (CNN) opened an online version of its news coverage on the World Wide Web called CNN Interactive. Within a year, CNN Interactive was receiving millions of "hits" by web cruisers, especially after big stories like the death of Princess Diana, and was able to break even financially by selling advertising on its web pages.[9]

All the major producers of small computers began building and selling machines that were capable of displaying high-resolution video images on the computer display in the mid-1990s. In 1996, Gateway Computers began to offer for sale a personal computer with a large (31-inch) monitor and a keyboard with an infrared interface that could be used either to watch TV or to cruise the Internet from the sofa in your living room.

In April 1997, Microsoft announced the purchase for $425 million of WebTV Networks of Palo Alto, California, a small firm that made set-top boxes for TV sets to permit TV owners to cruise the Web inexpensively. The basic idea was to simplify the interface between consumers and the Web by using a device very similar to a TV remote control. The WebTV box initially cost around $300 but soon dropped to the $150–$200 range.

Microsoft bought 11.5 percent of the shares in Comcast Corporation, a cable television operator, in June 1997. The investments in WebTV and Comcast were part of a larger shift in Microsoft strategy toward a more Web-oriented approach to software. Microsoft's CEO Bill Gates began talking about supporting a "Web lifestyle" with Microsoft products, especially after the phenomenal early success of Netscape Communications,

[9] Based on a presentation by Christine Ciandrini of CNN Interactive at a conference on "Toward a New Curricular Architecture: IPE, Telecommunications, and International Affairs Programs in a Networked Era" in Atlanta, Georgia, 26–27 September 1997.

a startup firm that battled Microsoft for control of the market for Web browsers and servers.[10]

There was a growing perception amongst key actors in the computer industry that home penetration of personal computers lagged behind that of offices because of the unwillingness of a substantial bloc of mostly lower-income consumers to pay more than $1,000 for a computer (or any other electronics device for the home). Since most households already owned a television, one idea was to produce an add-on device for the television that would give consumers computer-like capabilities to cruise the Internet without the expense and hassle of buying and setting up a computer.

After 1997, personal computer manufacturers began to produce PCs with price tags under $1,000 to get consumers who had previously been put off by higher price tags to buy one for their homes. This strategy was initially quite successful, but it caused some worries about the ability of computer chip and PC makers to maintain their traditionally high profit margins through sales of higher-priced models. Luckily for them, however, the demand for more and more powerful desktop PCs for offices and high-income homes remained strong, at least partly because of the increased importance of the Internet and the World Wide Web for business, recreation, and education and the resulting increase in demand for computers with faster processing speeds, faster peripherals (e.g., CD-ROMs), bigger memories, and better displays.

It is not an exaggeration to say that billions of dollars have already been invested in multimedia computing and digital convergence technologies, and there is more to come. The problem for this book is to identify the place of HDTV in this broader movement. We shall see in the chapters that follow that the major actors have readjusted their HDTV strategies a number of times to better position themselves to take advantage of digital convergence. Some actors, however, have been reluctant to do so, and why this is so raises a number of questions about the likely rapidity and depth of digital convergence.

High technology competition

Another reason for studying HDTV carefully is to learn more about the nature of competition in high technology industries, especially among the more industrialized countries of the world. With the end of the Cold

---

[10] Elizabeth Corcoran, "A Bit of Bill in Every Box: Gates's Vision of Microsoft's Future Moves from PCs to TV, Phones," *Washington Post*, 10 August 1997, p. H1.

War, the perceived importance of economic competition among the more industrialized countries has grown considerably.

An example of this would be the US debate over ratification of the North American Free Trade Agreement (NAFTA). Many supported NAFTA because they regarded it as necessary for maintaining US competitiveness in the face of growing competition from Japan, Europe, and the newly industrializing countries. Others opposed it because they believed that the United States might lose its competitive advantages in the region by removing barriers to trade with Canada and Mexico. Competitiveness was clearly on the minds of both supporters and opponents.

The Clinton Administration made increasing US competitiveness in high technology industries a major goal. They encouraged the development of new technologies for digital convergence by adding new programs to the existing ones. Very high on the list of priorities for this administration was promoting the building of a National Information Infrastructure (NII). The NII – at least in theory – would permit the delivery of all forms of digital information, including digital video, via the national infrastructure to homes, schools, offices, and factories. The federal funding for the NII remained quite modest, but there were a number of preexisting programs and new programs that were already aimed at enhancing technological development in this area.

The most important programs in HDTV were those administered by the Department of Defense through its Advanced Research Projects Agency (ARPA). ARPA funds research on advanced displays and advanced integrated circuits that may be used in HDTV equipment. It began doing this explicitly in 1988, but some DoD funding in this area has been going on for a lot longer. ARPA spent between 60 and 100 million dollars per year since 1989 on high definition systems. In 1993, the DoD announced its National Flat Panel Display Initiative, assembling approximately $550 million dollars in funding over five years for the purpose of promoting the development of the sort of high-resolution but less bulky displays that might lower the cost and improve the consumer appeal of HDTVs.

The factor that best explained this governmental effort was the American fear that the Japanese electronics industry was ahead of that of the US and that being behind Japan could hurt the US in both an economic and military/strategic sense. If digital convergence was really happening, then the inability to supply the computer and consumer products that permitted the viewing of high-resolution video, because of a lack of timely access to the latest technologies, would eventually hurt the US electronics industry. At least, this was the fear. In addition, weapons systems of various types were likely to use high-definition video technologies as soon as they were available. The question that US defense planners asked themselves was whether the US military would be able to integrate high-definition technologies into their weapons systems if there were no local suppliers of these technologies.

Previous work on international competitiveness in the steel, automobile, and semiconductor industries led me to take on the topic of advanced television (ATV) for the current work.[11] In *Rival Capitalists*, I focused on the United States, Japan, and Western Europe after World War Two. These countries are also the main focus here, with the main difference being the period of time under investigation. Whereas *Rival Capitalists* began with the end of World War Two and ended with the competitive situation of the late 1980s, this book begins with the late 1980s and ends in the late 1990s. Thus, there was a chance to see whether the countries investigated in *Rival Capitalists* learned any lessons from their earlier experiences, and, if so, how.

Changes in competitiveness were linked in *Rival Capitalists* to the way in which each country organized its government and the linkages between the government and large social groups – particularly business and labor. State–societal arrangements were linked to changes in competitiveness indirectly through their impact on the speed of innovation in new technologies. Whereas in steel, automobiles, and semiconductors Japan had emerged as a country that had increased its competitiveness in all three industries because its state–societal arrangements favored rapid technological change, in HDTV Japan was stymied in its attempt to dominate future HDTV markets by its choice of technologies. The United States, in contrast, which had done rather badly in remaining competitive in steel and automobile production, and only narrowly averted a similar fate in semiconductors, led the world in pushing for DTV. So, one of the major tasks of this book is to reexamine the premises of the argument made in *Rival Capitalists* in light of the ATV case.

Theories of regulation

Yet another reason for studying the ATV case is to use it to test prevailing theories of regulation. According to Robert Britt Horowitz, regulation is "a form of activity whereby a governmental authority formulates rules to mold private, usually economic conduct."[12] Digital convergence posed a number of difficult questions for inherited forms of regulation in the

---

[11] Jeffrey Hart, *Rival Capitalists: International Competitiveness in the United States, Japan, and Western Europe* (Ithaca, NY: Cornell University Press, 1992).

[12] Robert Britt Horowitz, *The Irony of Regulatory Reform: The Deregulation of American Telecommunications* (New York: Oxford University Press, 1989), p. 46.

industries associated with television broadcasting. Separate and distinctive regulatory regimes had evolved for content production, broadcasting, telecommunications, and computing in different countries. With digital convergence blurring boundaries among these industries, it was clear that these separate regulatory systems would have to be rethought.

Government agencies with regulatory authority emerged in the nineteenth century to deal with some of the consequences of the industrial revolution and the rise of industrial capitalism. Policies of these agencies were governed both by legislation and executive decree and by a body of internally generated rules that came to be called "administrative law."

Even prior to the nineteenth century, certain individuals and corporate entities were granted the right to pursue certain economic activities by the state in exchange for accepting certain obligations. For example, in eighteenth-century Britain, an individual was granted a monopoly in the region of Bath to provide postal services in exchange for contributions to the state treasury. In the same century, the French monarchy granted monopoly rights to salt production and to fine porcelain manufacturing in exchange for political favors. In a more economically benign set of arrangements, governments granted local monopolies to millers or bankers in exchange for guarantees of fair and equitable prices to users.

From the beginning of radio broadcasting in the early twentieth century, the granting of the right to be a broadcaster was associated almost universally with a set of responsibilities with respect to the government and civil society that went beyond those assumed by most other economic service providers. Frequently the broadcasters (even if initially private) became agencies of the state, using the model of regulation inherited from the postal and telegraphic monopolies. When they were parastatal or private entities, they were often closely regulated by a state agency with the specific responsibility to regulate broadcasting in the public interest. The definition of the public interest sometimes included the right of the public to hear many points of view with respect to political matters, even though this was far from a universal norm in early broadcasting regulation.

It became a matter of political controversy in the nineteenth century in most industrialized countries as to whether it was necessary for certain economic activities to be dominated by monopolistic producers, or indeed whether such government intervention in the economy was ever desirable. The liberal thinkers of the Scottish school of political economy were particularly influential and strong advocates of minimal government intervention and the social value of competition in unregulated markets.

In the late nineteenth and twentieth centuries, there arose a number of normative theories of regulation that provided answers to the question of when it was desirable to regulate an industry, and, if so, how to do it optimally. Much of this body of theorizing was strongly dependent on rational-choice theories of markets in economics, and much of it focused on market imperfections such as public or collective goods, externalities, and monopolies or oligopolies.

The political mobilization of interests in favor of regulatory reform and the rise of credible normative theories of regulation combined to form the basis of contemporary regulatory systems. Most modern regulation has to address the question of market structure – whether a particular market is competitive or monopolistic, or somewhere in between, and why that is the case – before it addresses the question of the desirable form of regulation. Antitrust and competition laws emerged to provide a basis for the regulation of market structure in most industrial countries in the twentieth century. Those laws depended strongly on normative economic theories that demonstrated the potentially bad consequences of monopolist and oligopolistic practices.

In the United States, a special form of capture theory emerged: the idea of an "iron triangle" of allies from the private sector, Congress, and the bureaucracy as protectors of a set of political compromises that benefited members of the alliance to the possible detriment of nonmembers.[13] Because of the general dispersion of decision-making power in the US government, it was possible for "special interests" to take appeals for specific policies to particular bureaucrats or particular committees or subcommittees of Congress where they could expect to receive the most favorable hearing. Over time, these triangular relationships would solidify into defensive fortresses that would defeat almost all attempts at policy change (unless acceptable to the coalition partners).

Thus it was that the general norm of maintaining competitive markets in all but a few exceptional cases became widespread in the industrialized capitalist world. However, empirical analysis of regulation by social scientists led one group of scholars to question the effectiveness of many forms of regulation, including antitrust laws, and to posit a "capture theory" of regulation in which regulated actors come to initiate and

---

[13] See, for example, Ernest Griffith, *Congress: Its Contemporary Role* (New York: New York University Press, 1961); Douglas Cater, *Power in Washington* (New York: Random House, 1964); Theodore Lowi, *The End of Liberalism* (New York: Norton, 1969); Thomas E. Cronin, *The State of the Presidency* (Boston: Little, Brown, 1975); Gordon Adams, *The Politics of Defense Contracting: The Iron Triangle* (New Brunswick, NJ: Transaction Books, 1982); Douglas R. Arnold, *The Logic of Congressional Action* (New Haven, CT: Yale University Press, 1992); and Raymond Vernon, Debra L. Spar, and Glenn Tobin, *Iron Triangles and Revolving Doors: Cases in U.S. Foreign Economic Policymaking* (New York: Praeger, 1991).

control their own regulation, using it to create higher barriers to market entry and thus to limit competition.[14]

Conclusions

This chapter provides an introduction to the major issues connected with the debates over HDTV and DTV that will be explored in detail below. These debates may tell us something useful about the broader transition from analog to digital technologies and will provide further evidence for testing the Schumpeterian framework for understanding large-scale socio-economic changes. The HDTV/DTV cases discussed below will also be used to test some of the author's own earlier ideas about the importance of national differences in explaining changes in international economic competitiveness over time. They may also provide some information about how to redesign regulatory regimes so that they are more appropriate for the digital age. Finally, I will argue that the HDTV/DTV outcomes were strongly influenced by the idea of "digital convergence" even though the outcomes themselves demonstrated continued divergence in national and regional practices.

[14] See Samuel Huntington, "The Marasmus of the ICC: The Commission, the Railroads, and the Public Interest," *Yale Law Journal*, 614 (1952), pp. 467–509; Marver Bernstein, *Regulating Business by Independent Commission* (Princeton, NJ: Princeton University Press, 1955); George Stigler, "The Theory of Economic Regulation," *Bell Journal of Economics and Management*, 2 (1971), pp. 3–21; Sam Peltzman, "Toward a More General Theory of Regulation," *Journal of Law and Economics*, 19 (1976), pp. 211–48; and Jean-Jacques Laffont and Jean Tirole, "The Politics of Government Decision-Making: A Theory of Regulatory Capture," *The Quarterly Journal of Economics*, 106 (November 1991), pp. 1089–127.

2   The institutional setting for advanced TV

Introduction

The choice of advanced TV standards in the United States, Europe, and Japan was strongly influenced by preexisting institutions, and especially by the broadcasting systems. Each region had its own pattern, with private broadcasting dominating in the United States, public broadcasting prevailing in Japan, and a mixture of private and public (tending toward further decline of public broadcasting) in Europe. The desire of public broadcasters to hold on to their niche in Europe and Japan played a very important role in the domestic and international politics of advanced TV.

Governmental regulation of broadcasting: general issues

Broadcasting systems are by their nature likely to be regulated by governments for a variety of reasons. First, there were historical precedents for state monopolies over postal and telegraphic systems. In many countries, the postal and telegraphic monopolies were simply expanded to include first radio and then television broadcasting as part of their mandate. There were a variety of political rationales for maintaining a public broadcasting monopoly, such as the transmission of elite-defined cultural values. But these political rationales were probably secondary to simple institutional inertia.

Second, the news and public affairs content of broadcast media made them important for the expression of ideas, and therefore susceptible to regulation because of the role of the media in the protection of free speech in a democratic society. This is the source of such policy innovations as "equal time" provisions in the United States that were designed to ensure relatively equal coverage of candidates during election campaigns. It is also a factor in the debates over the regulation of broadcasting content, for example, in laws governing obscenity and indecency.

Third, broadcasting itself is a "collective good" in some respects. For example, over-the-air television broadcasting produces a service to all individuals in the signal's path who possess a TV receiver. These individuals do not have to pay any fee for receiving the signal unless there are laws empowering the broadcasters to collect a fee from all owners of receivers. In the United States, the law authorizes no such fee collection. Even in countries like Britain and Japan, where fee collection is authorized, however, there is no way of excluding people who do not pay the fee short of seizing their TV receivers.

It is technologically possible to exclude non-paying customers by scrambling (encrypting) the signal. Then only paying customers are given the necessary technology to descramble (decrypt) the signal at the receiver end. This is how most cable and satellite pay-TV systems work.

If there were no advertising on unscrambled over-the-air TV broadcasts in countries where there is no receiver fee (like the United States), then (unless broadcasters are also in the business of manufacturing receivers) no one would invest in TV broadcasting because there would be no revenues to pay for programming and transmission costs. So the US government permits private over-the-air broadcasters to sell advertising, although the government limits the percentage of air time that can be devoted to advertising, to create an incentive for what some people call "free" over-the-air broadcasting. It is not really free, of course, since the people who buy the things that are advertised help to pay for the advertising that makes TV programs available to all set owners. Still, it is like a collective good in that consumers cannot be excluded because they have not bought an advertised product.

Television programs also have some characteristics of collective goods. The cost of producing a television program is independent of the number of people who will view it. However, the number of people who want to view a particular program may depend upon its "production values," the quality of the script, the direction, the actors, and the visual images, which in turn is likely to be reflected in the final cost of production. The recorded program, on film or tape, remains available and unchanged no matter how many times it is viewed. According to Bruce Owen and Steven Wildman, "Most entertainment is heavily infected with 'publicness' but is delivered to the consumer in or through a private good – a book, a magazine, a ringside seat, a theater chair. Television, however, has a public good as its delivery medium."[1]

TV programs and TV broadcasting are products that have high fixed costs and low marginal costs. To make a profit, the providers of TV programs must repeatedly exploit each product: that is, they must reach

[1] Bruce M. Owen and Steven S. Wildman, *Video Economics* (Cambridge, MA: Harvard University Press, 1992), p. 24.

the largest possible viewing audience and they must market the products in as many alternative forms as possible. This is the basic reason for the creation of the contemporary media conglomerates that include under one roof publishers of print media (books, magazines, newspapers, etc.), films, and electronic media (radio, television, audio and video tape recordings, etc.).[2]

As the number of ways of distributing TV programs increases over time and particularly as the number of channels available for over-the-air, cable, and satellite broadcasting increases, TV program delivery has become more of a private good. With the increase in the number of channels, the audience becomes more "segmented" and programs and attendant advertising are more carefully targeted toward a particular group of individuals. The mass audiences still tune in to certain types of programming – sporting events, news coverage of catastrophes, international crises, celebrity trials, etc. – but most of the time the audience is no longer a mass audience:

the new generation of video transmission technologies has undermined the concept of the national electronic hearth around which the national family gathers. Some of the new media are highly individual, such as videocassettes and records; others are local, such as cable television and low-power TV; still others are transnational, such as satellite transmission. Each rearranges the national audience into more specialized groups, just as magazine publishers have done, reaching different subgroups. Hence, television becomes transformed from the medium of national culture to that of subcultures, often cutting across frontiers, and from a nationally cohesive force to a differentiating, localizing, and internationalizing one.[3]

As program delivery becomes less of a public good, it becomes more and more difficult to defend government-owned or government-sanctioned broadcasting monopolies. That does not mean that public broadcasting monopolies have not been defended, however, and, as I will demonstrate below, there still remain significant variations in the mix of public and private ownership in broadcasting across and within geographic regions. This nearly universal struggle over the proportion of private broadcasting, however, is a key to understanding the politics of advanced TV.

The national broadcasting environments

It is a matter of national, and sometimes also local or regional, choice as to how to deal with the regulation of broadcasting and related industries.

---

[2] Elie Noam, *Television in Europe* (New York: Oxford, 1991), pp. 30–2.
[3] *Ibid.*, p. 25.

Some nations have chosen to maintain or preserve strong public broadcasting systems, while others have opted for minimal public broadcasting and a heavy emphasis on advertising-driven private broadcasting. Between these two extremes, there is a continuum of public–private mixes.

The United States opted for a private broadcasting-dominated environment. There are few countries in the world who have gone as far as the United States in this direction. Japan, in contrast, has maintained a broadcasting environment in which television broadcasting is dominated by a single public broadcaster, Nippon Hoso Kyokai (NHK). There are private competitors in Japan and their strength is growing, but NHK is still the dominant force. In Britain, the public broadcaster, the British Broadcasting Corporation (BBC), was a dominant force until the late 1980s, when it began to lose audience share to private broadcasting via satellite. In Italy, the dominant national public broadcaster was until recently RAI (Radiotelevisione Italiane). Now the three RAI channels are roughly equal in audience share to the private channels. In France and Germany, public broadcasting was divided between two national broadcasters: TF1 and A2 in France; ARD and ZDF in Germany.[4] In these two countries, there were also regional public broadcasters set up to add local and regional content to the signals of the national broadcasters. Now all the European public broadcasters face growing competition from private broadcasters delivering their signals via satellite or cable.

The rest of this chapter provides background material that is essential for an adequate understanding of the politics of advanced TV. The text below deals with the incentives and disincentives for broadcasters, public and private, to deploy advanced TV broadcasting systems. I will argue that the public broadcasters of Japan and Western Europe saw satellite transmission of advanced TV signals to be a way to protect their threatened quasi-monopolistic status. As a result, the nature and the timing of their technological choices made it extremely difficult for them to win international acceptance for their chosen advanced TV standards.

The broadcasting environment in the United States

The Italian inventor, Guglielmo Marconi, took his wireless telegraph equipment to Britain in 1896 to demonstrate it to officials of the British Post Office. A British corporation called Marconi Limited was formed in 1897, backed by a powerful investment group, and capitalized at £100,000. The 23-year-old Marconi received half of the stock in the

---

[4] TF1 was privatized in 1986; A2 became France 2 in 1992.

company and £15,000 in cash. He was also given a seat on the board of directors and put in charge of development.[5]

The new wireless technology was demonstrated at the 1889 America's Cup Race, but also figured in the announcement of the victory of Admiral George Dewey at Manila Bay in the Spanish–American war. In that same year, the Marconi Wireless Company of America (also called American Marconi) was incorporated under the laws of New Jersey with an initial capitalization of $10 million.

Radio broadcasting in the United States began in 1906, when the sounds of a woman singing, a violin playing, and a man reading the Bible were heard by wireless telegraphers on Atlantic ships. Lee De Forest, the inventor in 1907 of the "audion" tube, a vacuum tube which could amplify audio signals, started his own radio broadcasts in New York in 1910. By 1916, De Forest's broadcasts were on a regular schedule.[6]

At first, there were no restrictions on the operation of wireless broadcasting stations. Any amateur radio enthusiast could set up a transmitter and an antenna and add to the growing cacophony of the airwaves. The proliferation of would-be broadcasters led to the adoption of the Radio Act of 1912 requiring licenses for radio broadcasting. The responsibility for granting these licenses was given to the Secretary of Commerce and Labor. By the early 1920s, the spectrum was getting crowded enough that licenses were no longer granted automatically.[7]

American Marconi supplied radio equipment to the US military, but the fact that it was a subsidiary of a British firm bothered the US Navy. This irritation was compounded in 1912 when American Marconi bought out its only major competitor in the wireless business in America: United Wireless.[8] The Navy began to lobby for an American presence in the wireless industry to reduce dependence on British technology. Assistant Secretary of the Navy Franklin Delano Roosevelt was one of the supporters of this proposal.

A brief history of RCA

The 21-year-old David Sarnoff was the operator of a Marconi wireless receiver in 1912 when faint signals came to New York from the SS *Titanic* as it was sinking off the coast of Greenland. Sarnoff went on to become

---

[5] Erik Barnouw, *Tube of Plenty: The Evolution of American Television*, 2nd edition (New York: Oxford University Press, 1990), p. 9.

[6] *Ibid.*, pp. 13–15.

[7] William E. François, *Mass Media Law and Regulation* (Columbus, OH: Grid Inc., 1975), p. 287.

[8] Robert Sobel, *RCA* (New York: Stein and Day, 1986), p. 21.

the head of American Marconi and later of the Radio Corporation of America (RCA). He remained the chairman of RCA until 1969, at the age of 75, he became too weak physically to go to his office. Sarnoff was the single most important individual in shaping the evolution of the US broadcasting system. RCA was the beneficiary of an almost monopolistic position, which made it eventually a target of antitrust activity. RCA remained the dominant actor in the age of television because it used its profits from radio broadcasting to finance research in radio and television technology. Even after the settlement of successful antitrust suits took away some of RCA's market power, RCA remained the technological leader of the broadcasting and consumer electronics industries in America.

On Good Friday 1917 the US declared war on Germany after the sinking of four American ships by German U-boats. On that same day, President Woodrow Wilson directed the Navy to take over all wireless stations in the United States, including Marconi's ship-to-shore operations. During World War One, a great demand for radios and radio components arose as a result of the successful use of wireless technology in combat. American Marconi's manufacturing facility in New Jersey prospered, but other firms also began to supply the military with wireless components: notably, General Electric, Westinghouse, AT&T's Western Electric division, and a variety of smaller firms.

After Armistice Day, 11 November 1918, President Wilson was urged by his advisers to make the temporary acquisition of American Marconi permanent. Wilson asked Representative Joshua Alexander (D-Missouri) to sponsor legislation to authorize this. Hearings on the proposed legislation allowed the president of American Marconi to make the usual objections about nationalization of private firms, while the Secretary of the Navy, Josephus Daniels, argued that the Navy needed to control radio technology and would be better able than the private company to develop it further. No further action was taken at this time on Alexander's bill, but the handwriting was on the wall for American Marconi. The Navy purchased a large proportion of the radio transmission equipment that American Marconi had built and operated for the Navy during the war. The company was still left with its manufacturing facility, however, as well as a number of high-power radio stations to operate.

The Radio Corporation of America was formed in 1919. RCA took over the assets of American Marconi and responsibility for marketing the radio equipment produced by GE and Westinghouse. "Conceived as a 'marriage of convenience' between private corporations and the government for the development of wireless communications, RCA soon grew in a different direction."[9] By 1924, there were 2.5 million radio receivers in American homes (up from 5,000 in 1920) and RCA's revenues from radio sales far exceeded its revenues from wireless services.

The first commercial radio broadcasting station, KDKA in Pittsburgh, went on the air in 1920, with coverage of the Harding–Cox presidential election. KDKA was owned by one of RCA's manufacturing partners, Westinghouse. RCA's General Manager, David Sarnoff, had a vision of building the radio business by broadcasting entertainment into homes. As early as 1916, Sarnoff said: "I have in mind a plan of development that would make the radio a 'household utility' in the same sense as the piano or the phonograph. The idea is to bring music into the house by wireless."[10]

Sarnoff knew that the radio receiver had to be inexpensive in order for radio programming to be widely available. He estimated that the retail price of a "radio music box" would be $75. Thus, he supported the sales of radios by broadcasting events of great public interest and by building a national network of radio stations with a centralized source of programming. In 1926, RCA, GE, and Westinghouse bought WEAF in New York and made it the anchor station for the new National Broadcasting Company (NBC).

The federal government brought an antitrust suit against RCA in 1931. As a result of the suit, GE and Westinghouse withdrew from their partnerships with RCA, and Sarnoff began to diversify out of the radio business and into movie sound production systems and the ownership of movie theatres and a movie studio with an investment in RKO. In the midst of the Great Depression, RCA moved its headquarters from Los Angeles to New York into the Rockefeller Center complex and what came to be called Radio City.

RCA and early research on television in the United States

RCA began to fund development of television in the early 1930s. The American Telephone & Telegraph Company (AT&T) gave the first successful demonstration of television in the United States on 27 April 1927. This demonstration dismayed Sarnoff, because he wanted to be first in developing TV technology in the United States. Relations between AT&T and RCA had become strained in 1926 after Sarnoff's success in preventing AT&T from being allowed to get into radio broadcasting. He ordered

---

[9] Accessed via the World Wide Web at http://www.rca-electronics.com/story/ on 17 February 1997.
[10] *Ibid.*

his manufacturing partners, General Electric and Westinghouse, to double their research efforts to match those of AT&T.[11]

On 7 January 1927, a young man from Utah named Philo T. Farnsworth applied for a patent for an electronic television system that was distinctive from the others in using an electronic device, later to be called a camera tube, to turn visual images into electronic impulses. Sarnoff sent Dr. Vladimir K. Zworykin to investigate Farnsworth's device. (Zworykin also visited laboratories in Europe at around the same time.) Zworykin had experimented earlier with an electronic camera tube that used the same principles but did not work nearly as well as Farnsworth's. He had filed a patent on his device in 1923. Farnsworth showed Zworykin his laboratory. Sarnoff himself came to visit the lab shortly thereafter. He offered Farnsworth $100,000 for the whole works, but the latter considered this to be far too little and he turned the offer down. Farnsworth heard nothing further from RCA, but soon learned that Zworykin had basically copied his approach to fabricating camera tubes in the RCA laboratories. Farnsworth filed a patent infringement suit that was finally decided in his favor in 1939.

General Electric successfully demonstrated a TV system put together by a team under the direction of Zworykin and Dr. Frank Gray in 1928. Zworykin had purchased a picture tube in France that he thought was an improvement over the ones they had been using in the United States. When he told Sarnoff of his group's advances in camera and picture tubes, Sarnoff agreed to fund a new laboratory in East Pittsburgh. In April 1928, RCA applied for a permit to operate a television station in New York City. The RCA group was able to demonstrate a moving television image on 9 May 1929. All RCA television research was taken over by Zworykin in January 1930 and the lab was moved to Camden, New Jersey, where the Victor Corporation (recently purchased by RCA) had a plant. Sarnoff frequently visited the Camden lab to supervise Zworykin's work. Zworykin filed a patent for his picture tube, called the "iconoscope," in November 1931.

In July 1932, Randall C. Ballard of the RCA Zworykin Laboratory filed a patent for "interlaced" scanning. Interlacing solved the problem of reducing flicker in CRT images as well as reducing the amount of bandwidth required for sending TV signals. (Interlacing would become a major issue in the debates about advanced TV in the 1990s.)

---

[11] Albert Abramson, "The Invention of Television," in Anthony Smith (ed.), *Television: An International History* (New York: Oxford University Press, 1995); and "Big Dreams, Small Screen," program created for the *American Experience* series on PBS, first aired on 10 February 1997.

In the meantime, Farnsworth had gone to Philadelphia to work with Philco to develop his television technologies. He successfully demonstrated an all-electric system at the Franklin Institute in Philadelphia in the summer of 1934. Unfortunately, after the death of one of his children, he was forced to move back west, and was unable to continue the relationship with Philco. Farnsworth would spend the rest of his life trying to exploit his early discoveries. However, he was outgunned and outmaneuvered, legally, financially, and technologically (but mainly legally), by RCA until his death in 1971.[12]

Sarnoff was determined to pursue television commercialization as rapidly as possible, especially after the successful demonstration by RCA of TV broadcasting at the 1939 World's Fair in New York. However, the onset of World War Two impelled him to put aside his plans for marketing televisions. He demonstrated his political astuteness when he publicly pledged the resources of RCA and NBC for the war effort. Sarnoff was named a colonel in the Army Signal Corps and eventually was promoted to the rank of brigadier general. He insisted on being called "General Sarnoff" until his death in 1971.

A short history of CBS

The Columbia Broadcasting System (CBS) got its start in 1927 when the Columbia Phonograph company bought a failing radio company called United Independent Broadcasters, which operated an independent radio station, WCAU, in Philadelphia. One of the major investors in this new venture was Sam Paley, who was primarily in the cigar business. His company sold cigars made in Cuba under the "La Palina" (a Spanish neologism of "Paley") label and advertised the cigars on WCAU. Sam eventually relinquished control of the new radio network to his son, Bill, who went on to build CBS into a credible rival to Sarnoff's NBC.[13]

While both Sarnoff and Paley were of Russian Jewish ancestry, Sarnoff's parents were poor and had immigrated into the United States considerably later than Paley's. Sarnoff had risen from telegraph operator at Marconi to become the head of RCA. According to Sally Bedell Smith:

Paley was much that Sarnoff was not. Paley was American-born, handsome, gregarious, and charming. He was "Bill"; Sarnoff was the "general" or

---

[12] See Paul Schatzkin, *The Farnsworth Chronicles*, at http://songs.com/noma/philo/index.html; David E. Fisher and Marshall Jon Fisher, *Tube: The Invention of Television* (Washington, DC: Counterpoint, 1996); and "Big Dream, Small Screen," TV documentary, part of the *American Experience* series on PBS, aired on 10 February 1997.

[13] Sally Bedell Smith, *In All His Glory: The Life and Times of William S. Paley and the Birth of Modern Broadcasting* (New York: Simon and Schuster, 1990), pp. 57–9.

"Mr. Sarnoff." Paley also was wealthy from the beginning, the son of a million-aire Philadelphia family that owned the Congress Cigar Company . . . Paley was an impresario more concerned with the show than with the equipment used to transmit and receive it.[14]

Under Paley's leadership, CBS began to turn a profit and attracted the attention of people who wanted to invest in the new medium. In 1929, Adolph Zukor of Paramount Pictures purchased 50 percent equity (around 59,000 shares) in CBS for $5 million.[15] Paley, however, wanted to control the network himself, and with the help of financiers at Brown Brothers Harriman (including Averell Harriman and George Bush's father Prescott) bought back Paramount's shares for $5.2 million in 1932. At this time, Paley personally owned 40 percent of the stock.

In the 1930s, NBC and CBS competed for radio audiences by experimenting with various types and levels of quality in programming, hiring the most talented performers, and attracting advertisers who would pay for it all. After engaging in a series of bidding wars for talent, Sarnoff at NBC and Paley at CBS arrived at a "gentleman's agreement" not to poach on each other's territory.[16] Still the rivalry between the two firms and their heads continued and the gentleman's agreement was frequently broken. Sarnoff, for example, lost the services of Jack Benny, the comedian, to CBS during a raid on RCA's talent in 1948.[17]

NBC and CBS became the two largest radio networks in the United States in the 1930s and remained dominant in the transition to television broadcasting after the end of World War Two. The dominance of NBC and CBS attracted the attention of the "trust busters" in the Roosevelt administration who had mandated the divestiture by the Hollywood studios of their theatre chains in 1938.[18] Roosevelt appointed James Lawrence Fly as chairman of the FCC in 1939. "Fly was an ardent New Dealer, and he fully subscribed to Roosevelt's description of big businesses as malefactors of great wealth."[19] ABC was created in 1941 when the Federal Communications Commission directed NBC to sell off one of its two

---

[14] J. Fred MacDonald, *One Nation Under Television: The Rise and Decline of Network TV* (New York: Pantheon, 1990), p. 16.
[15] Smith, *In All His Glory*, p. 84.
[16] Sobel, *RCA*, p. 148; Smith, *In All His Glory*, p. 89.
[17] Sobel, *RCA*, p. 148; William S. Paley, *As It Happened: A Memoir* (New York: Doubleday, 1979), pp. 194–9.
[18] William Boddy, "The Beginnings of American Television," in Smith (ed.), *Television* p. 37.
[19] Andrew F. Inglis, *Behind the Tube: A History of Broadcasting Technology and Business* (Stoneham, MA: Focal Press, 1990), p. 178.

networks.[20] ABC did not become fully competitive with the other two networks until the 1960s. A fourth television network was created by TV manufacturer Allen DuMont in the 1940s, but it failed in 1958.

Early regulation of US broadcasting

The Radio Act of 1927 was "emergency legislation that provided temporary regulation to bring order to the airwaves."[21] There were so many private radio stations operating in urban areas that they were interfering with each other's signals. The Radio Act established a Federal Radio Commission with five members appointed by the president with the right to grant licenses for the right to operate radio stations. The key assumptions underlying the Radio Act of 1927 were that: (1) radio spectrum would not be owned by radio stations but licensed from the government; (2) licensees would have to operate their stations in the public interest; (3) there would be no government censorship of the air waves; and (4) radio service was to be equitably distributed among the states. The FRC started by abolishing all existing radio licenses and requiring all current license holders to reapply. It defined the standard AM broadcasting band at 550 to 1500 kHz. It created a system of specifying power, frequency, and times of operation for stations applying for new licenses. Within five years, the FRC had solved the interference problem and created a method for deciding how to allocate scarce radio frequency spectrum to broadcasters.[22]

According to Robert W. McChesney, the FRC's General Order 40 "laid the foundations for network-dominated, advertising-supported U.S. broadcasting system."[23] This outcome was opposed in the early 1930s by an odd coalition of nonprofit organizations, intellectuals, civic activists, educators, elements of the labor movement, religious leaders, and the press.

Nonprofit broadcasters and educators decried the rise of commercial broadcasting financed by advertising as wasting the power of the new medium to educate and uplift the public. They cited the examples of

---

[20] Ken Auletta, *Three Blind Mice: How the TV Networks Lost Their Way* (New York: Vintage, 1992), p. 30.

[21] Robert W. McChesney, *Telecommunications, Mass Media, and Democracy: The Battle for Control of US Broadcasting, 1928–1935* (New York: Oxford University Press, 1994), p. 253.

[22] Joseph R. Dominick, Barry L. Sherman, and Gary A. Copeland, *Broadcasting/Cable and Beyond: An Introduction to Modern Electronic Media*, 3rd edition (New York: McGraw Hill, 1996), p. 31.

[23] *Ibid.*, p. 254.

European nations, and particularly Britain, in keeping public control over the airwaves as part of a larger project of cultural enlightenment. The press was concerned about the encroachments of network news-gathering agencies into their bailiwick, and the potential for network news to reduce the public's access to competing viewpoints. Labor was concerned that private broadcasting tended to represent the interests of private business at the expense of labor and therefore favored the granting of broadcasting licenses to labor-affiliated groups.

Radio evangelism began as soon as commercial radio broadcasting did. Radio preachers like Father Charles E. Coughlin and Aime Semple McPherson used the new medium to spread the faith but also a rather nasty form of anti-semitism. The Catholic Church had been successful in protesting the immorality of Hollywood films in the 1920s, and had lobbied successfully for new censorship laws in state governments and local communities. The Hollywood Production Code, adopted voluntarily by the major studios in 1930, was designed to prevent further moves toward censorship of the movie industry.[24]

The Communications Act of 1934 was an effort to go beyond the Radio Act of 1927 in regulating the broadcasting industry. It replaced the Federal Radio Commission with a Federal Communications Commission composed of seven commissioners appointed by the president with the advice and consent of the Senate. The new FCC was given the responsibility of regulating both domestic and foreign wired and wireless communications, thus taking over the regulation of telephone and telegraph communications from the Interstate Commerce Commission. Like the FRC, the FCC had the power to grant or withhold licenses to broadcasters. Unlike the FRC, the new FCC "imposed minimum requirements for news or community programming" and "encouraged stations not to drench viewers with too many ads per hour."[25]

Senators Robert F. Wagner of New York and Henry D. Hatfield of West Virginia proposed an amendment to the Communications Act which would have nullified all existing radio licenses and then reassigned them, reserving 25 percent of all licenses for educational, religious, agricultural, labor, cooperative and not-for-profit associations. Unions, religious organizations, educators, and non-profit organizations supported this amendment. Strong lobbying against the Wagner–Hatfield Amendment by the National Association of Broadcasters, including personal interventions by Sarnoff and Paley, prevented its passage.[26] Defeat of the

[24] Black, *Hollywood Censored*, pp. 31–4.
[25] Auletta, *Three Blind Mice*, p. 30.
[26] Smith, *In All His Glory*, pp. 137–9; MacDonald, *One Nation*, pp. 28–9; McChesney, *Telecommunications*, pp. 200–7.

Wagner–Hatfield Amendment guaranteed continuation of a broadcasting system dominated by private broadcasters.

Regulation of TV broadcasting in the United States

The FCC accepted the recommendations of the National Television System Committee (NTSC) in 1941 for standards for television broadcasting. The NTSC recommended that black and white be transmitted with 525 interlaced lines scanned at thirty frames per second. The FCC issued a statement of policy and agreed to issue licenses for full-tune commercial TV stations.[27] By the end of the year, thirty-two stations had been licensed. World War Two interrupted the development of commercial television in the United States. The FCC banned TV station construction during the war. Immediately after the end of the war, however, the TV race began again in earnest.

In 1945, the FCC moved FM radio service to a different part of the spectrum, giving priority to development of TV on what was later called the VHF (very high frequency) band (channels 2 to 13). It then lifted the ban on the construction of TV stations it had instituted during World War Two and reinstated the standards adopted in 1941. CBS had argued against this, because it wanted new standards for color TV (the old standards dealt only with black and white or monochrome signals). CBS believed quite rightly that RCA had a significant lead in monochrome TV technology and wanted to delay the race so that the other TV equipment manufacturers could catch up with RCA. However, the arguments of CBS did not win the day, and newly constructed TV stations began to broadcast programming initially to a very restricted audience.[28]

By 1948, there were twenty-nine TV stations on the air, another eighty had been authorized, and applications had been filed for an additional 300 stations. While only 8,000 homes had receivers in 1946, there were 174,000 sets in homes by 1948. Four TV networks were operating at that time: NBC, CBS, ABC, and DuMont. Early TV service was marred by problems of poor quality signals and interference. The first sets sold had rather small screens and large cabinets. But demand remained strong and the FCC was unable to process the large number of applications for new licenses. In 1952, the FCC decided to set aside additional spectrum for TV broadcasting in the ultra high frequency (UHF) band,

[27] MacDonald, *One Nation*, pp. 18–19.
[28] Boddy, "The Beginnings," pp. 38–40.

channels 14–69. UHF channels from the start were generally less successful than VHF channels because, until 1963, manufacturers were not required to include UHF tuners in all sets and in any case the reception quality of UHF signals was usually greatly inferior to that of VHF signals.

The FCC dealt with interference problems by mandating minimum distances between broadcasting towers in the same and neighboring channels and by limiting the maximum power of signals. Thus was created the local over-the-air television service that became a virtually permanent fixture in the United States. Finally, the FCC set aside 242 channels (about 10 percent of available channels) for noncommercial stations in 1951 thanks to the vigorous efforts of Commissioner Frieda Hennock.[29]

The number of stations grew from 98 in 1950 to 1,693 in 1992. The percentage of households with TV sets grew from 9 percent in 1950 to over 99 percent in 1992.[30] In 1948, there were 66 manufacturers of TV sets, but about 75 percent of the market was controlled by just three firms: RCA, DuMont, and Philco.[31] By February 1955 there were 36 million sets in American homes.[32] By 1996, there were 97 million TV households, with an average of over two TVs per household.

This rapid growth in TV's penetration of mass consumer markets was driven by a combination of factors. First, the programming of TV stations was sufficiently interesting to consumers to justify the expense of purchasing a TV receiver. Initially receivers were about as expensive as automobiles, but the price declined rapidly as the number of sets sold went up. The networks were able to distribute programming nationally, first via the telephone network, then by the new microwave networks built by AT&T in the 1950s, and later via the telecommunications satellites that became available after the launching of the Telstar satellite in 1962.

The onset of satellite broadcasting of network programming made possible the construction of community antenna television (CATV) systems in communities that had previously been unable to receive terrestrial TV signals. Cable television services that supplemented the terrestrial broadcast services already available to consumers in urban areas was the next step for CATV providers. Finally, rural customers began in the late 1960s to be able to receive satellite signals in their homes directly via large dish-shaped antennas. This service was called DBS (direct broadcast by satellite), and was later to be transformed by the construction of

---

[29] Dominick, Sherman, and Copeland, *Broadcasting*, p. 58.
[30] *Ibid.*, p. 60.
[31] Boddy, "The Beginnings," p. 43.
[32] *Ibid.*, p. 58.

Table 2.1 *Cable systems and subscribers in the United States, 1952 to 1997*

Year	No. of cable systems	Thousands of cable subscribers
1952	70	14
1955	400	150
1960	640	650
1970	2490	3900
1975	3506	9197
1980	4225	17,672
1985	6600	39,873
1990	9575	54,871
1993	11,108	58,834
1994	11,214	60,495
1995	11,218	62,957
1996	11,119	64,654
1997	10,750	64,081

Source: New York Times 1998 Almanac (New York: New York Times, 1998) p. 409.

more powerful broadcasting satellites which made it possible to use much smaller dishes for receiving satellite signals.

In 1984, the Cable Deregulation Act was passed with the strong support of the Reagan Administration. The passage of this bill helped to accelerate the growth in the number of cable subscribers in the US. By 1997, the number of households subscribing to cable had grown to over 64 million, well over 60 percent of the television households in the United States.

TV broadcasting services in the United States started with terrestrial over-the-air services, which were subsequently supplemented with cable television and DBS systems. By the late 1970s, a significant number of households were also viewing prerecorded video programs on video-cassette recorders (VCRs). The rise of alternative means of delivering video signals to homes tended to cut into the audience shares of local terrestrial broadcasters and therefore of the major broadcasting networks. Cable providers, however, simply rebroadcast the terrestrial signals to their customers, so that network television maintained its position of dominance in the homes of the TV viewing public. The dominance of private broadcasting in the US system had two main pillars: the entertainment programming of national networks and the local news and sports programming provided by local terrestrial broadcasters.

The broadcasting environment in Europe

It would be hard to improve upon the fine description of the European broadcasting environment provided in Elie Noam's book, *Television in Europe*:

From the beginning, European governments participated actively in the control of broadcasting. They allocated radio frequencies, declared wireless transmission to be vital to military affairs, and kept a guiding hand on the new communications medium with its considerable political and economic potential . . . Although the organizational structures of West European broadcasting varied from country to country, there was much similarity. Typically, broadcasting was centralized in a public institution with a monopoly over television and radio. This organization provided two or three channels of television for the entire country, plus a handful of radio channels. It was (and still is) usually run not under direct government control, but through a semi-independent board appointed directly or indirectly by the government or, more frequently, by the national legislature (i.e., by the major political parties). This assured the major opposition parties of participation, but it was often associated with a heavy internal politicization along party lines. Financing derives from a periodic license fee on television and radio sets, supplemented by advertising revenues.[33]

Noam tells how and why this overarching pattern changed in the mid-1980s and afterwards to include greater participation by private broadcasters. He argues that the growing strength of private broadcasting was a product not just of changing technologies but also of pressures from a variety of social groups for deregulation of broadcasting to provide greater diversity of political viewpoints and greater choice in media programming. These changes were resisted by political actors who argued for the necessity of protecting national cultures by maintaining broadcasting monopolies, but who were also (not incidentally) defending the entrenched economic interests of the public broadcasters and their allies.

These changes affected the debates over advanced TV in Europe by forcing the public broadcasters into a set of defensive postures to protect their existing revenues and audience shares. We will see in chapter 6 that one of the tactics for doing this was to try to control advanced TV by forcing all advanced TV signal providers to broadcast a standardized signal over satellites controlled by allies of the public broadcasters. The number of channels that would be available to private broadcasters for this purpose would be limited. The public broadcasters allied themselves with the major manufacturers of TV equipment to assure this outcome. However, this plan for maintaining dominance was upset by a number of unforeseen and uncontrollable events. In chapter 6, that story will be

---

[33] Noam, *Television in Europe*, p. 3.

told in some detail. In this chapter, the focus will be on describing the environment that had evolved by the mid-1980s.

Britain

As mentioned above in the discussion of the history of American broadcasting, Britain was an early pioneer in both radio and television broadcasting. The Marconi Corporation, which held most of the key patents for radio technology,[34] was based in Britain and much of the early research on television technology took place in British laboratories. John Logie Baird, the Scottish inventor, was an important innovator in television technology who, at one point, teamed up with Philo Farnsworth in his struggle to defeat their larger foes. Just as Farnsworth was ultimately defeated by RCA, Baird was defeated by his larger opponent, Marconi–EMI.

Under legislation passed in 1904, wireless communication was put under the control of the British Post Office. Private radio broadcasting began in 1919.[35] The Post Office decided in 1923 to favor a state enterprise, the British Broadcasting Corporation, formed in October 1922, by licensing only those radios produced by a cartel of six radio manufacturers (Marconi, Radio Communication, Metropolitan Vickers, Western Electric, British Thomson Houston, and the General Electric Company) in association with the BBC.[36] John Reith became the managing director of the BBC soon after its foundation, and remained the guiding influence until his resignation in 1938. Reith articulated the idea of "public interest broadcasting" as a way of defining the BBC's mission, focused on creating quality programming that would be available to all British citizens. Reith's idea was broadly embraced by the British public (although the monopoly status of the BBC was contested from the very beginning).[37]

The Crawford Committee was appointed in 1926 to advise the British government on the permanent structure of British broadcasting. The Committee recommended maintaining the existing monopoly, arguing

---

[34] For an argument connecting British naval power to the early development of the radio industry, see Rowland F. Pocock, *The Early British Radio Industry* (New York: Manchester University Press, 1988).

[35] Noam, *Television in Europe*, p. 115.

[36] Mark Pegg, *Broadcasting and Society 1918–1939* (London: Croom Helm, 1983), p. 42. Note that the General Electric Company in the cartel was the British firm now frequently called GEC and not the General Electric (GE) company of the United States.

[37] See Paddy Scannell and David Cardiff, *A Social History of British Broadcasting: Volume One 1922–1939 Serving the Nation* (London: Basil Blackwell, 1991), especially ch. 1; Tom Burns, *The BBC : Public Institution and Private World* (London: Macmillan, 1977), ch. 2; and Burton Paulu, *British Broadcasting: Radio and Television in the United Kingdom* (Minneapolis: University of Minnesota Press, 1956), ch. 2.

that competition would inevitably result in a decline in the quality of programs. The Committee apparently believed that Britain should not emulate the United States. The Committee's report made this clear when it said that "It is agreed that the United States system of free and uncontrolled transmission and reception, is unsuited to this country, and that Broadcasting must accordingly remain a monopoly."[38]

In 1929, the BBC permitted John Logie Baird's company to transmit experimental TV signals created with his semi-mechanical TV system. In 1936, the BBC introduced regular TV services, which it called "high-definition television," from its Alexandra Palace studios in north London. There were initially only two hours of programming per day and the transmissions alternated between Baird's system and an all-electronic system put together by Marconi and EMI. The BBC accepted the Selsdon Commission's recommendation to drop the Baird system and the BBC continued broadcasting in the VHF bands with a signal that had 405 scanning lines. By 1939, there were 20,000 TV receivers in British homes.[39]

Television service was suspended during World War Two, as in the United States, to resume again shortly after the end of the war. A combined radio and TV license system was introduced in June 1946. The wedding of Princess Elizabeth and the Duke of Edinburgh was broadcast to the nation in November 1947. Between 1947 and 1956, the number of television licenses increased from 14,560 to over 5.7 million.[40]

The Television Act of 1954 authorized a newly formed Independent Television Authority (later renamed the Independent Broadcasting Authority) to license a private broadcasting competitor to the BBC. An independent private channel called ITV began broadcasting in the London area in September 1955. Its programming was livelier than that of the BBC and it soon attracted a sizeable share of the total audience. The BBC responded by pepping up their programming to match the more entertainment-oriented programming of ITV.

The election of a Conservative government in October 1951 had brought into power a group of leaders who felt that competition would help to increase the range of choice for TV viewers. Apparently, this was a popular issue for the Conservatives, who were more inclined than the Labour Party to favor an end to the BBC's monopoly. Winston Churchill made no secret of his contempt for the BBC and was a supporter of the Television Act, but many members of the Conservative Party questioned

---

[38] Paulu, *British Broadcasting*, p. 14.
[39] Noam, *Television in Europe*, pp. 117–18; a history of the BBC on their World Wide Web site at http://www.bbc.co.uk accessed on 5 March 1997.
[40] Paulu, *British Broadcasting*, p. 354.

the need for competition and it took strict enforcement of party discipline to assure passage of the bill in 1954.[41]

Part of the problem was the failure of the BBC to operate more than one channel. The British people were avid TV watchers from the very beginning, and they wanted greater variety in programming. The BBC belatedly opened a second channel called BBC2 in April 1964. The experimental color TV signal broadcast by BBC2 had 625 scanning lines. By 1965, the BBC had decided to adopt the PAL standard for its color transmissions (see the section on Germany below). A gigantic microwave relay tower, called the BBC Tower, was built in London and opened in October 1965.[42] From 1965 to 1974, all BBC programming was distributed either via microwave or cable. BBC2 began to broadcast regular color programming in 1967; BBC1 did so only in November 1969. After 1974, satellite distribution of BBC programming was added to microwave and cable.

In 1972, British Telecommunications was spun off from the Post Office and took control of public broadcasting. BT remained a state enterprise until its privatization in 1985 by the Thatcher government. All BBC commercial activities were brought together into a new entity called BBC Enterprises Ltd. in April 1986. BT remained the primary distributor of BBC signals but was no longer involved in program creation or broadcasting per se. The Independent Broadcasting Authority (IBA) remained the main agency responsible for regulating broadcasting (both public and private) in the British government.

A fourth channel was added to the British lineup (after the two BBC channels and ITV) during the Thatcher government. It was called Channel Four (an obvious choice). The new channel was intended to provide support for independent film and video producers in Britain, in the wake of the virtual collapse of the British film industry. Channel Four commissioned works both from British producers and from independent producers abroad (including Third World countries). According to Anthony Smith, Channel Four "provided a container, as it were, of a new pluralism, the resolution of a series of fresh cultural tensions."[43]

In 1986, the IBA awarded the contract for DBS broadcasting to a new entity called British Satellite Broadcasting (BSB). This venture had great financial difficulties because of high start-up costs and delays in the building of dishes and satellite receivers. Rupert Murdoch and his News Corporation created a strong competitor to BSB when they launched

---

[41] *Ibid.*, p. 46.

[42] The building is now called the British Telecom Tower.

[43] Anthony Smith, "Television as a Public Service Medium," in Anthony Smith (ed.), *Television: An International History* (Oxford: Oxford University Press, 1995), p. 87.

their Sky Television services using medium power satellites (see below). Sky TV had leased four channels on the Astra satellite and broadcast PAL signals; BSB was compelled to broadcast signals from an expensive new Hughes satellite with a PAL-incompatible standard called D-MAC. Sky TV was a commercial success; BSB was a bust. BSB and Sky TV merged on 2 November 1990 and the merged organization was called BSkyB. Murdoch's News Corporation owned 40 percent of the equity of BSkyB.[44]

From this point on, the BBC began to try to stave off the inevitable erosion of its audience share to BSkyB. For example, on 10 May 1994, the BBC formed a global alliance with Pearson PLC to develop its own satellite television channels.[45] In December 1995, the Office of Fair Trading (OFT) decided to initiate a review of the dominant market position of BSkyB in pay television. Later that year, Granada Television, one of the BBC's private competitors in the independent television (ITV) group, announced that it was forming a joint venture with BSkyB called GSkyB. Another member of that group, Carlton, had also approached BSkyB about satellite delivery of its programs. Even the BBC began to recognize the inevitability of this by the mid-1990s. In the fall of 1996, the OFT called off its review. In December 1996, the BBC called for curbs on the further expansion of BSkyB, admitting that it was powerless to stop the expansion of the Murdoch empire.[46]

The Broadcasting Act of 1990 replaced the IBA with an Independent Television Commission (ITC), which was empowered to promote private broadcasting by the auctioning of licenses. The ITC took over from the Cable Authority the right to grant cable TV franchises. In March 1991, the Department of Trade and Industry published a Duopoly Review White Paper "Competition and Choice: Telecommunications Policy for the 1990s" (Command 1461). Among other things, this document helped to establish greater freedom for cable operators. The promotion of cable TV in Britain in the 1980s was not a success despite strong support from the Thatcher government. In July 1990, for example, Oftel had taken action against four cable franchisees over delays in building their cable networks. Only 1.4 percent of British households were cable

---

[44] Information accessed via the World Wide Web at http://www.vbs.bt.co.uk/bt_bs/history.html on 5 March 1997. See also the detailed description of the BSB and Sky TV competition in William Shawcross, *Murdoch* (New York: Simon and Schuster, 1992), ch. 13.

[45] http://www.vbs.bt.com/bt_bs/history.html accessed on 20 February 1997.

[46] Stephen Barden, "Let's Get Digital: It's Not Too Late for British Companies to Join the Technological Revolution," *The Independent*, 8 December 1996, accessed via Nexis-Lexis. Stephen Barden was general manager of BSkyB in 1992 and chief executive of News International's New Digital Systems division from 1993 to 1995.

subscribers in 1990.[47] In July 1993, Oftel gave cable operators the option of offering voice telephony services along with cable television services as a way of inducing faster building of cable networks. This may be interpreted as an act of desperation, and an attack on the continuing power of British Telecom to delay the rollout of cable TV. In contrast, terrestrial and satellite broadcasting were doing very well indeed. By 1993, for example, over 2.6 million British households owned satellite receivers.[48] The big winner here was Rupert Murdoch and BSkyB.

Germany

Germany, like the other industrialized countries, was the source of much technological innovation in radio and television broadcasting. The cathode ray tube was invented by Karl Ferdinand Braun in Berlin in 1897. Braun was the first to coat the inside surface of a glass vacuum tube with phosphor so that it would glow when struck by electrons. The Braun tube was further developed in Germany by Max Dieckman and Boris Rosing in the first decades of the twentieth century. Vladimir Zworykin, the most important scientist working for RCA in the 1920s and 1930s, was a student of Rosing's.[49]

Development of broadcasting in Germany was delayed because of the upheaval caused by World War One and its aftermath. Many private individuals continued to experiment with electronics and radio technologies. Experimental broadcasts of concerts and operas started in December 1920 under the aegis of the German Post Office (the Reichspost). Germany was divided into nine broadcasting regions. Private broadcasters received licenses for a concessionary regional monopoly, but the Reichspost held a 17 percent equity share in each of the regional broadcasters.[50]

The German Ministry of the Interior tilted in the direction of public broadcasting in 1925 when it suggested the formation of the RRG (Reichs Rundfunk Gesellschaft). This society was funded by a portion of the radio license fees collected by the Reichspost for the regional private

---

[47] Hans Kleinsteuber, "Kabel und Satellit in der westeuropäischen Technologie-und Medienpolitik," *Rundfunk und Fernsehen*, 39 (1991), p. 513.

[48] Hans J. Kleinsteuber, "New Media Technologies in Europe: The Politics of Satellite, HDTV, and DAB," *Irish Communications Review*, 5 (1995), p. 13.

[49] Albert Abramson, "The Invention of Television," in Smith (ed.), *Television*, p. 16; and Inglis, *Behind the Tube*, p. 174.

[50] Noam, *Television in Europe*, p. 75; Donald R. Browne, *Comparing Broadcast Systems: The Experiences of Six Industrialized Nations* (Ames, IA: Iowa State University Press, 1989), pp. 180–2.

broadcasters and was responsible for regulating all program exchanges between radio stations. This gave the Ministry of the Interior considerable power over programming, while the Reichspost effectively became the regulatory agency for broadcasting. Radio stations were also required to accept the supervision of "cultural committees" that were appointed by the provincial (länder) governments and supervisory committees with representatives of both the central and provincial governments.

In 1932, the government passed radio reform legislation that centralized control of the medium by creating a new post for a radio commissioner in the Ministry of the Interior. This was an attempt to insulate the medium from the political struggles underway in Germany, but had the unanticipated effect of making it easier for the Nazis to control the media when they took power in 1933.

Hitler and his propaganda chief, Josef Goebbels, wanted to use radio to spread Nazi ideology and to secure Nazi control of German society. In 1933, control over broadcasting was transferred from the Reichspost to the Ministry of Propaganda. Just as Hitler wanted every German citizen to own a "people's car" (the origin of the word "Volkswagen" and the firm associated with it), he wanted them also to have a radio. The People's Radio Receiver (Volksempfänger) was designed to be inexpensive; it could receive only one or two frequencies so that Germans would not be able to listen to the broadcasts from neighboring countries. Listening to foreign broadcasts was illegal under the Nazi regime. These sets sold quite well, and by the end of the 1930s, the Germans had the largest number of radios in Europe. The Nazi government increased the power of existing transmitters and kept the annual license fee low so that everyone who could afford a set would be able to listen to broadcasts without difficulty.

Television broadcasting began under the Nazis in 1935. Hitler decided to put television broadcasting under the control of Hermann Göring, who was in charge of the German air force at the time, instead of Goebbels. Initially, the broadcasts could only be viewed on receivers set up in public places. The picture was crude, with only 180 scanning lines, but that system was replaced with a new system with higher resolution images in 1937 when a 441-line system was introduced. The prices of sets remained high through the outbreak of World War Two, when set production was ended, but broadcasts continued through 1944.[51]

After the end of World War Two, the resumption of national broadcasting services under the Allied occupation was one of the many issues that eventually led to the Cold War. The Soviet zone contained

---

[51] Noam, *Television in Europe*, pp. 76–7; Browne, *Comparing Broadcasting Systems*, pp. 181–6.

the remnants of the national broadcasting system, while many of the regional broadcasting stations had been badly damaged during the war. The Americans, French, and British wanted to be able to broadcast information to the whole country using the national broadcasting facilities in the Soviet zone. The Soviets opposed this, however, so the other Allies were forced to rebuild the regional broadcasting systems.

One of the consequences of Germany's defeat in World War Two, especially in the western part of the country, was a strong desire to avoid the kind of centralization of authority that made it possible for the Nazi regime to lead the nation into calamity. Strong support for a more federalized system emerged after the war. This was reflected in the decision to devolve control over broadcasting to the provincial governments and to separate broadcasting from the post office, even in the Soviet zone. The provincial legislatures proceeded to pass laws to govern broadcasting, subject to the approval of the occupation authorities. The result was a broadcasting system quite unlike the one Germany had developed prior to World War Two.

One distinctive feature of the new regime in the western zones was that each provincial broadcasting law had to make provisions for an advisory council of citizens representing different interests in society – for example, labor, business, education, cultural organizations, and religious groups. Representatives were selected by the groups themselves, not by either the broadcaster or the government. These councils were given extensive powers, including the ability to hire and fire station managers, oversee the setting of annual budgets, and, in some cases, veto certain types of expenditures.

When the occupation ended in 1949, further changes in the regime occurred. In 1950, the state-owned broadcasting stations created the Arbeitsgemeinschaft der öffentlichrechtlichen Rundfunkanstalten Deutschlands (ARD) (Working Group of German Public Service Broadcasting Organizations) to serve as a formal channel for the exchange of programs and other forms of cooperation. In 1951, Chancellor Konrad Adenauer attempted to establish a private national broadcasting system that was independent of the ARD. The first attempt was unsuccessful. Adenauer's party, the CDU, felt that ARD was too left-wing, and wanted it counterbalanced with a more conservative broadcaster.

In 1959, the CDU-led government tried again to establish a private national television broadcasting system through proposed legislation, and this time it was successful. However, the legislation was challenged by the provincial governments, and the Federal Constitutional Court subsequently ruled in their favor. In 1961, they formed the Zweites Deutsches Fernsehen (ZDF) (Second German Television). A new studio for the production of programs for the entire ZDF system was built in the city of Mainz in 1974. However, each province is responsible for the broadcasts in its territory, and each has a television council (fernsehrat), similar to the broadcasting councils of the ARD system. Thus, Germany wound up with two public television broadcasting systems, both largely under the control of the provincial governments. As a result, the CDU continued to push for private broadcasting.

Financial difficulties struck the ZDF in 1964, and a group of publishers offered to take over the network. As a result of this effort, two government panels were established to investigate the media, but the ZDF remained a public broadcaster. Efforts were mounted in Saarland and Bavaria to set up private competitors to the state broadcasters in the late 1960s, but these were largely unsuccessful.

The controversial media law passed in the Saarland in 1967 became the subject of a lengthy constitutional deliberation on the part of the Federal Constitutional Court. In 1981, that court finally decided that private broadcasting was not unconstitutional, as long as the proper legal framework was set up. In particular, such broadcasters would need to ensure that a diversity of opinions would be expressed in broadcasts and that supervisory institutions, similar to those governing the public broadcasters, were established. This decision became the basis for future broadcasting reforms.[52]

In the 1970s, there were intense debates within Germany over the introduction of cable television. The initiative in favor of cabling Germany came from the Deutsche Bundespost, the German postal, telegraphic, and telecommunications agency. The Bundespost proceeded to set up pilot projects and then to begin cabling major German cities. In 1977, the Federal Cabinet of the government of Chancellor Helmut Schmidt decided to oppose the further cabling of the country unless there was "acute public demand," but since the Bundespost was allowed to decide whether such demand existed, the decision had relatively little effect on its behavior. In 1984, the prime ministers of the provincial governments agreed on a framework for delivering television programming via cable, on the model established in the Ludwigshafen cable pilot project. ARD and ZDF began to deliver their signals via cable at this time. A new commercial cable channel called Sat1 was developed for the Lundwigshafen cable project. The two main stakeholders in Sat1 were Leo Kirch, best known for his licensing of the rights to air Hollywood films in Germany, and Springer Verlag, the publishing firm run by Axel Springer and his family. Once the cable system developed to a certain point, then the

---

[52] Noam, *Television in Europe*, pp. 80–4.

question arose as to whether the Bundespost would be allowed to license cable channels to other private broadcasters.

The public broadcasters had a stake in avoiding competition from private broadcasters and hence opposed the use of the Bundespost cable system by private broadcasters. Those in favor of private broadcasting found themselves defending one public monopoly against another for pragmatic reasons. Since the public broadcasters controlled all the terrestrial antennas for over-the-air broadcasts, then private broadcasters would have to set up satellite delivery systems to get their signals economically to the cable systems or directly to homes, so the battle over private vs. public broadcasting expanded into space in the 1980s.

In the early 1980s, the Compagnie Luxembourgeoise de Télévision (CLT) in Luxembourg proposed to deliver both French and German language televisions programs via satellite to France and Germany. The service was to be called RTL (Radiodiffusion-Télévision Luxembourgeoise) plus. One of the early investors in CLT was the Banque Bruxelles Lambert. Later, the Bertelsmann and WAZ (Westfälisch Algemeine Zeitung) publishing groups in Germany would become major stakeholders also. In 1983, a group of private investors, including Clay Whitehead, who had headed the Office of Telecommunications Policy in the Nixon Administration, proposed the launching of an intermediate power broadcast satellite to deliver programming to European listeners, primarily via cable systems. This was the GDL-Coronet project (GDL stands for Grand Duchy of Luxembourg). Whitehead lined up financial support from the investment banking firm, Salomon Brothers, and programming support from Home Box Office (HBO).

The French government strongly preferred the RTL project to Coronet. In the meantime, CLT and the government of Luxembourg began to argue over CLT's claim to a contractual monopoly for broadcasting in Luxembourg (in order to block the Coronet project). The European PTTs (postal, telegraphic, and telecommunications agencies) came to the defense of CLT. The issue began to be framed in terms of resisting an American cultural invasion, and key politicians like François Mitterrand and Helmut Kohl weighed in on the side of CLT. After the 1984 elections in Luxembourg, the new Prime Minister, Jacques Santer, and his government decided to form a new satellite company, the Société Européenne des Satellites (SES), to replace Coronet. SES took over all of Coronet's assets, bought out Clay Whitehead's financial interest, and took over Coronet's contract for an RCA satellite.[53]

[53] *Ibid.*, pp. 301–3.

In 1987, the Bundespost launched its first high-power direct broadcast satellite, the SAT-1. The satellite failed soon after launching. Its solar panels did not unfold. SAT-2 was launched in 1989, but it also experienced a series of technical difficulties. In contrast, the Astra 1A satellite was launched successfully in December 1988 by the SES. Rupert Murdoch had already announced in June 1988 that he intended to use the Astra satellite as the means for delivering his new Sky Channel programming (see the section on the UK above). Whereas SAT-1 and SAT-2 were BSS (Broadcast Satellite Services) satellites, the Astra 1A was an FSS (Fixed Satellite Services) satellite which required less power for its transmission but somewhat larger satellite dishes on the receiver end. In addition, SAT-1 and SAT-2 signals had to be transmitted in the MAC (multiplexed analog components) format, while the Astra satellite could deliver signals in the PAL (phase alternation by line) format – which was already the standard for television signals in Germany. This meant you didn't have to buy a converter or a new receiver to display Astra signals on your television. Both sets of satellites could deliver signals to households either directly (to homes with dishes and satellite receivers) or via cable systems.

Right from the start, Astra was a commercial success. All sixteen of its transponders were leased out quickly. Its signal covered around 15 million European households by the early 1990s. Astra channels initially included among others: Sky Television, Sat.1, RTL Plus, MTV Europe, Screen Sport, Lifestyle, and the Children's Channel. As SES launched additional satellites, it added channels to its cable and DBS lineup. Leo Kirch's movie channel, Pro7, for example, was an early addition to the Astra lineup. Astra offered more channels and a greater variety of programming than either the German or French DBS satellites. 3Sat, a tripartite alliance of ZDF with the Swiss and Austrian public broadcasters, leased a transponder on Astra in 1990. So did Eins Plus, the satellite channel of ARD. ARD and ZDF dropped their transmissions on SAT-1 and SAT-2 in 1993. As a result of this experience, the two public broadcasters became strong supporters for prolonging the life of the PAL standard in Europe and determined opponents of the MAC standard and its variants. By 1994, SAT-1 and SAT-2 no longer carried any television broadcasts.[54]

---

[54] Kleinsteuber, "New Media Technologies in Europe," pp. 12–14; John Peterson, "Toward a Common European Industrial Policy: The Case of High Definition Television," Department of Politics, University of York, no date, p. 12; and Peter Humphreys, *Media and Media Policy in Germany: The Press and Broadcasting Since 1945*, 2nd edition (Providence, RI: Berg, 1994), pp. 270–1.

France

Radio transmission was developed in France[55] under the partnership of the army, the PTT, and the private wireless company Compagnie Sans Fils (CSF). In 1919, the government passed a law giving the French PTT control over public wireless telegraphy. CSF became the first radio broadcaster in France in 1921. By 1923, there were a large number of private radio broadcasters and the PTT confronted the problem of dealing with congestion in the radio spectrum. In 1931, the government purchased the CSF Radio-Paris transmitter and replaced it with a powerful station located in central France. Competition from this powerful station and other government restrictions made it difficult for private radio stations to establish themselves financially. In 1933, under pressure from newspaper publishers, the government prohibited advertising on state-owned stations and began directly funding state broadcasting through a listener license fee. The government used the fee to expand the reach of public broadcasting signals to the entire nation.

In 1935, the French PTT developed a television service with 441 scanning lines. Private radio stations were required under a new law passed that year to have councils of management directly elected by the listeners. The leftist Popular Front government extended the scope of governmental control over both public and private broadcasting between 1936 and 1939. It decreed a ban on all local radio and television broadcasting and, in 1938, instituted a system of censorship. By the beginning of World War Two, fifteen hours of TV programming per week were broadcast over the public television service.

During World War Two, the broadcasting system was divided into two main parts: the northern part of France was controlled by the Nazi occupiers, the southern part by the Vichy regime. Both used radio primarily for propaganda purposes, and strictly limited the ability of private stations to operate independently from the government. When Paris was liberated from German control in June 1944, the broadcasting system was in shambles. The new government of General Charles de Gaulle revoked all private radio broadcasting licenses in March 1945. Some owners of private stations were accused of Nazi collaboration, others simply had their licenses terminated and then were compensated for their losses. In November 1945, the government established by decree Radiodiffusion-Télévision Française (RTF) as a broadcasting monopoly for both radio and television. This monopoly lasted until 1982.

---

[55] This section relies heavily on the descriptions of the French broadcasting environment in Noam, *Television in Europe*, ch. 7; Browne, *Comparing Broadcast Systems*, ch. 2; and Jean Cluzel, *La télévision après six réformes* (Paris: J. C. Lattès et Licet, 1988).

During the presidency of Charles de Gaulle, between 1958 and 1964, there were daily meetings between the RTF and an arm of the Ministry of Information to plan each day's television news broadcast. In 1964, the RTF was reorganized into the Office de Radiodiffusion-Télévision Française (ORTF). Under this new organization, broadcasting became a bit more open and opposition candidates were actually allowed to appear on television broadcasts. It was still difficult, however, for non-Gaullists to get their viewpoints expressed on official radio or television channels. The system was not altered substantially after the upheavals connected with the leftist uprisings of May 1968. During the uprisings, the ORTF general staff and journalists went on strike to protest governmental interference in news reporting. Once general order was restored, the government dismissed or transferred a large number of broadcast journalists, but also increased the number of representatives of ORTF employees on the ORTF's board of governors.

A referendum held in 1969 forced de Gaulle to retire from office and Georges Pompidou was elected president in the ensuing elections. Pompidou abolished the Ministry of Information (although it reappeared a few years later) and placed the ORTF directly under the control of the prime minister. Two separate news teams were created for each of the two ORTF television channels, one headed by a Gaullist and the other by a liberal journalist. For a while, this helped to create some space for opposition views in broadcasting, but a crisis developed in 1971 when it was discovered that ORTF personnel were planning to insert commercials into noncommercial programs and to mention brand names of products in the middle of regular programming. The government dismissed the director general of the ORTF and proposed a new law to govern broadcasting.

The debate over the broadcasting law of 1972 revealed the desire of both the rightist and leftist parties to permit the entry of private broadcasters and to introduce greater diversity of political perspectives into television programming. Neither was satisfied with the new broadcasting law. Further reform was put off until the election of Valéry Giscard d'Estaing in 1974 to the French presidency.

Giscard abolished the Ministry of Information in 1974 and broke up the ORTF into seven separate companies, none of which was financially viable. Two of the new companies dealt with the two national television channels (TF1 and Antenne 2). A third company was formed to administer the regional stations (FR3). A fourth company was in charge of program production, a fifth dealt with transmission issues, and the remaining two with radio and common services respectively. He also appointed his son-in-law in 1976 to head the Haute Conseil de l'Audiovisuel – an advisory body also created in 1974 with members appointed by both the executive and legislative branches of government that was to become eventually an independent regulator of French broadcasting. Giscard also promoted the "telematics" initiative of 1978, which established the basis for the French Minitel system and the TDF-1 DBS satellite. Both were seen as part of a larger strategy of promoting the electronics industry, however, and not as regulatory reforms for broadcasting.

When the Socialist presidency of François Mitterrand began in 1981, much more serious efforts at reform were initiated. Mitterrand put media liberalization high on his agenda. The Socialists had had to rely on pirate radio stations to air their views in the late 1970s (as did striking steelworkers in Lorraine), so the granting of licenses to private radio broadcasters was one of the earliest reform initiatives of the new government. The broadcasting law of 1982 established a regulatory body called the Haute Autorité (HA) that was empowered to grant licenses to private broadcasters. The HA would have nine members: three appointed by the president, three by the chief French legal/constitutional bodies, and three by the Conseil National de l'Audiovisuel.

One of Mitterrand's strongest political supporters was André Rousselet, head of L'Agence Havas, an advertising agency that was founded in 1835, nationalized in 1945, and privatized in 1987.[56] Rousselet convinced Mitterrand in 1983 to permit the establishment of a new pay television channel call Canal Plus with Rousselet as its first president. Canal Plus specialized in airing recently released movies licensed from major movie studios. Its encrypted broadcasts were carried on the TDF-1 satellite to homes with satellite dishes, decoders, and receivers. Because the signal was delivered via satellite, over 80 percent of French households were potential subscribers. Even though the monthly subscription charge for the Canal Plus service was around $32, the number of its subscribers in Europe grew quickly to 7 million by mid-1996.[57]

In 1984, the French government committed itself to lease two channels of the TDF-1 broadcasting satellite, which was to be launched in 1986, to the Luxembourg broadcasting firm CLT-RTL. It reversed this decision in 1985 when it gave a broadcast license instead to a consortium of French and Italian interests which included Silvio Berlusconi, the Italian TV mogul. Jean Riboud, former president of Schlumberger, and Jérôme Seydoux, grandson of Marcel Schlumberger and partial owner of the left-leaning magazine *Nouvel Observateur*, were also members of

---

[56] For a history of Havas, see http://www.havas.fr.
[57] "Canal Plus Sees Digital TV in Belgium This Year," *The Reuter European Business Report*, 30 May 1996, accessed via Nexis-Lexis.

the consortium and political friends of Mitterrand. The license was to become the basis for the creation of a new television channel called "La Cinq" (Channel 5).[58]

Two other TDF-1 transponders were promised at this time to a consortium that included as partners Berlusconi, Seydoux, Robert Maxwell, and Leo Kirch. Maxwell was a British media mogul, competitor to Rupert Murdoch, and Kirch was a German mogul (see the section on Germany above). This eventually became the basis for a sixth channel, TV6 or Le Six, that was dedicated to entertainment programming. All three of the private channels formed during the Mitterrand presidency – Canal Plus, TV6, and La Cinq – "relied heavily on films and series imported from the US."[59]

The March 1986 elections resulted in a partial defeat for the Socialists and their coalition. A period of cohabitation began with Mitterrand as president and Jacques Chirac, leader of the Gaullists, as prime minister. The Chirac government announced that it would abolish the HA and replace it with a body called the Conseil Nationale des Communications et Libertés (CNCL). They privatized Agence Havas: which meant an indirect privatization of Canal Plus and RTL. They also privatized the public channel TF1 and announced their intention to privatize FR3. TF1 was purchased by Francis Bouygues, formerly the owner of a public works group. The deal for La Cinq was restructured so that Robert Hersant, conservative publisher and owner of a chain of radio stations, could join the consortium. Channel 6 was reallocated also to include Luxembourg's CLT (as a 25 percent owner), Lyonnaise des Eaux (25 percent), and a variety of smaller stakeholders. TV6 was turned into a more music-oriented channel called M6.

When Michel Rocard became prime minister in July 1988, the CNCL was disbanded over alleged licensing scandals and replaced temporarily with a group of seven experts, which subsequently became the Conseil Superieur Televiseur under a new broadcasting law passed in 1989.[60] The privatized public channels Antenne 2 (A2) and FR3 merged in 1989, and, in 1992, A2 became France 2 and FR3 became France 3. The merged organization was renamed the France Television Group.[61]

---

[58] At this point, there were three major public television channels under the control of the ORTF: Télédiffusion de France 1 (TF1), Antenne 2 (A2), and France Regionale 3 (FR3).

[59] Susan Emanuel, "Culture in Space: The European Cultural Channel," *Media and Culture*, 14 (1992), p. 284.

[60] Raffaele Barberio and Carlo Macchitella, *Europa delle Televisioni* (Milan: Il Mulino, 1989), p. 97.

[61] Information accessed via the World Wide Web at http://www.france3.fr/ on 8 March 1997.

In the 1980s, the French broadcasting system moved toward the building of both cable and direct broadcast satellite (DBS) delivery systems. France Télécom was responsible for the building of cable infrastructure. It initially favored using fiber optics, but, after conducting some research on optical fiber, decided instead to use coaxial cable. Demand for cable services was not strong, however, and there were only 300,000 paid subscribers by 1991.[62] The TDF-1 satellite was launched in October 1988 by France Télécom. Unfortunately, four of its five transponders were inoperable. TDF-2 was launched successfully in August 1989. The six working transponders on the two satellites were allocated to La SEPT (a new channel geared to European cultural interests),[63] Canal Plus, Canal Plus Allemagne, Sport 2–3, Canal Enfants, Euromusique, Radio France, and Radio France Internationale. In 1990, only 40,000 French homes were able to receive the DBS broadcasts of the satellites and only 278,000 (1.4 percent of French households) were wired for cable.[64]

The French TDF satellites were burdened, as in the case of the German SAT satellites, with the requirement of using MAC formatted signals. Consumer reluctance to purchase expensive and hard to find MAC receivers combined with the availability of the Astra satellite services (see the section on Germany above) greatly limited the commercial appeal of TDF services. As in Germany, the French public and private broadcasters began to deliver their signals in PAL format over the Astra satellite. This helped struggling channels like La SEPT to survive. The French government, in addition, helped La SEPT by encouraging FR3, the third public channel, to provide time for La SEPT's programs on its terrestrial over-the-air services.

In October 1990, the provincial governments of Germany and the central government of France signed a treaty to create a European cultural channel called ARTE with its headquarters in Strasbourg. ARTE automatically included the ongoing activities of La SEPT in Paris, but also a new television production facility in Baden-Baden operated jointly by ARD and ZDF. ARTE commenced broadcasting in 1992. The signing

---

[62] Henry Ergas, "France Telecom: Has the Model Worked?" paper prepared for a seminar organized by the Royal Norwegian Council for Scientific and Industry Research on The Interplay of Government, Industry, and Research in France, Oslo, 29 January 1992, p. 9.

[63] See Susan Emanuel, "Culture in Space." SEPT is short for Société Européenne de Programmes de Télévision.

[64] Kleinsteuber, "Kabel und Satellit," p. 513; Emanuel, "Culture in Space," p. 291; Jean-Pierre Jezequel and Guy Pineau, "French Television," in Alessandro Silj (ed.), *The New Television in Europe* (London: John Libbey, 1992), p. 444; and Paul Slaa, "High Definition Television in Europe: The Risk of Picking a Loser," paper prepared for delivery at the International Communications Association, Miami, May 1992.

of this treaty was part of a larger effort to build up bilateral ties between France and Germany, and particularly to deepen cooperation in high technology areas. It was also evidence of the continuing desire of continental European elites to resist the cultural erosion that they believed attended the growing dominance of English-language electronic media in world media markets.[65]

Italy

Although Italy was the birthplace of one of the key inventors of radio technology, Guglielmo Marconi, radio broadcasting came late to that country. The government of Italy granted a six-year renewable concession to the privately owned Union Radiofonica Italiana (URI) in 1924. In 1929, the Fascist government transformed URI into the Ente Italiano Audiozioni Radiofoniche (EIAR), a semigovernmental enterprise with supervision divided between the government and local Fascist party organizations. In 1931, the EIAR was put under the control of the Societá Idroelettrica Piemontese (SIP), than an electric utility which later became the state telephone company. The name was changed to Radio Audironi Italiane (RAI) in 1944. During World War Two, state control over the broadcasting system was tightened further.

After the end of World War Two, RAI continued to exist but SIP sold its financial stake to the Istituto per la Ricostruzione Industriale (IRI), a government holding company that also held financial stakes in heavy manufacturing industries like construction, shipbuilding, and iron and steel.

Television broadcasting began in 1954, supported by license fees and advertising. A second channel, RAI-2, was launched in 1961. The programming and particularly the news reporting of RAI was by necessity oriented toward the preferences of the ruling party, the Christian Democrats. As the Christian Democrats lost electoral strength in the 1970s, some of the control over RAI content shifted from the Cabinet to Parliament, and the programmers were encouraged to permit the broadcasting of more diverse political viewpoints than had been the case in the 1950s and 1960s. In 1975, the Christian Democrats and the Socialists agreed to split control over the two RAI channels, with the Christian Democrats getting RAI-1 and the Socialists RAI-2. This resulted in the politicization of all sorts of related broadcasting decisions, including personnel questions. A

[65] Emanuel, "Culture in Space"; and Hans J. Kleinsteuber, "The Federal Republic of Germany: The Media System," in *The Media in Western Europe* (London: Sage, 1996), p. 13.

third RAI channel was created in 1979 to provide regional programming, and was dominated by the Italian Communist Party. By 1987, it had become a national channel with a reputation on par with the other two RAI channels.

The RAI was a bit slow to convert over to color broadcasting; it did not do so until 1977. While RAI was able to produce many high quality programs for Italian audiences, the lack of professionalism and the politicization of RAI management hurt the reputation of the broadcaster in the eyes of the viewers. In 1975, Italian Law 103 made it possible for private cable operators to set up operations in competition with the public terrestrial broadcasters. Although licenses were initially hard to obtain, many pirate stations were set up in 1975 to provide programming for local cable systems. The Italian Constitutional Court ruled in 1976 that the RAI monopoly was unconstitutional, thus paving the way for the legalization of the existing pirate stations and making it easier for new private operators to establish services.

The Socialist Party responded to the cable challenge initially by backing a fourth channel for RAI under the control of a private broadcaster (on the model of ITV in Britain), but it switched later to supporting private broadcasting. The Socialist leader, Bettino Craxi, developed close personal ties with Silvio Berlusconi, who was emerging as Italy's "media mogul." The Communists also did not oppose private broadcasting, although they preferred a greater degree of government regulation and the mandating of locally produced programming for all private broadcasters.

The private broadcasters were not allowed to link up with each other to form a national network. The number of private TV stations grew rapidly from 90 in 1976 to 1,319 in 1985. As a result, Italy has become one of largest markets in Europe for television programs. While this meant rapid growth in the importation of foreign television programs it also resulted in a booming domestic television production industry.

Berlusconi entered broadcasting in 1980 after the initial growth phase of private broadcasting in Italy. His first station was Canale 5 in Milan, which became the flagship of his three networks: Canale 5, Italia-1, and Rete-4. Berlusconi's empire grew on the basis of his ability to outbid other broadcasters for talent and on investments in high-quality terrestrial transmission facilities. After securing the financial success of Canale 5, Berlusconi purchased Italia-1 from the Rusconi publishing group, and then Rete-4 from the Mondadori publishing group in 1983. It was from this Italian base that Berlusconi began to diversify his broadcasting holding into the rest of Europe. As mentioned earlier, Berlusconi was a key investor in La Cinq in France, but he also invested in the Tele-5 networks in Germany and Spain. His company, Fininvest, has also pursued ventures in Russia, Poland, Hungary, and Czechoslovakia. By 1986, Berlusconi's networks held roughly the same audience share as the three RAI channels.

In 1990, the Italian Parliament finally passed a bill (which had been under consideration for five years) that extended antitrust rules to broadcasting, forcing Berlusconi to divest one of his newspapers (*Il Giornale* in Milan) to maintain his interests in the three television networks. He was also forced to sell his interests in Tele-piu (a pay TV channel) and in two smaller TV networks: Italia-7 and Junior TV.

RAI responded to the Berlusconi challenge by improving the quality of its programming and by launching Italy's first pay TV service in July 1990. RAI suffered some financial difficulties in the early 1990s, but this was resolved by shifting some of RAI's assets to IRI. Thus, by the early 1990s, the Italian broadcasting scene was marked by two m in players of roughly equal strength, one public and one private.[66]

Japan

In 1896, the Ministry of Communications began research on wireless telegraphy in its Electrical Experiment Center. Wireless telegraphy was successfully demonstrated the next year at Tsukishima Beach on Tokyo Bay. Six years later, the same research group was able to send a wireless signal from Nagasaki to Hawaii. Wireless telephony research began in 1907. Uichi Torigata invented a working wireless telephone system in 1912. The first legislation governing wireless transmissions was passed on 19 June 1915: the Wireless Telegraphy Law. Under that law, the Ministry of Communications was authorized to be the regulator of wireless telegraphy, but not wireless radio broadcasting. In the early 1920s, the Ministry was able to convince the rest of the Japanese government to interpret the law in such a way that radio broadcasting also came under its purview.

The initial idea of the Ministry of Communication was to promote radio broadcasting by regulated private broadcasters with local or regional monopolies. In 1924, the Ministry called for the establishment of one station in each of Japan's three largest cities: Tokyo, Osaka, and Nagoya. Actual broadcasting was scheduled to start in 1925, but the Ministry changed its mind about having private regional broadcasters and asked the three urban companies to merge into a single firm with stringent limitations on profits, a ban on advertising, and censorship of broadcasting

---

[66] Noam, *Television in Europe*, ch. 9.

content. The new national broadcaster was called NHK (Nippon Hoso Kyokai, which means Japan National Broadcasting).

Governmental control over NHK's operations was extensive. The Ministry issued instructions on forbidden content, which were regularly updated. The NHK radio stations were required to install circuit breakers so that any broadcast could be immediately interrupted by a radio inspector. Not only the Ministry of Communication but also other government agencies could petition for inclusion of items on the list of forbidden subjects. NHK did not initially develop its own news-gathering capability because of objections from the newspapers. All news broadcasting was done on the basis of newspaper reports. NHK tried to avoid political subjects, partly as a result of the desire of government officials to restrict the access of extremist political factions (particularly on the left) to mass audiences, but obviously it was not always possible to do this.

The Ministry of Communication put a number of its own former employees on the managing board of NHK from the start of operations. It insisted on having a say in the hiring and firing of key personnel, including radio performers. It pursued a policy of enabling listeners with relatively inexpensive crystal radios to hear NHK broadcasts. In 1928, listeners paid an annual fee (listener contract) of 12 yen to NHK to pay for radio programming and broadcasting costs. The Ministry of Communication and the local governments raked off a small percentage of these fees as a sort of tax on broadcasting.[67]

Beginning in 1928, NHK employees began to visit the homes of listeners to collect the annual contract fee. Later on, listeners were permitted to pay the fee at their local post office but the tradition of sending fee collectors to homes has continued to the present. The salaries paid to fee collectors have remained a major percentage of NHK's total annual expenditures to the present day.

On 18 September 1931, fanatical officers of Japan's Kwangtung Army had plotted to blow up a section of the South Manchurian Railway line in order to precipitate a war against China. Radio reporting of the Manchurian incident demonstrated the power of news broadcasting, and scared Japanese newspapers into another campaign against radio news reporting. But public officials were convinced by the incident that radio was a potentially powerful tool for the government to rally domestic support and counteract negative reporting abroad, and so the Ministry of Communications was given greater control over the operations of NHK nationwide.

[67] Gregory J. Kasza, *The State and the Mass Media in Japan, 1918–1945* (Berkeley, CA: University of California Press, 1988), ch. 4; and NHK, *Fifty Years of Japanese Broadcasting* (Tokyo: NHK, 1977), pp. 10–42.

By the late 1930s, "radio became the principal means of communication between the Japanese state and its subjects."[68] The number of radio receivers increased from 2.9 million in 1936 to 6.6 million in 1941. Over 45 percent of all households owned a radio. License fees were reduced and sets were distributed free of charge to communities in the poorer rural regions in order to hasten the diffusion of radio information throughout the country. Responsibility for censorship shifted from the Ministry of Communication in the late 1930s to the Cabinet Information Bureau. The military-dominated government attempted to insulate the Japanese public from the views of both leftists and religious leaders.

When the war with China broke out in July 1937, radio broadcasting was well entrenched as a key propaganda tool of the military-led government. As in Germany, "decadent" music like jazz was outlawed. Patriotic and nationalist programming was developed and aired, even for children. Japanese citizens were not allowed to own short-wave radios, which meant that they could not listen to foreign broadcasts. Initially, the resources needed to prosecute the war made it difficult to continue the pre-1937 rate of growth of radio receivers and radio contract fees. In 1938, however, NHK designed and marketed a standard receiver that was less expensive than existing models and contract fees resumed their previous growth path. By the end of World War Two, there were over 7 million licensed receivers in Japan, but a lot of them were not working because of war-inflicted damage.

During the occupation, the US occupation authorities first considered and then rejected the idea of establishing a national private broadcaster to compete with NHK. Instead, they pushed for a postwar NHK that would be a public broadcaster independent of the government but regulated by an agency called the Radio Regulatory Commission (RCC) that, like the FCC in the United States, would be empowered to grant licenses to private broadcasters. In December 1950, four private radio broadcasting licenses were approved – two in Tokyo, and one each in Osaka and Nagoya. After the end of occupation in 1952, the RRC was absorbed into the Ministry of Posts and Telecommunications (MPT).

Television research began in the 1920s. Kenjiro Takayanagi of the Hamamatsu College of Engineering succeeding in reproducing the Japanese character "i" (ee) on a reception tube in 1927. Research continued at NHK until the cancellation of the 1940 Tokyo Olympics.[69] Television broadcasting began in 1953. NHK inaugurated its TV operations

[68] *Ibid.*, p. 252.
[69] Nobuo Otsuka, "Japan," in Lynne Schafer Gross (ed.), *The International World of Electronic Media* (New York: McGraw-Hill, 1995), p. 302.

in February; Nippon Television Network Corporation (NTV) started broadcasting in August. NTV was a commercial venture pioneered by Matsutaro Shoriki, former president of *Yomiuri Shimbun*, a leading daily newspaper, and supported initially by US Senator Carl Mundt. NTV received its license the day before the RRC was merged into the MPT. The main investors in NTV initially were Japan's three largest newspaper companies: Asahi, Mainichi, and Yomiuri.

In 1954, there were only 16,000 TV receiver contracts in Japan; the monthly fee was 200 yen. Televisions were expensive. In November 1953, MITI announced a policy of assisting Japanese manufacturers of television receivers. Import restrictions were imposed and MITI helped Japanese firms to license patents for the manufacturing of foreign-designed products.[70] NTT was given the responsibility for constructing a national network of microwave relay towers in order to deliver network television programs to seven major cities: Sapporo, Sendai, Tokyo, Nagoya, Osaka, Hiroshima, and Fukuoka. By 1956, NHK was able to deliver TV signals to about 38 percent of Japanese households. With lower priced sets and more hours of broadcasting, Japanese families began to purchase sets at a rapid rate. By the end of 1956, there were 300,000 receiver contracts in Japan.

In June 1957, the MPT announced its "First Channel Plan." The purpose of the plan was to increase the number of channels to eleven, so as to allow for nationwide distribution of NHK signals and to permit the establishment of local commercial stations. Thirty-four companies received licenses to start thirty-six local broadcasting stations in 1957. By 1961, there were sixty-one of these stations operating. The rules set out for private broadcasting in 1957 included restrictions on the ownership of multiple stations and the ownership of stations by newspapers. NHK was enjoined to increase its educational programming. Licenses were made conditional on the establishment of close ties between local communities and local broadcasters.

Japan was the second nation in the world to introduce regular color television broadcasts. NHK and six commercial stations in Tokyo and Osaka began color broadcasting on 10 September 1960. The CBS color wheel system was used experimentally, but the broadcasters soon switched to the RCA system. The 1964 Tokyo Olympic games were a major impetus in the conversion to color broadcasting. Thanks to the rapid economic growth of the country in the 1960s, advertising revenues of the commercial stations soared. The local stations started to set up national program exchanges, first for news programs and later for general

---

[70] Browne, *Comparing Broadcast Systems*, p. 318.

programming. Eventually, the two national stations – NHK and NTV – were supplemented by the Asahi and Fuji national networks, and the Tokyo Broadcasting System (TBS) also offered its programming to local stations. NHK expanded its offerings to two channels: the first was devoted to general programming, the second focused on educational programming.[71]

Concerns over the quality of television programming became a political issue, especially in the 1960s, and a bill to revise the Broadcast Law was introduced in the Japanese Diet in 1965. Among other things the revised law was designed "to prevent the undesirable influence of vulgar programs on young people." Although the bill did not pass, the message was received and the Japan Broadcasting Federation, which included NHK, the Federation of Commercial Broadcasters, and NTT, established a program improvement committee.[72]

By the early 1970s, TV ownership had spread to almost all households. Color TVs rapidly displaced black and white sets. The number of NHK listener contracts peaked at around 33 million and has remained at that level more or less to the present. While the Diet approved a fee increase in 1976, the steady rise in programming costs and stable revenues resulted in chronic budgetary deficits for NHK. NHK's news coverage is considered the best in the nation, and has the largest audience share for its time slots – over 50 percent. Its general programming is less popular, with audience shares ranging from 30 to 40 percent. NHK executives admitted in interviews that NHK combines some of the world's best transmission facilities with some of the world's worst programming.[73] This creates a problem because as NHK loses audience share to the private broadcasters it has greater difficulty collecting the receiver fees, especially from those households that watch very little of NHK's programming.[74]

Only 550,000 Japanese households were cable subscribers in 1992, and these were mostly in rural areas where reception of terrestrial signals was bad.[75] Cable systems in Japan have a limited number of channels and are notorious for high cost and bad service. A typical installation fee is over $500 and the minimal monthly fee is around $25 for twelve channels or less. The cable operators were upgraded to thirty-channel capability only in the mid-1990s. Tokyo residents were finally offered cable services in the

[71] NHK, *Fifty Years*, pp. 236–9, 251–3.
[72] Browne, *Comparing Broadcast Systems*, pp. 322–3.
[73] Interviews at NHK by the author in September 1989; lecture by Ellis Krauss on NHK at Indiana University, Bloomington, 12 February 1992.
[74] Browne, *Comparing Broadcast Systems*, p. 326; Peter Dunnett, *The World Television Industry: An Economic Analysis* (London: Routledge, 1990), ch. 8.
[75] Otsuka, "Japan," pp. 306–7.

early 1990s with new programming which could make urban cable more competitive with terrestrial and satellite services, but again the prices were high and many people were satisfied with the other services. In short, cable networks and cable operators, who played an increasingly important role in other countries, most notably the United States, Germany, and the smaller European countries like Belgium, played almost no role in the Japanese broadcasting environment. In contrast, private terrestrial and satellite broadcasters were slowly encroaching on the audience share and therefore the primacy of NHK.

NHK dominated broadcasting in Japan but faced increased competition from private broadcasters. One of NHK's competitive strategies to reduce transmission costs, to increase subscriber revenues, and to limit competition from private broadcasters was to move from terrestrial to satellite transmission.

The first Japanese DBS satellite, the BS-1, was launched from the Kennedy Space Center in April 1978. This satellite was used for experimental broadcasts of wideband Hi-Vision signals. The second DBS satellite, the BS-2a, was launched by NHK with funding from the Japanese Space Agency from a Japanese launch site in January 1984. The BS-2a was intended mainly to provide signals to rural areas that were not covered by terrestrial broadcasts (that is, it did not have a "footprint" that covered the entire country) and did not provide twenty-four-hour services. It simply repeated the signals that were sent terrestrially and did not present new types of programs. The BS-2a was quickly disabled by transponder failures, but not before some experimental testing of both NTSC and HDTV broadcasts could be done.

Regular nationwide satellite broadcasts began in July 1987 with the successful launching of the BS-2b satellite. The BS-2b had a two-channel capability, and NHK used both of them to provide new programming that was not available on the terrestrial channels. Satellite Channel 1, for example, provided additional news services, while Satellite Channel 2 presented cultural and entertainment programs.[76] NHK used BS-2b to broadcast NTSC programs for twenty-four hours a day. The Ministry of Posts and Telecommunications changed the rules on the use of original programs for satellite transmission in June 1987, which made it possible for NHK to put original programs on Satellite Channel 1 and to mix the general and educational programs of terrestrial Channels 1 and 2 for

---

[76] "Broadcasting in Japan and the Status Quo [sic] of HDTV," a special issue of *The Telecom Japan*, 15 April 1991, pp. 1–3. *The Telecom Japan* is published in Tokyo by the *The Dempa Times*. This special issue was prepared for an HDTV exhibit at the National Association of Broadcasters meeting in Las Vegas in May 1991.

Satellite Channel 2. When NHK began to experiment with HDTV transmission in June 1989, it used Satellite Channel 2 of the BS-2b satellite to broadcast one hour of HDTV programming per day.

The private broadcasters objected to NHK's monopolization of the DBS satellites, so the next satellite that was launched, the BS-3a, which was placed into orbit in August 1990, had three channels, one of which was to be used by a consortium of commercial broadcasters called Japan Satellite Broadcasting (JSB). The BS-3a was launched successfully, but the solar battery system failed immediately after launching, so a supplementary satellite, the BS-3h was launched in April 1991. When the BS-3h also failed, the future of DBS in Japan began to seem uncertain. However, in August 1991 a third BS-3 satellite, the BS-3b, was launched successfully and pay satellite TV was put into service one month later, followed the next month by an increase in NHK's HDTV broadcasting from one hour to eight hours per day.

At the end of 1990, about 3 million households had registered satellite receivers in Japan. By October 1991, there were 4 million receivers, and 550,000 subscribers to the JSB satellite services. It was expected that the number of receivers would increase to 5.7 million by the spring of 1992 and JSB subscribers would increase to 1 million. After the launch of BS-3b, televisions and VCRs built for the Japanese market increasingly had DBS tuners incorporated into the units.[77]

NHK delivered video programming on two terrestrial channels and two direct broadcast satellite (DBS) channels.[78] There were 6,917 NHK terrestrial broadcasting stations in the forty-seven prefectures of Japan. The large number of stations reflected the mountainous terrain of the country and the need, therefore, to have that many antennas to get national coverage with over-the-air broadcasts. NHK competed typically with two or three private programmers in each of its major broadcast areas, although the competition got weaker the further one went from large cities.

The four main private broadcasters in Japan were Nippon Television Network (NTV), Asahi National Broadcasting, Fuji Television, and Tokyo Broadcasting System (TBS). Unlike NHK, these private broadcasters could not collect receiver fees and were dependent therefore on commercial advertising for most of their revenues. For this reason, they tried to increase their audience shares (at the expense of NHK) to give advertisers an incentive to buy broadcasting time for ads. TV advertising

---

[77] "New Media," in *Japan Electronics Almanac '92* (Tokyo: Dempa, 1992), pp. 254–5.

[78] In addition to the four television channels, NHK has four radio channels and a nationwide teletext service.

accounted for about 30 percent of all advertising in Japan in 1990, totaling around $89 billion. Sports broadcasting (especially baseball) was
particularly popular in Japan, and as a consequence TV advertising during sporting events was the most expensive. The commercial stations also
were more likely to air foreign movies and TV programs than NHK, and
acted over the years to undermine attempts to limit the amount of time
devoted to advertising and to end broadcasts at midnight.[79]

The Japanese bureaucracy favored public broadcasting from the start
as a way of protecting Japan from cultural imperialism and controlling
the Japanese public's access to politically relevant information. For example, political advertising was controlled by NHK. Not only did NHK
produce the actual advertisements, it also controlled the time allocated
for broadcasting them. Time slots were not available for purchase, they
were allocated on a "fair use" basis.[80]

In addition, there was an elaborate system of social relationships between TV and print media journalists and the various Japanese bureau-
cracies that permitted government bureaucrats to control the flow of news
and to limit access to journalists who did not conform to the rules of the
group. There were "reporters' clubs" for each of the major governmental agencies: MITI, Finance, MPT, Agriculture and Fisheries, etc. The
result was that there tended to be an overrepresentation in news coverage of bureaucratic actions; the news often covered related governmental
decisions from the perspective of different agencies (which can get a bit
boring to watch unless you are a political scientist). The reporters were
generally not very critical of agency decisions and often simply presented
the agency's views in their stories.

Conclusions

This chapter contains descriptions of the changes in the broadcasting
environments in six large industrialized nations since the beginning of
radio broadcasting: the United States, Britain, Germany, France, Italy,
and Japan. It shows how they started from strikingly different institutional solutions to address the problem of encouraging and regulating
broadcasting – with the United States being the only country to begin
and end with a system dominated by private broadcasters. In Britain,
Germany, France, Italy, and Japan, state-owned or state-dominated public broadcasters were put in charge of radio broadcasting in the 1920s

---

[79] A. C. Pinder, "Japan," in *Television and Video Almanac 1990* (New York: Quigley Publishing, 1990), pp. 612–13.
[80] Discussion with Ellis Krauss, 12 February 1992. See also Ellis S. Krauss, *Broadcasting
Politics in Japan: NHK and Television News* (Ithaca, NY: Cornell University Press, 2000).

and 1930s. Prior to World War Two, the main changes in broadcasting environments were connected with the rise of fascist regimes in Italy, Germany, and Japan. Although all three of these countries had already established public broadcasting monopolies of one sort or another prior to the age of dictatorships, the latter increased the centralization of control over broadcasting in order better to use the new media for propaganda purposes. After World War Two, the defeat of the dictatorships and post-war American hegemony led to new broadcasting institutions less susceptible to government control (with the notable exception of Gaullist France). While the US government pushed for private broadcasting to be established in Germany and Japan during the postwar occupation of those two countries, it had only limited success. In the late 1950s and early 1960s, television broadcasting began in earnest, together with a rapid diffusion of television receivers in all six countries. The legal and institutional arrangements established for radio broadcasting were modified only slightly to accommodate the new medium.

Private television broadcasting came slowly but surely to the Western European countries and Japan. There were three main factors contributing to the increased role of private broadcasting: (1) changes in technology; (2) the economics of the media and the desire of consumers for greater diversity in programming; and (3) the nearly total market penetration of TV receivers and hence the stabilization of receiver license fees.

With the rise first of cable television and then of satellite broadcasting, it became less and less easy to argue that there needed to be a public monopoly in order to maintain the quality and integrity of national broadcasting. Media firms began to see the value of repackaging content in as many forms as possible. Consumers in all the industrialized nations saw the benefits of having a greater range of choice in programming that the addition of new commercial broadcasting provided and did not seem to mind the advertising that came with it.

For private broadcasting to establish a foothold, however, it was necessary for powerful domestic interests, usually print media publishing firms, to lobby effectively for the establishment of commercial stations. These interests often found allies in the political parties and governments of their nation who, for one reason or another, did not like the political positions taken by public broadcasters. In Britain, the most important political ally was Winston Churchill; in Germany, it was Konrad Adenauer in the 1950s and Helmut Kohl in the 1980s; in France, it was François Mitterrand; in Italy, it was Bettino Craxi.

An additional factor was the slowness with which the public broadcasters realized that greater diversity in programming was necessary to reduce the political pressures for privatization. They were caught in a difficult bind. Their revenues were tied to user fees that were based on the purchase of television receivers. When almost all homes had at least one receiver, the license fee revenues stabilized while programming and transmission costs continued to rise. The public broadcasters in Europe and Japan were able to get their governments to permit them to supplement their incomes with advertising, but they were not able to raise as much advertising revenues as the private broadcasters without endangering their status as public service providers. In addition, although they increased the proportion of their programming that was popular entertainment and decreased their commitment to news broadcasting and cultural and educational programming in order to match the offerings of the new private competitors, they were constrained in how far they could go in this direction since their very existence depended upon a rationale that linked public broadcasting with a broader cultural mission.

This was the situation the public broadcasters found themselves in at the end of the 1980s, when the issue of making a transition to HDTV arose. It is understandable, therefore, that the public broadcasters in Europe and Japan would be looking for ways to shore up their positions. In Japan, the main approach taken by NHK, as we will see in chapter 4, was to try to dominate satellite broadcasting and to control the technologies associated with the transition to HDTV in alliance with the major manufacturers of consumer electronics. In Europe, the public broadcasters tried a similar strategy in alliance with the PTTs and the two largest electronics manufacturers in Europe: Philips and Thomson (see chapter 6). The European public broadcasters were notably less successful in this than NHK because of the greater political power of private broadcasting interests in Europe than in Japan, but all suffered from a continued decline in audience shares in spite of their efforts. While NHK was more successful in its HDTV strategy than the European public broadcasters, nevertheless it failed to win broad public acceptance of its analog version of HDTV and found itself again on the defensive politically with the switch to digital television in the United States. Similarly, the Europeans had to adjust to the US decision to adopt a digital television standard after 1993. This is the story that will be told in chapters 7–9.

3   Digital convergence: consumer electronics

Introduction

One of the key arguments in this book is that the idea of digital convergence played a key role in the politics of HDTV and digital television. Digital convergence is the progressive blurring of the boundaries between the consumer electronics, computer, and entertainment (especially television and film) industries made possible by the digitalization of signal delivery systems of all sorts (e.g. telephone, broadcast television, cable, and satellite infrastructures). The power of the idea of digital convergence derives partly from its interpretation and use by important stakeholders in the debates over advanced television. Three important industries – consumer electronics, computers, and entertainment – are powerful stakeholders in these debates. The focus in this chapter will be on the consumer electronics industry, with the primary purpose of explaining the Japanese HDTV initiative as a response to the shift of high-volume consumer electronics production from Japan to other East Asian countries.

The consumer electronics industry

The consumer electronics industry is an important member of the family of electronics industries. The two main categories of products in the consumer electronics industry are audio and video equipment, but an increasing share of consumer electronics sales has been in a residual category that includes video games and home computers. Another name for the residual category is "multimedia" because of the increased incorporation of digital audio and video content on software for video games and home computers.

What used to be a simple distinction between consumer electronics and computers is breaking down because of digital convergence. Part of the reason for this is the increased use of digital circuitry in all types of electronic systems. Until the last decade or so, very few consumer electronics devices required the use of digital circuits. Most consumer devices relied on analog circuits, because analog circuitry was the only available way to handle the high bandwidth requirements of radio and television. Now it is routine to find digital microprocessors and digital memory devices in telephones, radios, televisions, and even in vacuum cleaners. Many newer consumer electronics devices – such as CD players, DVD players, and MP3 players – are completely digital until the final stage of output to speakers and displays.

In recent years, there has been rapid growth in "home information systems." These systems integrate devices that were previously stand-alone products – putting them under some sort of centralized control. Further miniaturization of circuitry and displays is making possible a new set of consumer electronics products called "personal electronics"– such as notebook computers and personal digital assistants (PDAs) – which are relatively inexpensive and highly portable. These products bring to the individual consumer capabilities previously available only to larger business customers.

The development of cellular telephone networks and other "wireless" digital data transmission systems is likely to make the market for advanced portable electronics more important at home, at work, and at play. Some of the boundaries between "consumer" and "industrial" products are breaking down thanks to the increasing use in both of digital circuitry and their connection to telecommunications networks. It will eventually become necessary to think of the market in terms of portable and non-portable products rather than in terms of the location (home, factory, or office) of end-users of those products.

Rapid growth and technological change have characterized the consumer electronics industry since the 1950s. The main beneficiaries of growth in the last two decades have been Japan and the newly industrializing countries (NICs) of Asia. The consumer electronics industry in the United States went from a position of global dominance after World War Two to its current position of extreme weakness (to be explained below). The consumer electronics industry in Europe experienced strong competitive pressures from Asian producers in the 1970s and responded with a combination of highly concentrated ownership, government subsidies for R&D, and barriers to trade and inward investment (including the use of incompatible European standards).

The next round of competition in consumer electronics products is likely to involve a new set of advanced television technologies (including both HDTV and DTV). HDTV receivers will differ from the current generation of televisions by doubling the horizontal and vertical resolution of video images, and by providing a wider screen and digital stereo sound. Advanced television technologies are going to be more similar

Table 3.1 *World sales of consumer electronics, 1995–9, in billions of US dollars*

	Video products	Audio products	Information and telecom products	Total
1995	76.2	50.3	66.7	193.2
1996	76.4	48.0	73.8	198.2
1997	71.6	43.2	76.2	191.0
1998	69.0	41.0	79.5	189.5
1999	71.1	41.8	90.0	202.9

Source: Euromonitor.

to those found in computers and telecommunication equipment than were the technologies underlying previous generations of video equipment. For this reason, all the major industrial countries are interested in enhancing their advanced television capabilities and are trying to compensate for whatever weaknesses they have in this area.

Demand for consumer electronics products

Consumer electronics products are very diverse. They range from the simplest electronic calculators and watches up to the almost professional-quality equipment purchased by audiophiles and videophiles. The Consumer Electronics Show held each year in Las Vegas by the Consumer Electronics Manufacturers Association (CEMA) of the Electronic Industries Association (EIA) has thousands of exhibitors from dozens of countries. Each year hundreds of new products are introduced as some company or individual entrepreneur finds yet another way to apply microelectronics technology to meet some kind of consumer demand. A new product introduced in 1989, for example, was the notebook computer, essentially a small hand-held computer with a tiny keyboard and a liquid crystal display (LCD). In 1991, palmtop computers were introduced which were so small that they required the use of a pen or stylus instead of a keyboard as the main input device. Palmtop computers like the Palm Pilot, sold by 3Comm, are almost as ubiquitous now as desktop and notebook computers.

In 1999, world sales of consumer electronics totaled around $202 billion. Information and telecommunications products increased their share of the consumer electronics market considerably in the late 1990s (see Table 3.1). World sales of both video and audio products declined both relatively and absolutely during this period.

The world market for televisions increased to 120 million units in 1996 from around 70 million units in 1988. In the 1980s, Europe and the United States accounted for over half of the world demand for televisions. But the share of the rest of the world grew rapidly in the 1990s, especially in China.[1] High consumption of TVs and VCRs in the United States and Europe and limited local production meant that these two regions would be major net importers of consumer electronics. Neither the United States nor Western Europe exported much, while Japan remained a major exporter. Most of Japan's limited imports of consumer electronics came from other Asian countries (see the section on Japanese production and trade below).

The United States

The largest national market for consumer electronics was the United States. Sales increased from about $8 billion in 1977 to over $88 billion in 2000 (see Table 3.2). The largest single sub-market within consumer electronics in 2000 was personal computers at $16.4 billion (included in Table 3.2 under the "Other" category). Home computers surpassed color televisions as the number one earner of consumer electronics sales in 1992. Over $9 billion worth of televisions were sold in the United States in 2000; about $6 billion of these were analog direct-view color TVs; the remainder were projection TVs, TV/VCR combinations, and digital TVs.

The market for VCRs in the United States was about $1.9 billion in 2000, down from a peak of over $4.7 billion in 1985.[2] Unit demand remained fairly strong but average prices declined rapidly. Sales of video products (TVs, VCRs, camcorders, etc.) made up less than 14 percent of the total market for consumer electronics in the United States in 2000, down from about 30 percent in 1990. Sales of digital products such as home computers, CD players, DVD players, and other digital devices increased rapidly in the 1990s.

The US trade deficit in consumer electronics increased rapidly in the 1980s and 1990s. In 2000, for example, the United States had a trade deficit of $18.7 billion in consumer electronics, up from $7.9 billion

---

[1] BIS Mackintosh as cited in Jane Rippeteau, "Whose Hand Will Be On the Horizontal Hold?" *Financial Times*, 21 April 1988, p. 17; Stanford Resources, Inc., *Television Systems: Market and Technology Trends in a Digital World* (San José, CA: Stanford Resources, 1998).

[2] All the statistics cited in this section come from the Consumer Electronics Manufacturers Association, which is part of the Electronic Industries Association of the United States.

Table 3.2 US factory sales of consumer electronics, 1977–2000, in millions of dollars, including imports

Year	Mono TV	Color TV	VCRs	Audio systems	Audio components	Home radio	Portable radio	Car audio	Other	Total
1977	530	3,289	180	606	1,275	523	1,208	534	0	8,145
1978	549	3,674	326	748	1,143	436	1,649	582	0	9,107
1979	561	3,685	389	748	1,178	436	1,739	623	0	9,359
1980	588	4,210	621	809	1,424	468	1,403	1,368	0	10,891
1981	505	4,349	1,127	720	1,363	501	1,157	2,000	569	12,291
1982	507	4,253	1,303	573	1,181	530	971	2,100	2,659	14,077
1983	465	5,002	2,162	630	1,268	565	1,102	1,900	4,228	17,322
1984	419	5,538	3,585	976	913	661	1,191	2,500	5,236	21,019
1985	328	5,565	4,738	1,372	1,132	379	1,140	2,761	7,658	25,073
1986	373	6,040	3,978	1,370	1,358	408	1,389	3,135	9,428	27,479
1987	341	6,303	3,442	1,048	1,715	409	1,469	3,523	10,773	29,023
1988	236	6,277	2,848	1,225	1,854	377	1,547	3,937	11,946	30,247
1989	156	6,530	2,625	1,217	1,871	379	1,595	4,125	13,168	31,666
1990	132	6,376	2,439	1,270	1,935	360	1,645	4,292	14,488	32,937
1991	61	5,979	2,454	1,264	1,805	310	1,780	4,107	22,848	40,608
1992	47	6,591	2,947	1,370	1,586	324	2,096	4,457	25,770	45,188
1993	40	7,316	2,851	1,464	1,635	307	2,187	4,803	30,091	50,694
1994	38	7,225	2,869	1,703	1,686	306	2,495	5,123	37,569	59,014
1995	34	6,798	2,767	1,677	1,911	284	2,506	5,031	43,522	64,530
1996	29	6,492	2,815	1,537	1,808	291	2,149	4,326	48,619	68,066
1997	27	6,023	2,618	1,688	1,606	300	2,033	4,521	53,100	71,916
1998	23	6,122	2,409	1,754	1,448	300	2,146	4,439	57,085	75,726
1999	20	6,199	2,333	1,843	1,442	348	2,086	4,767	62,637	81,675
2000	15	6,140	1,861	1,863	1,523	351	1,640	4,869	69,890	88,152

Source: Electronic Market Data Book (Washington, DC: CEMA, various years). 1991 to 2000 figures are from the Electronic Market Data Book (Arlington, VA: eBrain Market Research, 2001).

in 1983.[3] About 23 million VCRs were sold in the United States in 2000, over 90 percent of which were imported directly, mainly from Mexico, Japan, and Korea. Less than 10 percent of the VCRs sold in the United States were assembled in the United States. Since larger TVs were increasingly assembled or manufactured in the United States, a large part of the US trade deficit in consumer electronics was attributable to imports of other video products: e.g., camcorders, DVD players, and VCRs.[4]

Japan

Domestic demand for consumer electronics peaked in 1988 at 2.15 trillion yen. The Japanese overall trade surplus in consumer electronics peaked at around 3.5 trillion yen in 1985, but declined steadily to less that 0.9 trillion yen in 1996 (see Table 3.3). The United States was by far the single most important destination for Japanese exports.[5] The main sources of imports into Japan were other East Asian countries like Korea, Taiwan, and Hong Kong.

Japanese exports of consumer electronics were hurt by the revaluation of the yen in 1985; but the main damage to domestic production in the 1990s was caused by the decline in the Japanese growth rate, the so-called "bubble economy." In 1985, exports of consumer electronics peaked at around 3.5 trillion yen. By 1996, they had dropped to around 1.3 trillion yen. Most of the decline in the value of consumer electronics production and export revenues in Japan was due to a combination of the bubble economy, falling prices of older products, and the offshoring of production by Japanese companies to lower wage countries. Imports remained low, however, and most domestic demand was still serviced by domestic production.

Western Europe

Sales of consumer electronics in Western Europe increased from 30 billion euros in 1986 to over 41 billion in 1990 and then declined to less

---

[3] *Electronic Market Data Book* (Washington, DC: Electronic Industries Association, 1988), p. 124; *Electronic Market Data Book* (Arlington, VA: eBrain Market Research, 2001), p. 38.

[4] Allen Lenz, "Slimming the US Trade and Current Account Deficits," *The AMEX Bank Review, Special Papers*, No. 16 (October 1988).

[5] This figure is base on statistics from the Japanese Ministry of Finance as reported in *Facts and Figures of the Japanese Electronics Industry '91* (Tokyo: Electronic Industries Association of Japan, 1991), pp. 36–7 and 40–1.

Table 3.3 *Consumer electronics production, exports, imports, trade balance, and domestic demand in Japan, 1978–96, in trillions of yen*

Year	Production	Exports	Imports	Trade balance	Domestic demand
1978		1.352	.021	1.331	
1979	2.290	1.480	.037	1.443	0.847
1980	2.932	2.047	.038	2.009	0.923
1981	3.668	2.600	.033	2.567	1.101
1982	3.506	2.508	.026	2.482	1.024
1983	3.834	2.702	.020	2.682	1.152
1984	4.719	3.306	.023	3.283	1.436
1985	4.912	3.519	.024	3.495	1.417
1986	4.434	2.601	.032	2.569	1.865
1987	3.971	1.939	.060	1.879	2.092
1988	4.260	2.208	.098	2.110	2.150
1989	4.191	2.287	.145	2.142	2.049
1990	4.436	2.618	.113	2.505	1.931
1991	4.696	2.696	.136	2.560	2.136
1992	3.564	2.258	.156	2.102	1.462
1993	3.059	1.752	.172	1.580	1.479
1994	2.772	1.542	.238	1.304	1.468
1995	2.434	1.313	.333	0.980	1.454
1996		1.283	.410	0.873	

Note: Domestic demand = production plus imports minus exports.
Source: EIAJ, *Facts and Figures of the Japanese Electronics Industry* (various years).

than 30 billion in 1997 (see Table 3.4).[6] The last three years of the 1990s witnessed a return to positive growth. Germany, the UK and France accounted for more than 60 percent of total sales in the European Union during most of this period.

The European market for color televisions was around 30 million units in 1996, up from 15.9 million units in 1986. Color TVs accounted for over 35 percent of total consumer electronics sales in 2000. Sales of widescreen televisions were particularly strong in the late 1990s. In the UK alone, for example, sales of widescreen TVs increased from around 350,000 units in 1998 to around 650,000 units in 1999. Britain, France, Germany and Italy accounted for around 70 percent of the total European demand for

---

[6] The main source of statistics in this section is the European Association of Consumer Electronics Manufacturers (EACEM). European consumer electronics sales figures, unlike those in the United States and Japan, do not include estimates of sales of home computers. The main categories included are: color TVs, VCRs, DVD players, camcorders, static and portable audio equipment, car audio, and recording media.

Table 3.4 *Consumer electronics sales in Europe, 1986–2000, in billions of euros*

Year	Sales
1986	30.0
1987	32.9
1988	35.3
1989	37.4
1990	41.1
1991	40.3
1992	38.3
1993	34.4
1994	33.1
1995	31.4
1996	30.2
1997	29.6
1998	30.7
1999	31.6
2000	33.7

Source: European Association of Consumer Electronics Manufacturers (EACEM).

televisions.[7] Sales of VCRs remained high in unit volume but declined in value as average prices declined. As sales of DVD players increased, sales of VCRs began to decline in absolute terms.

World production of consumer electronics equipment

North America and Europe were the two largest regional markets for consumer electronics, although Japan's domestic market was also sizeable. Most of the consumer equipment sold in the United States was either imported or manufactured locally by foreign firms. Most local manufacturing was assembly only. In Europe, a much larger percentage of consumer electronics products were manufactured locally and the local content (value-added) of those products was on average higher than in the United States. Almost all the consumer electronics sold in Japan were still made in Japan, although imports from other Asian countries began to increase in the mid-1980s.

---

[7] *Consumer Europe 1988* (London: Euromonitor, 1988), pp. 394–9; Stanford Resources, *Television Systems.*

Table 3.5 *Production of consumer electronics by region, 1984–93, in billions of dollars*

Year	USA	Japan	W. Europe	NICs	Total
1984	6.4	19.9	7.0	n/a	33.3
1985	5.7	20.4	7.1	6.0	39.2
1986	6.3	26.1	10.1	7.7	50.2
1987	6.1	27.2	12.1	10.6	56.0
1988	7.2	33.2	12.5	12.9	65.8
1989	6.2	30.5	12.1	13.3	62.1
1990	6.4	30.6	12.3	13.6	62.9
1991	7.6	34.8	15.4	13.2	71.0
1992	7.9	29.7	13.9	13.0	64.5
1993	8.2	29.2	14.3	12.5	64.2

Sources: EIAJ, *Facts and Figures on the Japanese Electronics Industry*; 1988 (p. 17), 1991 (p. 115), and 1994 (p. 109). The EIAJ stopped publishing these data in 1993.

According to the Electronic Industries Association of Japan (EIAJ), world production of consumer electronics totaled $64.2 billion in 1993 (see Table 3.5).[8] This represented around 11 percent of world production in electronics. Consumer electronics production grew at an average rate of 10.6 percent per year between 1985 and 1990. Growth in sales and production of traditional consumer electronics equipment was slower in the 1990s; sales and production of digital devices like personal computers grew more rapidly.

Japan had the largest share of global consumer electronics production, around 49 percent in 1990. Western Europe and the Asian NICs had roughly equal shares, around 20 percent each, in that year. The United States produced a little over 10 percent of the global total of consumer electronics equipment. Of the three industrialized regions, the biggest gap between production and consumption of consumer electronics was in the United States.

Production in the United States

While only a little more than 12 percent of the US television market was supplied by US-owned firms in the late 1980s, it was estimated that

---

[8] It should be noted that the EIAJ uses a somewhat narrower definition of what constitutes consumer electronics equipment than does the EIA: radios, monochrome televisions, color televisions, video tape recorders, prerecorded disks and tapes, and audio equipment. It does not include home computers or video games, which makes its figures somewhat smaller than those of the EIA.

approximately 70 percent of the value of TVs sold on the US market was domestic in origin. Asian and European firms had set up plants in the United States to manufacture picture tubes and cabinets and assembled large-screen televisions locally. The tubes and cabinets combined with local labor costs were the main contributors to the domestic content of TVs sold in the United States. The circuitry contributed only about 5–7 percent of the manufacturing costs of an average television. Very little of this circuitry was produced in the United States. By the late 1990s, however, most of the manufacturing value-added moved to Mexico after both US and foreign firms moved their assembly operations south of the border.

The major Japanese producers established US final assembly operations in the following sequence: Sony in 1972, Matsushita in 1974, Sanyo in 1976, Mitsubishi in 1977, Toshiba in 1978, Hitachi and Sharp in 1980. With the exception of Matsushita's purchase of Motorola's Quasar division in 1974, all of the Japanese facilities were new ones. The Korean firm, LG, built an assembly plant in California in 1981. Philips and Thomson established their presence in the United States mainly through acquisitions of US firms. Philips purchased Magnavox in 1975 and Sylvania in 1981. Thomson bought RCA/GE consumer electronics from GE in 1987. Thus, every major supplier of consumer electronics to the United States had at least one assembly operation in the United States by the late 1980s. Some – like Philips, Sony, and Thomson – had major research facilities as well as manufacturing operations in the United States.

Production in Mexico

The largest source of television and VCR exports to the United States by the 1990s was Mexico. Most of these exports came from the so-called *maquiladora* plants of multinational firms in Northern Mexico. Under Mexican law, firms that assembled products solely for export did not have to pay import duties on imported components. Under Sections 806.30 and 807.00 of the US tariff code, firms that established plants overseas for production of exports to the United States did not have to pay export duties on components and only paid import duties on the value added abroad. Accordingly, all the major firms involved in supplying consumer electronics products to the United States located assembly plants below the border with Mexico to take advantage of both US and Mexican laws. The primary incentive for doing this was to reduce direct labor costs in the assembly phase of manufacturing.

In 1987, there were about 1,250 maquiladoras employing 330,000 workers.[9] Japanese firms owned only thirty of them, but they employed about 19 percent of all maquiladora workers.[10] Zenith had large maquiladora plants in Reynosa and Matamoros that produced around 60 percent of all the TVs Zenith sold in the United States. After the closure of its remaining assembly plants in the United States in 1992, Zenith's Mexican facility would assemble *all* the TVs Zenith sold in the United States. Both Philips and Thomson also had Mexican plants. Thomson closed its last remaining US assembly operation in 1997.[11]

Production in Japan

Production of consumer electronic equipment in Japan rose dramatically between 1967 and the mid-1980s (see Table 3.2). Even though domestic production declined in the 1990s, overseas production of consumer electronics equipment by Japanese firms more than offset the decline in domestic production. In 1967, Japanese firms produced 1.3 million color TVs. In 1985, production peaked at 17.9 million units but fell back to around 14 million for the next two years.[12] Japanese firms began to move upmarket to deal with growing competition from TV producers in Korea and Taiwan. In addition, they made major investments in new products like VCRs, camcorders, and DVD players. Because Japanese firms were able to dominate VCR and audio equipment markets in the 1980s, they were able to increase overall production of consumer electronics even though unit production of TVs stabilized and the overall value of TV production declined with lower average unit prices. The value of VCR production in Japan first exceeded the value of TV production in 1981. By 1987, the value of VCR production was almost twice the value of TV production. VCR revenues began to decline in the mid-1980s despite the fact that volume continued to increase because of lower average prices.

The largest consumer electronic firms in Japan were Hitachi, Matsushita, Mitsubishi, NEC, Sanyo, Sharp, Sony, and Toshiba. All of these firms, with the possible exception of Sony, were vertically integrated

---

[9] Mexican National Chamber of Industry and American Chamber of Commerce in Mexico as cited in the *San Francisco Chronicle*, 29 February 1988, p. A6.

[10] Larry Rohter, "Plants in Mexico Help Japan to Sell to US," *New York Times*, 26 May 1987, p. 25; John Eckhouse, "Japan Finds Mexico a Profitable 'Back Door' to US," *San Francisco Chronicle*, 1 March 1988, p. A8.

[11] All of the chassis for Thomson's televisions are assembled in its plant in Juarez, Mexico. Only cabinets and tubes are manufactured in the United States.

[12] *Facts and Figures on the Japanese Electronics Industry* (Tokyo: Electronic Industries Association of Japan, 1988), p. 51.

electronics companies with ties to other firms via *keiretsu*.[13] Japanese consumer electronics companies all produced a significant proportion of the semiconductor components used in their own consumer products, but only some of them were self-sufficient in cathode ray tubes (CRTs). Sharp, for example, depended on other Japanese firms for its supply of CRTs. This dependency on others for CRTs gave Sharp a strong incentive to invest in alternative display technologies, which was the origin of Sharp's early and large investments in liquid crystal displays (LCDs). Japanese strength in semiconductors and LCDs was an important reason for the continued health of their consumer electronics business in the face of growing competition from other East Asian countries.

Production in other East Asian countries

The reduced trade surplus in Japanese consumer electronics in the late 1980s was due mostly to increased competition from producers in East Asia, especially in Korea and Taiwan. The largest increase in Japanese imports from Asia between 1985 and 1987 was in audiocassette recorders, but increases also occurred in color TVs and VCRs.

Most of the production for export to Japan in Asia was by subsidiaries of Japanese firms or by local makers under OEM contracts.[14] Exports to the rest of the world, however, were not so closely tied to Japanese ownership or contractual arrangements. The Asian NICs were globally competitive in consumer electronics. They combined favorable labor market conditions (high skill-base and relatively low wages) with successful transfer and adaptation of semiconductor and electronics assembly technologies from Japan and the United States. As they came under competitive pressure from lower-wage countries in Asia and elsewhere, the Asian NICs, like Japan, moved upmarket into more sophisticated and more expensive products, thus increasing the pressure on Japan to promote new generations of consumer products like HDTV.

The three largest Korean firms – LG (formerly called Lucky Goldstar), Samsung, and Daewoo – produced their own designs under their own labels, unlike the smaller electronics firms of Hong Kong and Taiwan. Each of these firms had their own semiconductor operations. They all

[13] *Keiretsu* are alliances of firms in unrelated markets clustered around a lead bank. The members of a keiretsu tend to hold shares in other members, a practice called cross-shareholding. The cross-shareholding gives the members of a kereitsu a major incentive to cooperate with one another. In Japan, most competition is between firms that belong to different keiretsu. The keiretsu system guarantees a high level of domestic competition in Japan while insulating Japanese firms from hostile takeovers.

[14] *Japan Electronics Almanac 1989* (Tokyo: Dempa, 1989), ch. 9.

produced their own CRTs for televisions and computer monitors. Korea began their own program to develop HDTV technologies in the early 1990s and funded it initially at around $200 million per year.

The two largest Taiwanese firms – Tatung and Sampo – also manufactured color televisions. Tatung began manufacturing VCRs in 1982. Taiwanese electronics strategy was focused more on information technology than on consumer electronics. Taiwan dominated world production first of assembled printed circuit boards for personal computers, then for laptop/notebook computers, and later for assembled laptops and notebooks. In the 1990s, Tatung's Chunghwa Picture Tubes (CPT) Division challenged the Japanese and Korean firms for dominance of world markets for TV picture tubes and computer displays.

Hong Kong, in contrast to both Taiwan and Korea, focused on the production of small consumer items like portable black-and-white TVs, portable radios, audiocassette recorders, hand-held video games, and the like. Hong Kong producers tended to be small firms working under contract with larger distributors.

After 1987, the People's Republic of China (PRC) started to become a major producer of consumer electronics equipment. The opening of PRC markets to international trade produced initially a major influx of consumer items from Japan and other Asian countries to meet domestic demand for TVs and VCRs. Eventually, foreign firms began to set up first assembly and then full manufacturing facilities in the PRC in order to service both the Chinese domestic market and foreign markets. Philips, for example, negotiated a joint venture with Novel of Hong Kong and China National Huadong of the PRC to produce 1.6 million color TV tubes per year in Jiangsu province. Philips also worked with PRC firms on joint ventures for VCRs and bipolar integrated circuits.[15] All the Korean and Taiwanese firms had Chinese subsidiaries by the late 1990s.

The success of the Asian NICs in becoming internationally competitive in consumer electronics resulted in a number of attempts by the Western countries to erect new barriers to imports. A series of antidumping cases were brought against Asian producers in the United States and in the European Community, some of them resulting in the imposition of dumping duties, "voluntary" export restraints, and quotas. The continued access of East Asian producers to North American and West European markets of the wealthy countries increasingly depended on concessions their governments made to open domestic markets to foreign competition.

---

[15] "N.V. Philips Enters China Color TV Tube Venture," *Electronic News*, 23 November 1987, p. 7.

Production in Western Europe

A major difference between Europe and the United States was that the major European consumer electronics firms were able to survive in the presence of Asian competition. They did so primarily on the basis of extensive government assistance in various forms including R&D subsidies, the promotion of mergers and acquisitions, the granting of exclusive patent rights for European standards, and a variety of trade and investment barriers designed to keep out Asian competitors.[16]

The two most important European firms – Philips and Thomson – produced televisions and VCRs in high volume in both Europe and North America. Philips purchased two large American TV firms: Magnavox in 1975 and Sylvania in 1981. Thomson purchased the consumer electronics operations of RCA/GE in 1987, making it the number one producer of televisions in the United States. Thomson marketed and assembled Japanese-designed VCRs for Europe and North America; only Philips had the capability to manufacture its own VCRs as of the late 1980s.

Japanese firms supplied only 14 percent of the European color TV market in 1986. The Japanese firms were kept out of the market in the 1960s and 1970s by restrictions on the licensing of patents for PAL and SECAM technologies. In more recent times Japanese firms have avoided local production of televisions because the Europeans made it clear that they would not make it easy for Japanese firms to establish a manufacturing presence in Europe. No Japanese producer could be sure that products assembled in Britain, for example, would be considered sufficiently European to be exported freely to France. Since it was still possible to make money by exporting and licensing the production of VCRs and camcorders, the Japanese firms focused their European activities in these areas.[17]

European firms were weaker in VCR and camcorder markets than they were in color televisions. Japanese firms supplied about 40 percent of the European VCR market in the 1980s. Other than Philips, which developed its own VCR technologies in collaboration with Sony, the European firms all had to produce VCRs under joint ventures with Japanese firms. Examples are JVC–Thomson, Matsushita–Bosch, Amstrad–Funai, and Hinari–Shintom.

---

[16] See, for example, Alan Cawson, Peter Holmes, and Anne Stevens, "The Interaction Between Firms and the State in France: The Telecommunications and Consumer Electronics Sectors," in Stephen Wilks and Maurice Wright (eds.), *Comparative Government–Industry Relations* (Oxford: Clarendon Press, 1987); Rhonda J. Crane, *The Politics of International Standards: France and the Color TV War* (Norwood, NJ: Ablex, 1979).
[17] Interview by the author with a representative of the Electronic Industries Association of Japan in Düsseldorf, Germany, June 1987.

The rapid decline of the US television industry

The American television industry, which led the world into the television age, was only a shadow of its former self by the mid-1980s. At the beginning of the 1950s, there were 140 domestically owned firms in the industry; only fifty remained by 1956, twenty-seven by 1960, five by 1980, virtually none by 2000.[18] The number of workers in the industry declined from a high of 100,000 in 1966 to 33,000 in 1984.[19] As of 1986, only three US-owned firms – Zenith, RCA, and Curtis Mathes – manufactured TVs in the United States. In 1987, RCA's TV manufacturing facilities were sold to General Electric (GE) and then sold again in January 1988 to Thomson CSF, a French firm. After 1987, the only high-volume manufacturer of televisions that remained under US ownership was Zenith.

In the late 1980s and early 1990s, Zenith operated its TV manufacturing operations at a loss, because low prices in the industry as a whole made it impossible for it to make money on TVs. Thomson suffered financial losses in the US market for the same reason, although it had some financial success with the introduction of a new DBS system in the early and mid-1990s. Zenith sold its more profitable computer business (Zenith Data Systems) to Groupe Bull of France in 1990 in order to stay in the television business. It solicited new investments in 1991 from a Korean firm, Lucky Goldstar (now called LG), to ward off a hostile buyout by a New Jersey-based air-conditioner company. In 1999, Zenith became a wholly owned subsidiary of LG.

Some of the relative decline of the US television industry could be attributed to increased production in lower-wage countries in East Asia and Mexico. This was particularly true of lower-priced audio equipment and TVs. But the world leader in consumer electronics production by the early 1980s was Japan, no longer a low-wage country, and production grew rapidly in other East Asian countries, particularly in Korea and Taiwan, that had experienced a rapid rise in wages. Japan's share of global consumer electronics production in 1990 was 49 percent. Of the top ten firms producing color TVs in the early 1980s, five were Japanese.[20]

---

[18] James H. Wooster, "Industrial Policy and International Competitiveness: A Case Study of US–Japanese Competition in the Television Industry," Ph.D. dissertation, University of Massachusetts, February 1986, p. 35; Ira C. Magaziner and Robert B. Reich, *Minding America's Business: The Decline and Rise of the American Economy* (New York: Vintage, 1982), p. 171.

[19] David H. Staelin, "The Decline of US Consumer Electronics Manufacturing: History, Hypotheses and Remedies," Consumer Electronics Working Group, Commission on Industrial Productivity, MIT, Cambridge, MA, April 1988, p. 18.

[20] The five largest Japanese color TV producers in 1982 were: Matsushita, Sony, Toshiba, Hitachi, and Sanyo. See BIS-Mackintosh data cited in Jacques Pelkmans and Rita Beuter,

Japanese firms continued to lead the world in the production of higher-priced TVs, VCRs, and camcorders, although increasingly those products were assembled in Mexico and other East Asian countries and not in Japan itself.

The success of Japanese consumer electronics products in world markets was the result of a variety of intelligent technological and marketing strategies on the part of Japanese firms, along with some predatory pricing (documented in a series of successful antidumping investigations).[21] Of primary importance was the early replacement of tubes with semiconductors. Sony Corporation sold the first all-transistor monochrome TV in 1959. Soon after, all the major Japanese consumer electronics firms introduced transistorized monochrome receivers. A US manufacturer, Motorola, developed the first prototype solid-state color television in 1966, but Hitachi was the first to produce solid-state color TVs in high volume. Hitachi introduced it to the market in 1969. By 1970, 90 percent of all color TVs produced in Japan were solid-state.[22]

Japanese firms began to market TVs in the United States in the early 1960s. They confined themselves mainly to smaller units (with less than nineteen-inch screens) and sold them through department stores or large electronics retailers rather than through licensed distributors. At first, these sets sold simply because they were cheaper than their American-made counterparts. They used tubes and the circuit designs were inferior to US products. But the Japanese were quick to replace tubes first with transistors and then with integrated circuits, while continuously improving circuit designs. As large-scale integrated (LSI) circuit technology allowed semiconductor manufacturers to put more transistors on a single device, Japanese TV producers were able to reduce the parts counts in TV sets substantially.

Not only did Japanese TV producers reduce the parts counts faster than US firms thanks to the rapid introduction of semiconductors, but they were also faster in automating assembly of circuit boards. Tube technology, because of the fragility of the components and the importance of hand-wiring to assure quality control, required a great deal of labor-intensive work. Semiconductor technology was more amenable to automation of assembly, but the key to automation was to develop devices

"Standardization and Competitiveness: Private and Public Strategies in the EC Colour TV Industry," paper prepared for an INSEAD Symposium, "Product Standardization as a Tool of Competitive Strategy," 9–10 June 1986, p. 26.

[21] See David Yoffie, *Zenith and the Color Television Fight*, Harvard Business School, Case No. 9-383-070, May 1984 revision.

[22] James E. Millstein, "Decline in an Expanding Industry: Japanese Competition in Color Television," in John Zysman and Laura Tyson (eds.), *American Industry in International Competition* (Ithaca, NY: Cornell University Press, 1983), pp. 117–18.

for automatically aligning and inserting semiconductor components on circuit boards.

Japanese firms pioneered automated insertion equipment in the late 1960s. The first generation of such equipment was operating by 1968, and it was manually rather than automatically controlled. A second generation was produced in 1972 that was much faster but was also manually controlled. The third generation was about ten times faster than the first generation and allowed for limited numerical or computer control of the insertion process.[23] This gradual and incremental improvement of insertion equipment provided an interesting parallel with the incremental improvement of semiconductor manufacturing equipment by Japanese firms later in the 1970s.[24]

Japanese TVs became more reliable and required less maintenance and servicing *because* they used semiconductors rather than tubes. During the mid-1970s, for example, US-made color TVs were failing at five times the Japanese rate.[25] By 1977, the number of production faults were 1.4 to 2.0 per set in the United States and only 0.01 to 0.03 in Japan.[26] The greater reliability and durability of Japanese sets made it possible to sell them widely without building an extensive service network. The service networks of the US manufacturers were thus converted from a barrier to entry for foreign firms to a financial liability.

The third key to improved Japanese competitiveness was their more rapid reduction of the number of circuit boards in TVs. For example, it was only in the mid-1980s that General Electric was able to put all the circuitry for its color TVs on a single board, whereas Japanese firms had been doing this since 1976. The switch to a single-board chassis further reduced the labor time required for assembly.[27]

US firms located new production facilities offshore

In the late 1960s, most of the major US television manufacturers began to take advantage of sections 806.30 and 807.00 of the tariff code

---

[23] Wooster, "Industrial Policy," pp. 162–3.

[24] See Jay S. Stowsky, "Weak Links, Strong Bonds: US–Japanese Competition in Semiconductor Production Equipment," in Chalmers Johnson, Laura D'Andrea Tyson, and John Zysman (eds.), *Politics and Productivity: The Real Story of Why Japan Works* (Cambridge, MA: Ballinger, 1989).

[25] Wooster, "Industrial Policy," p. 146.

[26] Staelin, "The Decline of US Consumer Electronics Manufacturing," p. 17.

[27] Wooster, "Industrial Policy," pp. 140 and 161. Wooster breaks this down as follows: of the total drop in assembly labor time between 1974 and 1978, 55 percent was accounted for by reduction in component counts, 33 percent by automation of assembly, and 14 percent by reduction in the number of circuit boards.

to locate final assembly offshore in lower-wage countries (mainly in Mexico). Under sections 806.30 and 807.00, firms that established assembly plants overseas for production of exports to the United States did not have to pay export duties on parts sent to those plants and only paid import duties on the value added abroad. All production of monochrome receivers was soon relocated offshore, while production of color receivers remained, for the most part, in the United States. The offshore products were converted more quickly to semiconductor components than the domestic products, which had the unfortunate effect of creating expertise in manufacturing transistorized TVs outside the United States.

One of the reasons for the slow introduction of automated insertion equipment and the single-board chassis in US manufacturing was the heavy reliance on offshore "board stuffing" operations to keep assembly costs down. The offshore board stuffers, mainly in Mexico and East Asia, were not considered sufficiently reliable for single-board chassis assembly. In addition, the engineers of US firms believed that integrated circuits would not be as reliable as tubes, and wished to avoid the high maintenance costs that would be associated with the repair of a single-board chassis, so they were perhaps overly cautious about reducing the number of circuit boards in sets.

US firms spent more effort than was called for in maintaining the distributor networks in the belief that their main customers would continue to demand larger sets with higher quality pictures, which would necessarily require more servicing, than their Japanese or East Asian competitors were offering. They believed that consumers did not care about semiconductor components as much as they cared about the size and quality of the picture. They did not believe that semiconductors would be as reliable as tubes.

US firms, therefore, kept color TV production onshore after they moved black-and-white TV production offshore. They were slow to introduce semiconductor components and to reduce the number of circuit boards. They were not sufficiently worried about Japanese competition – they underestimated the ability of Japanese firms to produce TVs with semiconductor components and to move up from simple black-and-white sets to small color sets and finally to larger color sets. In this respect, they resembled their colleagues in the automobile industry who were willing to concede the market for low-priced subcompact vehicles to Japanese competitors in the belief that they would continue to have production-cost and distribution advantages in high-priced vehicles. But in actuality, Japanese firms quickly applied the lessons they learned in competing in the low-end markets to higher-end products, while US firms were cutting themselves off from this important source of learning.

The stillbirth of the US video recorder industry

Had a few US firms been able to shift their activities from television to VCR production in the 1970s, the consumer electronics industry might still have been able to hang on, despite the mistakes made in TV production. The story of the video recorder industry in the United States is a sad one.[28] One company, Ampex Corporation, owned all of the patents required for producing video recorders and used those patents to dominate the markets for professional video recording equipment (sold mainly to TV broadcasting stations). But it was unable to turn that technological advantage into a commercial one in the vast consumer market for videocassette recorders (VCRs) that arose in the 1980s. The result was that no US firm produced VCRs in the 1980s – instead they marketed products made in Japan. Only RCA continued to design VCRs, but even RCA was unable to manufacture them. The failure of US firms to match Japanese technology in VCRs made it virtually impossible for them to take advantage of the growing video camera and camcorder markets as well.

In 1968, a Vice President of Ampex, Richard J. Elkus, Jr., produced an internal report calling for a strategic shift toward producing a video recorder for the consumer market. He recommended scrapping the development a new machine, the VR-7700, in favor of a machine he called the "Instacorder" which used half-inch tape, and was compact, easy to use, and self-loading. In other words, Elkus proposed that Ampex should build something like a videocassette recorder (VCR). The Instavideo project was given the go-ahead by top management, and while the engineers in California and Illinois attempted to create a prototype, Elkus proceeded with a number of business plans for financing and marketing the product.

Ampex had difficulties obtaining a Japanese patent for its professional video recorders. Like many US firms in similar circumstances, Ampex was tempted to get around its patent and marketing problems in Japan by forming a joint venture with a Japanese firm. The first joint venture was with Sony, signed in July 1960. The terms of the venture called for Sony to produce a portable version of the Ampex professional recorder in exchange for Japanese production of Ampex recorders for nonbroadcast customers. This venture was of only limited success, especially after Sony

---

[28] The rest of this section relies heavily on two sources: Richard S. Rosenbloom and Karen J. Freese, "Ampex Corporation and Video Innovation," in Richard Rosenbloom (ed.), *Research on Technological Innovation, Management and Policy*, 2 (Greenwich, CT: JAI Press, 1985), pp. 113–85; James Lardner, *Fast Forward: Hollywood, the Japanese and the VCR Wars* (New York: Norton, 1987).

introduced a transistorized recorder, the SV-201, in 1961. CEO William Roberts was concerned that Sony was too capable of stealing Ampex's technology, so he let the agreement lapse.

In 1964, Ampex and Toshiba formed a joint venture called Toamco. This venture manufactured Ampex-designed professional tape recorders and computer tape units, which were sold by Toshiba in Japan and by Ampex elsewhere. Toamco was not doing well financially in the late 1960s, so CEO Roberts gave it the task of producing the Instavideo. This decision was governed by concerns over cash and engineering personnel shortages in Ampex, by the desire to avoid a deal with a US firm who could become a domestic competitor, and by the need to produce a machine which was compatible with the emerging standard for video recording tape, a half-inch format called the EIAJ-Type 1, which had been pioneered by the Japanese.[29]

The first Instavideo machine was demonstrated at the Americana Hotel in New York on 2 September 1970. The machine used an automatic-loading cartridge system – rather than a cassette – with a tape capacity of sixty minutes' extended play. It weighed less than sixteen pounds, and included a monochrome TV camera. The tape was compatible with the EIAJ-Type 1 standard. The unit with camera was priced at $1,500; without at $1,000. The demonstration was a smashing success. Ampex stock increased in value by 45 percent and the firm was able to use the enthusiasm about its new product announcement to ward off financial difficulties for a few more months.[30]

By the beginning of 1971, Toamco was having difficulties producing enough Instavideos, while Ampex was experiencing severe financial difficulties. In addition, Matsushita had marketed a cheaper video recorder at about that time, taking some of the luster off the Ampex Instavideo announcement. By the end of 1971, Ampex reported a loss of $12 million. Its sales of magnetic tape and consumer audio equipment plummeted as cheaper imports had come onto the market. It became overly dependent on debt capital to finance some of its acquisitions. CEO Roberts resigned

[29] US equipment and tape producers did not think that half-inch tape would ever be able to match the high quality standards they expected and did not attempt to create a standard format. The Japanese firms, in contrast, knew that they needed a narrower tape if they were going to be able to market a video recorder for home use and figured they did not need to build such equipment to studio- or industrial-level standards. On the battle within Japan between Beta and VHS advocates, see Gregory W. Noble, "The Japanese Industrial Policy Debate," in Stephan Haggard and Chung-in Moon (eds.), *Pacific Dynamics: The International Politics of Industrial Change* (Boulder, CO: Westview Press, 1989), pp. 73–7.

[30] Presentation by Richard Elkus at a meeting on HDTV at the American Electronics Association, Santa Clara, California, 6 June 1988.

at the request of the board of managers, and was succeeded by Richard Elkus, Sr., the father of Richard J. Elkus, Jr. The senior Elkus proceeded to cut back Ampex's expenditures and investments in order to restore the firm to fiscal health. That such austerity clearly was called for is not in doubt: the firm reported a loss of $90 million in 1972. One of the projects cut was the Instavideo project. The death of Instavideo ended the chances for any US-owned firm to participate in the breathtaking growth of the home video recorder market.

The inability of Ampex to commercialize its lead in video recorder technology, therefore, was primarily a function of its financial weakness. Its financial weakness was primarily the result of poor management. Ampex made a particularly unfortunate joint venture arrangement with Toshiba that hastened the diffusion of VCR technology to Japan. Apparently, Magnavox approached Ampex prior to deciding to go with the joint venture with Toshiba, but it decided (ironically) that the Toshiba deal was better because the Japanese firm was less likely to be a serious competitor in the future.[31]

Larger US firms, such as RCA, GE, or Zenith, did not have the vision to see the future of VCR markets and did not attempt to acquire Ampex or to salvage the Instavideo project by purchasing the VCR technology. The subsequent failed efforts of RCA in the late 1970s to produce a videodisc system that could only play but not record video programs, suggested that even RCA, the most capable US consumer electronics company, had not developed a proper understanding of the nature of consumer demand for home video recording systems. GE apparently did not perceive a great future for its consumer electronics operations, as evidenced by the sale of its TV division to Thomson in 1987. In contrast, Japan's earlier successes in cameras and optical equipment together with its growing strength in TVs and VCRs paved the way for success in camcorders and projection TVs in the 1980s.

Explanation of US decline: a summary

The US consumer electronics industry declined because there was a failure of vision on the part of the managements of US firms. Their analysis of the Japanese threat in consumer electronics focused too much on labor costs and not enough on the incorporation of new technologies. They failed to see the importance of new components technologies

[31] Presentation by Richard Elkus at a conference on "Seizing Opportunities of Change – Strategic Electronic Markets for Semiconductors," sponsored by Dataquest and the Semiconductor Industry Association, Santa Clara, California, 29 September 1988.

in television, and they failed to see the market potential for VCRs. US television firms tried to get around their higher labor costs by manufacturing in low-wage countries. While this was rational in the short run, it put the firms on a technological trajectory that was disastrous in the long run.

Japanese firms were engaged to some degree in the dumping of consumer electronics products on US markets from the early days of their entry. Japanese markets were closed to US producers by high tariff and nontariff barriers during this period, and no US-owned TV firm was permitted to establish a manufacturing presence in Japan. Even though Japanese trade/investment barriers and weak enforcement of trade laws by the US government speeded the decline of the US industry, greater reliability and lower production costs were at the root of increased Japanese global competitiveness in consumer electronics. US firms lacked the vision to match Japanese innovations in component and assembly technologies.

The impact of the decline of the US consumer electronics industry on US competitiveness in electronics

The decline of the US television industry hurt the ability of US firms to compete in follow-on products like VCRs and video cameras. In addition, the loss of the consumer electronics industry eventually handicapped the US semiconductor industry in its efforts to compete with Japanese firms. Semiconductor producers in the US were not able to keep up with the state of the art in high-volume CMOS process technology, nor were they able to match the developments in opto-electronics (and particularly CCDs or charge-coupled devices), liquid crystal displays (LCDs), and consumer-oriented analog circuitry.[32]

One important result of the failure of US consumer electronics was to reduce the proportional importance of consumer demand in total demand for semiconductors. Whereas consumer end-use accounted for more than 40 percent of total consumption of semiconductors in Japan in 1988, the same figure for the United States was around 7 percent.[33] To the extent that the structure of consumption of semiconductors in Japan differed radically from that of the United States, it remained difficult for US firms – which had specialized in products for the computer, telecommunications, industrial and automotive markets – to penetrate

---

[32] See Adam Watson-Brown, "Towards the Triumph of the Matt Black Box," *Intermedia*, 16 (January 1988), p. 24.

[33] Data provided to the author by the Semiconductor Industry Association.

Japanese markets. The Japanese firms used this fact to explain why US penetration of the Japanese semiconductor market remained less than 15 percent, despite a 30–40 percent share of the European market.[34]

Weakness in consumer production had other repercussions besides reducing the volume of domestic demand for electronic components like CMOS integrated circuits and LCDs, however. By exiting consumer markets, US electronics firms missed an important opportunity to learn how to implement new production methods for high-volume production of electronic systems. High-volume consumer electronics production in Japan drove innovations not only in automated insertion for assembly of printed circuit boards (as mentioned above), but also in successor technologies like surface-mount technology (SMT), tape-automated bonding (TAB), amorphous and polysilicon processing, and chip-on-glass (COG) technology.[35]

Summary and conclusions

Consumer electronics markets experienced rapid growth and technological change in the 1980s and 1990s. East Asian governments understood the importance of consumer electronics as a generator of wealth, jobs, exports, and technology and focused their industrial policies on providing support to local consumer electronics producers. In the developing world outside Asia, Mexico was the primary beneficiary of growth in demand for consumer electronics in North America thanks to the maquiladora program and subsequently NAFTA. The failure to appreciate the dynamism in the demand for and the technology of consumer electronics products badly hurt many European and US firms. The US firms all eventually abandoned the field. The European industry consolidated into three major survivors: Philips, Thomson, and Nokia.[36] Europe was in a much stronger position than the United States in consumer electronics in the 1980s, but it remained vulnerable to competition from Japan in high-end analog devices, from the United States in digital devices, and from East Asian countries in low-end products. Japanese firms, in turn, were vulnerable to increasing competition from other East Asian firms, particularly from Korean and Taiwanese firms, in low-end products and from the United States in digital products.

---

[34] See Jeffrey A. Hart, "The Origins of the US–Japan Semiconductor Dispute," in Haggard and Moon, *Pacific Dynamics*.

[35] Michael Borrus and Jeffrey Hart, "Display's the Thing," *Journal of Policy Analysis and Management*, 13 (Winter 1994), pp. 21–54.

[36] Although ITT is nominally a US-owned corporation headquartered in the Bahamas, its operations and personnel are heavily oriented toward Europe.

The purpose of this chapter was to provide background information on why the Japanese government and electronics industry put such a high priority on creating a new generation of video technologies. It also helps to explain US and European perceptions of the Japanese competitive threat. The main difference between Europe and the United States in this was that Europe still had a few surviving consumer electronics producers to defend by the late 1980s, while the United States had only one, and a shaky one at that. The industry had begun to change in the 1980s by moving assembly operations closer to markets and by offshoring manufacturing and assembly of lower-priced components and final products to lower-wage countries. In the 1990s, substantial investments by European and Asian television producers in North America and by American, Japanese and European electronics firms in East Asia further globalized the industry. As the 1990s progressed, demand shifted away from analog to digital devices, reducing the perceived threat of Japanese competitiveness. US and European firms discovered that, by allying themselves with corporate partners in East Asia, they could become more internationally competitive. Most importantly, HDTV technology became less of a concern to everyone as consumer demand shifted markedly toward digital devices, especially toward networked personal computers, and away from analog products.

4   HDTV in Japan

The global story of HDTV begins with the decision of Japan's national public broadcaster, NHK (Nippon Hoso Kyokai), to begin research on next-generation television technologies. Prior to and during the 1964 Tokyo Olympics, there was a major jump in TV sales in Japan. The dissatisfaction of engineers at NHK's Technical Laboratories with the quality of television coverage of the Tokyo Olympics and the improved ability of NHK to finance television research were the two main reasons why NHK Laboratories began to do research on advanced television technologies in 1964. From that point on, NHK was the key actor pushing for HDTV in Japan. NHK's leadership depended critically on its control over the core technologies for Japan's version of HDTV. Because NHK was enjoined by law not to engage directly in manufacturing activities, it began in 1970 to assemble a coalition of manufacturers to support its work on HDTV technologies. NHK then used its coalition to win support for national HDTV standards. It did not succeed in winning sufficient support for its approach to HDTV outside of Japan, however, for reasons to be explored in later chapters.

NHK's research on MUSE/Hi-Vision

Two NHK laboratories were established in 1930: one for broadcasting issues (including viewer surveys) and the other for technical issues. NHK Science and Technical Research Laboratories (NHK Labs for short) were supposed to investigate scientific and technical issues with the potential to have long-term effects on broadcasting. The annual budget of NHK Labs in 1989 was 2.5 billion yen (around $25 million), which represented only about 0.7 percent of NHK's total budget. With a research staff of around 260 scientists and engineers, NHK Labs became the most important center for HDTV research in Japan. Dr. Takashi Fujio, Director General of NHK Labs, was in charge of the research.

Leland Johnson identifies three main reasons for NHK's decision to initiate research on HDTV: (1) the perceived obsolescence of NTSC,

84

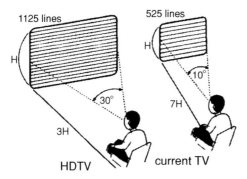

Figure 4.1   Comparison of HDTV and current TV

PAL, and SECAM standards; (2) Japan's previous successes in penetrating color television markets; and (3) consistency with Japan's emphasis on the promotion of high-technology, export-oriented businesses in its overall industrial policy.[1]

Beginning in 1970, NHK conducted detailed studies on visual perception to determine their options for improving the quality of television broadcasts. They learned that viewers preferred images that were higher in resolution and permitted a wider angle of vision than NTSC television. The average person could get the subjectively most satisfying picture from an NTSC standard color television at a viewing distance of about seven times the height of the screen: i.e., if the screen is 20 inches high, the optimal viewing distance for an NTSC image is 140 inches away from the screen. If a viewer moved closer to the screen, the scanning lines and other artifacts became visible. If a viewer moved farther away, the image became too small. This viewing distance combined with the 4:3 aspect ratio resulted in an angle of vision of about 10 degrees.[2]

NHK researchers experimented with wider and sharper images and determined that their subjects strongly preferred images that produced a 30-degree angle of vision at a distance of 3.3 times the height of the screen (see Figure 4.1).[3] Wider and sharper images produced a greater feeling of viewer involvement in the action on the screen and a closer

[1] Leland L. Johnson, *Development of High Definition Television: A Study in US-Japan Trade Relations* (Santa Monica: Rand, 1990), pp. 7–8.

[2] Michel Dupagne and Peter B. Seel, *High-Definition Television: A Global Perspective* (Ames, IA: Iowa State University Press, 1998), p. 73. Scott D. Elliott assisted the authors in writing their chapter on HDTV in Japan.

[3] Jerry Whitaker, *DTV: The Revolution in Digital Video*, 2nd edition (New York: McGraw-Hill, 1999), p. 13.

Table 4.1 *Aspect ratios for various video and film systems*

Name of system	Aspect ratio
NTSC, PAL, SECAM	4:3 or 1.33:1
35 mm photographs (4″ by 6″)	3:2 or 1.5:1
initial Hi-Vision	5:3 or 1.66:1
modified Hi-Vision	16:9 or 1.78:1
Vistavision	1.85:1
Panavision	2:1
70 mm Wide Scope	2.2:1
Cinemascope	2.35:1

Source: Talk delivered by Eiji Kaneko, director of Giant Technology Corporation at the annual meeting of the Society for Information Display, Anaheim, California, 7 May 1991.

approximation to everyday visual reality – what some video engineers call "telepresence."

Movie producers had already taken advantage of this preference by moving to larger screens with wider aspect ratios and to films with higher resolution. Thirty-five mm films shown in movie theatres were at least twice as sharp as the pictures produced by the expensive NTSC monitors in television studios, and hence much, much sharper than pictures seen on television sets at home. Most movies today are shown in widescreen formats (see Table 4.1). NHK researchers, like the movie industry before them, found that increasing the angle of vision beyond 30 degrees actually diminished the perceived quality of images because of the need to move the head to take in the entire screen.

In order to get at least a 30-degree angle of vision at a viewing distance of three times the height of the screen, it was necessary to increase the aspect ratio of the display from 4:3 to 5:3. So initially, the image format for HDTV in Japan was set at an aspect ratio of 5:3. In addition, NHK researchers decided to pursue the goal of improving picture resolution on the wider screens by increasing the number of scanning lines in video production cameras from 525 (the NTSC standard) to 1,125.[4] They believed that at least 1,000 lines were necessary to match the resolution of 35mm still photographs, and 1,125 was a useful number because it

[4] Dupagne and Seel report that NHK reduced the number of lines from 1,241 (the optimal number in their view) to 1,125 in order to win support for their approac 1.

would facilitate down conversion of HDTV images to both NTSC and PAL/SECAM images.[5]

In addition, NHK selected a field rate of 60 Hz (60 fields per second) for the display of HDTV images. This was slightly higher than the 59.94 Hz rate used in NTSC televisions. The NHK researchers determined that the 50 Hz rate common to PAL and SECAM televisions was not fast enough to prevent "flicker" in the image and that it would impose a limit on the brightness of the display.[6]

NHK begins to work with Japanese manufacturers

After 1970, NHK approached private electronics manufacturers in Japan to ask them to work jointly in developing technologies for HDTV. Sony Corporation and Ikegami Communication Device Company, Ltd., the two main competitors for television production equipment in Japan, were early to sign on. These two firms were strongly dependent on orders from NHK for television production equipment and hence needed to stay on good terms with an important customer. Other manufacturers – in particular, Toshiba, Hitachi, Matsushita, Sharp, Sanyo, and Mitsubishi – joined the NHK-led efforts after several major technical problems were solved.

At first, NHK worked informally with individual manufacturers. Later on, it decided to put the collaboration in a more structured format. In 1981, NHK established a nonprofit subsidiary called NHK Engineering Services (NHK-ES). Until 1989, all the members of NHK-ES were Japanese-owned companies. NHK-ES was created to permit NHK to continue to work with manufacturers as they moved closer to commercialization of Hi-Vision products without violating the legal restraints against involvement in manufacturing activities. Its main purposes were: (1) to obtain patents, copyrights, and trademarks on Hi-Vision technologies created by NHK Labs or with NHK funding; (2) to license those technologies preferentially to members of NHK-ES; and (3) to educate NHK-ES members and prospective members about the Hi-Vision technologies that it controlled.

The first technical problems to be tackled were connected with the building of prototype cameras, monitors, and recorders for HDTV video production. Also, because of the obvious advantages of HDTV over NTSC in displaying movies, NHK-industry teams worked on developing machines called "telecines" that are used to convert films to HDTV video.

[5] Johnson, *Development of High Definition Television*, pp. 8–9.
[6] Whitaker, *DTV*, p. 13.

Later on, NHK and the manufacturers worked together on equipment to convert Hi-Vision/MUSE signals so that they could be displayed or recorded on NTSC televisions and VCRs.

High definition cameras could not provide higher resolution images until new camera imaging tubes were developed. The camera imaging tubes for NTSC cameras, called Vidicons, could be stretched to produce higher resolution tubes (called Plumbicons and Saticons), but only at the expense of requiring much higher levels of lighting, especially for studio shooting. So NHK and private industry researchers went to work developing a new generation of camera tubes that produced higher resolution images without requiring more light.

In 1987, NHK Labs discovered a new type of tube called a HARP (High Gain Avalanche Rushing Amorphous Photoconductor Target) tube that produced HDTV-quality images with very little lighting. Since this was obviously a desirable quality for commercial video cameras independently of HDTV, it was not surprising that NHK got a significant amount of cooperation from private firms in incorporating HARP tubes in HDTV cameras.

The main challenge in HDTV monitors was in producing inexpensive, large-area displays. The initial approach was simply to scale up existing CRT-based direct-view and projection monitors, and to begin production of prototypes with 16:9 aspect ratios at various screen sizes. Industry leaders in high-resolution monitors like Sony and Ikegami did much of the early work. Later, the other major manufacturers of consumer electronics established facilities for manufacturing 16:9 widescreen CRTs. In addition, NHK and the manufacturers began to work on alternative display technologies including large-area flat panel displays and LCD projectors. NHK Labs focused on a wall-sized plasma display technology, which was not particularly successful. The manufacturers, together with the Giant Electronics Corporation, an R&D consortium set up under the Key Technology rubric, focused for a short time on large-area active-matrix LCD flat panel displays. Both MITI and MPT established large-area display programs with MITI focusing on flat panels and MPT on projectors.

In the area of video tape recorders (VTRs), used primarily in TV studios and by producers of broadcast-quality video programs, NHK worked with Sony, JVC, Matsushita, Mitsubishi, NEC, Sanyo, Sharp, Hitachi, and Toshiba to build first analog base band recorders and then digital VTRs for HDTV. The first experimental one-inch digital VTR was displayed in 1979. Sony, Hitachi, and Toshiba moved later to develop half-inch versions of the one-inch machines, and to further miniaturize them so that they could be sold on the mass consumer market.

MUSE: video compression comes to Hi-Vision

By 1984, the outlines of a potentially successful Japanese HDTV strategy could be discerned from the successes that NHK and its private partners had already achieved. The system they would pursue into the early 1990s was coming to be called "Hi-Vision." Its essence was a television picture with twice the resolution of NTSC pictures and with about 25 percent greater width. It also featured CD-quality digital stereo sound. The key remaining technological challenge was to take the 30-megahertz base band signal which came out of Hi-Vision studio camera equipment and compress it so that it could be stored easily on VCRs and delivered economically on existing over-the-air, cable, and/or satellite transmission systems.

Between 1980 and 1984, accordingly, NHK focused its research efforts on video compression techniques. In 1984, Masao Sugimoto – head of HDTV research at NHK Labs – announced the discovery of a type of signal encoding called MUSE, short for Multiple Sub-Nyquist Sampling Encoding, that could reduce the bandwidth necessary for transmitting Hi-Vision signals. An unencoded or base band Hi-Vision signal requires 30 megahertz, while a MUSE-encoded signal requires only 8.1 megahertz. While NHK was able to send base band Hi-Vision signals for experimental purposes over its earlier DBS satellites, the use of so much bandwidth would have added greatly to the expense of delivering HDTV signals and would have ruled out sales of HDTV VCRs to consumer markets. So NHK planned to deliver a MUSE-encoded HDTV signal via DBS when it moved beyond the experimental stage.

MUSE technology, unlike some of the other technologies that NHK worked on, was strongly protected from the start. NHK-ES owned the patents and copyrights for MUSE circuitry and software and would not make the circuit designs available to nonmembers. Later US applicants to NHK-ES, like National Semiconductor, reported that NHK-ES asked for payments of over $100,000 from companies who wanted just to look at the MUSE circuit designs before deciding to pay considerably more for membership in NHK-ES, and therefore the right to design chips incorporating parts of the MUSE circuitry. NHK continued to maintain, somewhat inconsistently, that it was interested mainly in obtaining inexpensive equipment from its suppliers and was indifferent to their national origin. However, clearly they felt a need to protect their Japanese manufacturing partners from excessive competition from foreign suppliers, and did so by limiting access to NHK-ES.

MUSE compression was important for making both transmission and reception of Hi-Vision signals practical. Because NHK had already decided to move its main broadcasting activities over to DBS, it did not matter to them that the 8.1 megahertz signal did not fit into the 6 megahertz channels used for terrestrial NTSC broadcasts. The 8.1 megahertz bandwidth of MUSE signals later proved to be a crucial impediment to winning the acceptance of MUSE/Hi-Vision in the United States.

Satellite delivery of MUSE/Hi-Vision signals

From the beginning, NHK and the Ministry of Posts and Telecommunications (MPT) planned to deliver HDTV signals by direct broadcast satellites (DBS). There were a variety of reasons for this. The official reasons included the desire to provide an upgraded HDTV service on top of the continued terrestrial over-the-air delivery of NTSC signals, the need to provide earthquake-proof broadcasting in case of emergencies, and the desire to preserve scarce spectrum for other types of broadcasting.

There were other reasons that were not so clearly in the public interest. First, NHK was worried about the tendency of its NTSC stations to lose audience share to private broadcasters. Since NHK depended almost entirely for its revenues on user fees, and since the Japanese Diet had refused to increase those fees in recent years (at a time when expenses continued to rise), NHK felt the necessity to create new revenue streams. Providing a new service like HDTV over satellites would provide a rationale for increasing user fees.[7] Also, royalties and license fees for HDTV technology might also provide an additional source of revenue.

Japanese consumer electronics manufacturers were attracted to the idea of delivering HDTV signals that could not be received on existing NTSC TVs. To receive the MUSE Hi-Vision signals, consumers would have to purchase satellite dishes, satellite tuners, HDTV receivers or "down converters" that enabled NTSC sets to display HDTV signals. This at a time when sales of both televisions and VCRs were tapering off and the market shares of Korean and Taiwanese firms were increasing.

The BS-3a satellite was to be the first satellite capable of broadcasting MUSE Hi-Vision signals. The Japanese Diet gave the MPT control over this particular operation in a bill passed in April 1988. About $75 million was appropriated for the MPT's Telecommunications and Broadcasting Satellites Organization, which would collect fees from

---

[7] Interviews by the author in Tokyo with Japanese informants in 1989.

NHK, the private broadcasters, and the consumer electronics firms to finance the satellite launching and maintenance. The BS-3a was put into orbit in August 1990, but a solar battery failed soon after launch so a supplementary satellite, the BS-3h, was launched in April 1991. The BS-3h also failed, however, so the BS-3b was launched in August 1991. This time the satellite worked and NHK was able to increase the amount of MUSE Hi-Vision programming from one to eight hours per day.[8]

NHK as the architect of Japanese industrial policy in HDTV

NHK's efforts to build and maintain an alliance with Japanese equipment manufacturers created an impression in the minds of both European and US actors that NHK was acting in the time-honored fashion of Japanese governmental agencies like MITI, and more recently MPT, by providing "administrative guidance" to Japanese firms for the sake of Japanese international competitiveness.

The scale of the HDTV effort in Japan fed into already existing fears of total Japanese world domination in the area of consumer electronics manufacturing. Between 1970 and 1989, NHK Labs, the Japanese government, and the major electronics companies spent approximately $700 million developing the technologies necessary for implementing the Hi-Vision system. NHK Labs accounted for roughly 21 percent of that total (see Table 4.2).[9] Most of the important MUSE and Hi-Vision technologies were created in NHK Labs and were controlled by NHK-ES. Until 1989, only Japanese firms were members of NHK Engineering Services.

Because NHK was legally excluded from actually manufacturing HDTV equipment and because its strategy for HDTV could not succeed without plentiful and reasonably cheap HDTV equipment, it had to enlist the support of the Japanese manufacturers in pursuing its strategy. It did so by subsidizing private HDTV research and by providing intellectual property protection for allied manufacturers through NHK-ES.

---

[8] Eiji Kawabata, "Relative Technological Superiority, Domestic Institutions, and HDTV Development in Japan and the US," paper prepared for delivery at the annual meeting of the International Studies Association, Los Angeles, California, 15–18 March 2000, p. 4.
[9] See Corey Carbonara, "The Evolution of High Definition Television," *HDTV Proceeding for 1991* (Washington, DC: National Association of Broadcasters, 1991); Norm Alster, "TV's High-Stakes, High-Tech Battle," *Fortune*, 24 October 1988, p. 166; and Jon Choy, "Developing Advanced Television: Industrial Policy Revisited," *JEI Report* (Washington, DC: Japan Economic Institute), No. 2a, 13 January 1989.

Table 4.2 *R&D spending on HDTV in Japan, 1970–1989, in millions of dollars*

Source of spending	Amount
NHK	148
MITI	116
Private Companies	444
Total	**708**

Source: Robert B. Cohen, "An Economic Evaluation of Japan's Public Policy Initiatives in Support of High Definition Systems," in Richard J. Elkus, Robert B. Cohen, Birney D. Dayton, David G. Messerschmidt, William F. Schreiber, and Lawrence E. Tannas, Jr., *JTEC Panel Report on High Definition Systems in Japan* (Baltimore, MD: Loyola College, February 1991), p. 117.

It can be argued that the interests of Japanese consumers were not carefully considered in the strategy's adoption and implementation. The imagery of global domination, exclusion of foreign manufacturing interests, and an apparent lack of concern for protecting the interests of consumers became a fatal problem for NHK as it moved from building its Japanese coalitions to creating an international coalition of supporters for Hi-Vision/MUSE.[10]

The role of MITI and MPT in promoting Hi-Vision

Unlike many other areas of high technology development, the development of HDTV technology was almost entirely under the control of NHK and not government ministries like the Ministry of International Trade and Industry (MITI) or the Ministry of Posts and Telecommunications (MPT). This did not prevent the governmental ministries from attempting to piggyback on top of NHK's efforts in order to pursue their own agendas. Occasionally, the government ministries attempted

[10] See Jeffrey A. Hart, "The Use of R&D Consortia as Market Barriers: Case Studies of Consortia in the United States, Japan, and Western Europe," *The International Executive*, 35 (January/February 1993), pp. 11–33.

to score points against each other and NHK while scrambling for HDTV turf.

In March 1987, the MPT established a Round Table Conference Concerning HDTV Promotion. In May of that year, they set up a Hi-Vision Promotion Office within the Broadcasting Bureau to prepare policies for the promotion of Hi-Vision. Finally, MPT helped to set up a quasi-public Hi-Vision Promotion Association (HPA)[11] – with representatives from major consumer electronics and broadcasting firms – in September to recommend specific measures for encouraging the commercialization of HDTV.

Norio Ohga of Sony was the first President of the HPA; Morio Kumabe of NHK was its first Vice President. Three private broadcasters – Fuji Broadcasting, NTV, and JCSAT – belonged to the HPA. All the major consumer electronics firms, trading companies, communications firms and banks joined also. The private firms put up both cash and in-kind resources to help pay for various promotions.

The Hi-Vision Promotion Association planned and executed demonstrations of Hi-Vision during the Seoul Olympics in 1988. Large HDTV displays were set up in train stations and other public places so that Japanese audiences could view broadcasts of Olympic events in Hi-Vision. NHK estimated that around 3.7 million people were able to see these broadcasts.

MPT started a Hi-Vision Cities program in 1988 to create "a city-wide video information network providing high-quality images as the core, which aims at 'creating a charming and intellectually stimulating city.'" Out of seventy-one applications submitted to the MPT in 1989, fourteen cities were chosen to participate.[12]

MITI also established an advisory committee on HDTV in January 1987. Theirs was called Future Prospects for HDTV. MITI set up the New Visual Industry Office and an affiliated promotion organization called the Hi-Vision Promotion Center in July 1988.[13] One of the Hi-Vision Promotion Center's more ambitious activities was to upgrade the Gifu Museum of Art by adding Hi-Vision displays and visual databases as a showcase for HDTV technologies. MITI matched MPT's Hi-Vision Cities Program with its own Hi-Vision Communities initiative. Most importantly, MITI used "administrative guidance" to ensure that Japanese banks would make available no-interest and

---

[11] Originally called the Hi-Vision Promotion Council, it was later renamed the Hi-Vision Promotion Association.
[12] Dupagne and Seel, *High-Definition Television*, pp. 86–7.
[13] Greg Noble, "The Politics of HDTV in Japan," paper presented at the annual meeting of the American Political Science Association, Chicago, Illinois, August 1992.

low-interest "policy loans" to private firms for the purpose of promoting Hi-Vision business. One estimate was that these loans totaled around $4.3 billion.[14]

Despite the continued bureaucratic rivalry between MPT and MITI, it was clear that the primary responsibility for coordinating Japanese Hi-Vision efforts belonged to NHK. While the two government agencies controlled considerable resources, their primary concern was to use those resources to best advantage in maintaining the support of politicians from different regions within Japan. This explains the competing Hi-Vision Cities and Communities programs. NHK, in contrast, controlled the key enabling technologies for Hi-Vision and hence was likely to remain more influential than either MPT or MITI with respect to both consumer electronics manufacturers and the private broadcasters.

NHK goes global

In the mid-1980s, NHK began to build bridges to powerful American interests who could serve as a base of foreign support for NHK's efforts to internationalize Japan's HDTV standards. One of NHK's principal interests in doing this was to reduce the cost of obtaining high-quality programming for HDTV broadcasting in Japan. It made sense to work with the Hollywood studios that would have to agree at minimum to allow their film libraries to be converted to HDTV video formats for broadcasting and VCR viewing. The US television networks and the independent film and video studios were major potential sources of new programming material as well, and would also be purchasers of HDTV production equipment.

But, just as importantly, part of the NHK strategy for internationalizing Hi-Vision was to argue for the need to have a single global standard for HDTV, in contrast to the multiple standards for color TV (NTSC, PAL, SECAM, and the MAC standards). In 1989, NHK issued a policy statement in which that argument was made:

In the world today, TV broadcasting services are operated under three different systems, viz., NTSC, PAL, and SECAM. This has always been the cause of great inconvenience to broadcasting organizations everywhere, having an inhibiting effect on the promotion of international exchanges of TV programs and international co-production of programs.

The efforts being made toward setting up a single worldwide standard for HDTV and the worldwide spread of this new technology are considered to be

---

[14] *Ibid.*

fully justified by the great many advantages that will be brought about as a result; the promotion of international exchanges of TV programs and international co-productions and the spread of HDTV broadcasts, given momentum by the re-duction in operational costs as a result of shared use of equipment and facili-ties, becoming feasible among the broadcasters of the world. And this, in turn, is expected to bring favorable results in the production of programs that con-tribute to the development of world broadcasting and enhancement of cultural ideals.[15]

These were concerns strongly shared among the network and film pro-duction communities, especially as high production and distribution costs had begun to erode the profitability of media businesses.

People who made films or video for a living were tired of having to worry about compatibility problems and paying the costs of conversion across regional standards boundaries. In addition, they were eager to reduce the post-production costs of editing films and adding special effects to them, often done by converting film to digital video (the mainstay of post-production firms like George Lucas's *Industrial Light and Magic*) and then back to film. The studios hoped that this could be accomplished less expensively by shooting more of the original "footage" in HDTV video formats. So NHK's vision of a unified, global standard for HDTV had a lot of appeal for the film industry.

NHK argued that the unified, global standard for HDTV produc-tion should be Hi-Vision because all the existing equipment for HDTV was being built (in Japan) to those standards. It was the only game in town. When standards were adopted for color TV, the American stan-dard, NTSC, prevailed in Asia and America, because that was the only option. So why should it matter that this time the technologies were Japanese?

NHK showed prototypes of Hi-Vision equipment at the 1981 meeting of the Society for Motion Picture and Television Engineers (SMPTE). Since these prototypes were pre-MUSE, they were not taken very se-riously. Nobody in the United States was interested in broadcasting a signal that required 30 megahertz of bandwidth.[16] SMPTE had formed a study group on HDTV as early as 1977. In 1982, the Columbia Broadcasting System (CBS) began to experiment with HDTV be-cause of its investments in DBS technologies. CBS gradually developed very close ties with Sony Corporation. Sony was later to purchase the

[15] "NHK's Policy for Worldwide Spread and Promotion of HDTV," *HDTV Newsletter* (February/March 1989), p. 14.
[16] Joel Brinkley, *Defining Vision: The Battle for the Future of Television* (New York: Harcourt Brace, 1997), pp. 15–16.

recordings division of CBS and later would buy Columbia Pictures, but even as early as 1982, CBS and Sony already shared an interest in HDTV.

Joseph Flaherty, then Vice President for Engineering at CBS, became a key player in a new organization set up in that year, the Advanced Television Systems Committee (ATSC). The charter members of the ATSC were the National Association of Broadcasters (NAB), the Electronic Industries Association (EIA) of the United States, the Institute of Electrical and Electronic Engineers (IEEE), the National Cable Television Association (NCTA), and SMPTE.[17] The ATSC, in other words, represented primarily the interests of the domestic broadcasting and program production communities the mostly foreign-owned consumer electronics producers (Japanese and European) in the EIA. The American electronics firms who belonged to the American Electronics Association (AEA) did not feel that they were adequately represented on the ATSC.[18]

NHK modifies Hi-Vision to win American support

NHK's dealing with the ATSC and SMPTE resulted in an important change in the Japanese approach to HDTV. NHK came to the United States with a Hi-Vision system that had (among others) the following parameters: 1,125 scanning lines, 59.94 fields per second for interlaced displays, and a 5:3 aspect ratio for displays. American film and video engineers convinced NHK to alter these parameters somewhat. The former argued that a refresh rate of 60 fields per second was more likely to be acceptable to the Europeans than the proposed rate of 59.94 because it was different from both the current European and the American field rates. In addition, they suggested an aspect ratio of 16:9 was more appropriate than 5:3 for display of widescreen motion pictures (see Table 4.1 above).[19] NHK altered the Hi-Vision

---

[17] Carbonara, "Evolution of High Definition Television," p. 13.

[18] See the section on the American Electronics Association below. William Schreiber reports that the formal vote on Hi-Vision in the ATSC in 1987 achieved the required two-thirds majority only because seven Japanese-owned companies voted in favor of the measure. He argues further that the measure would have been defeated had the vote been delayed, because a number of ATSC members were in the process of changing their minds. See William F. Schreiber, "Withdrawal of United States Support for the NHK HDTV System as an International Standard," comments submitted to the National Telecommunications and Information Administration of the US Department of Commerce, 1 March 1989, p. 6.

[19] Based on interviews by Ellis Krauss with Masao Sugimoto, Managing Director of NHK Labs in May 1991 and US representatives to the CCIR in March 1989. See Ellis Krauss,

parameters accordingly and the American National Standards Institute (ANSI) approved the modified 1125/60 system – now also designated as SMPTE 240M – as a "voluntary consensus standard."[20] This effort at compromise was to come back to haunt NHK as others came to see the modifications as efforts to make Hi-Vision totally incompatible with NTSC and PAL/SECAM systems.

The fact that NHK won significant support in the ATSC and SMPTE for its approach to HDTV helped NHK and its allies to convince officials of the Department of State to formally adopt the modified Hi-Vision approach to HDTV production as the US position in April 1985, despite objections from at least one large American manufacturer, RCA.[21] The State Department later led the US delegation at the plenary meeting of the CCIR (Consultative Committee on International Radio) in Dubrovnik in 1986 (see the next section). At that meeting, the US government supported the Japanese proposal for making Hi-Vision a global HDTV production standard.[22]

Modified Hi-Vision goes to Dubrovnik

In international standards forums, the Japanese government adopted a stance of global leadership, arguing for the need to replace the divisive multiple standards of the contemporary color TV world (NTSC, PAL, and SECAM) with a new unified global standard based on Hi-Vision. Important groups outside Japan, including movie producers and video programmers in Hollywood and New York, supported this stance. Unfortunately for the Japanese, influential groups in Europe and the United States perceived the Japanese proposal to be part of a general effort to consolidate Japan's global position of hegemony in consumer electronics and therefore proceeded to block the NHK initiative.[23]

At the CCIR meeting in Dubrovnik, the Europeans strongly opposed acceptance of Hi-Vision as a global standard. The reasons for this are

Competition Among Japan, the US, and Europe Over High-Definition Television, Pew Case Studies.

[20] See Johnson, *Development of High Definition Television*.

[21] Schreiber, "Withdrawal of United States Support," p. 5.

[22] For a detailed analysis, see Suzanne Chambliss Neil, "The Politics of International Standardization Revisited: The United States and High Definition Television," paper prepared for the Seventh Bi-Annual Conference of the International Telecommunications Society, 29 June–1 July 1988.

[23] Meeting of the author with NHK officials, including Executive Director-General of Engineering, Yoshiro Nakamura, 26 September 1989, Tokyo.

complex, but in essence, they sprang from European concerns that their consumer electronics, film, and television production firms would lose out to US and Japanese producers by the acceptance of a Japanese production standard for HDTV. The Europeans believed that even though the CCIR was being asked only to endorse the Hi-Vision production standard, such a decision would eventually translate into a general adoption of Japanese HDTV transmission and reception standards. Their own earlier strategy of survival in consumer electronics had depended on maintaining incompatible regional color TV standards (PAL and SECAM).[24] In addition, Europe was trying to get beyond multiple standards within Europe by migrating away from both PAL and SECAM to a new set of satellite broadcasting standards based on the idea of multiplexed analog components (MAC). The MAC standards were well suited to signal delivery via direct broadcast satellites – the preferred method for both France and Britain – and they could be upgraded easily to produce higher resolution and widescreen images. But the MAC standards were incompatible with Hi-Vision, because they were based on multiples of 625 scanning lines and a field rate of 50 Hz. Europe was committed to maintaining their current system of 50 Hz for video systems (partly because AC power in Europe is 50 cycles, while AC power in the United States and Japan is 60 cycles), and would have had to pay large sums to down convert 1125/60 video to 625/50 video for display on European PAL, SECAM, and MAC receivers.[25]

But much more importantly it would be difficult to continue the strategy of harmonization of broadcasting within the region while excluding foreign TV manufacturers if Europe went on record as supporting Hi-Vision as a global production standard. The European manufacturers did not want to make things easier for their Japanese competitors in consumer electronics. Strangely enough, though, it was not the manufacturers but rather bureaucrats from the European Commission who flagged the CCIR discussions of HDTV standards as an important issue for the Community. The European delegates to the CCIR were instructed to delay the acceptance of Hi-Vision as an international standard by calling for "more studies." They also submitted a proposal for an alternative "standard" based on speculation about Europe's ability to build a

---

[24] On this topic, see Rhonda J. Crane, *The Politics of International Standards: France and the Color TV War* (Norwood, NJ: Ablex, 1979).

[25] At first the Europeans claimed that down conversion was impossible, but then argued – after seeing working Japanese prototype down converters – that it was just too expensive.

system with 1,250 scanning lines and 50 fields per second. This effectively postponed further CCIR consideration of the Japanese proposal for four more years.[26]

---

[26] It should be noted that the American National Standards Institute (ANSI) adopted a modified version of Hi-Vision 1125/60 as SMPTE 240M in 1988. However, ANSI withdrew its approval of SMPTE 240M in 1989 after Capital Cities/ABC appealed the original decision. See Leland L. Johnson, *Development of High Definition Television*, pp. v–vi. The CCIR met again in 1990 to consider HDTV productions standards, and again delayed a decision for four more years.

5   HDTV in the United States

Introduction

In the 1960s and 1970s, there was a rapid retreat of US firms from consumer electronics markets under intense competition from Japan. The US consumer electronics industry was in a very weak position in the early 1980s. The US semiconductor industry was having increased difficulty competing with the larger and more integrated Japanese electronics concerns. When the European Community reacted negatively in 1986 to a Japanese effort to have its version of HDTV technology recognized as an international standard, many Americans in information technology industries looked to the US government to respond with special "industrial policies" for HDTV. Why such policies were proposed but for the most part not adopted in the United States is one of the main questions to be addressed in this chapter. This chapter also begins to explore the reasons why the Federal Communications Commission recommended rejection of the Japanese HDTV standard and adoption instead of a digital TV (DTV) standard in the late 1980s and early 1990s.

The HDTV issue comes to the United States

The HDTV issue appeared on the national agenda when NHK asked the Department of State in March 1985 to support its system as an international HDTV standard. NHK and other national actors also approached a variety of broadcasters and video production organizations to find out whether they would support the system. Initially, these groups were favorable toward the Japanese system. However, certain difficulties arose which prompted a reexamination of that earlier stand.

In June 1985, the Federal Communications Commission (FCC) initiated a proceeding on the sharing of ultra high-frequency (UHF) spectrum for land-mobile applications. UHF frequency was until that time reserved for television applications. Land-mobile applications, particularly for cellular telephones, were growing at a rapid pace and needed more spectrum to continue their expansion. The connection with HDTV was that the FCC knew that there was some possibility that HDTV would require additional spectrum, so it wanted to make sure that both land-mobile and HDTV would be accommodated in any reallocation of spectrum.

HDTV was still somewhat of a mystery to people in the United States at this point even though a few groups in broadcasting had established working groups and minor research programs in the early 1980s. The Society for Motion Picture and Television Engineers (SMPTE) formed a study group on HDTV as early as 1977. NHK showed prototypes of Hi-Vision equipment at the 1981 meeting of SMPTE. In 1982, the Columbia Broadcasting System (CBS) began to experiment with HDTV because of its investments in direct broadcast satellite (DBS) technologies. CBS gradually developed close ties with Sony Corporation. Sony was later to purchase the recordings division of CBS, but even as early as 1982, CBS and Sony already shared an interest in HDTV.

An executive from CBS, Joseph Flaherty, became a key player in a new organization set up in that year, the Advanced Television Systems Committee (ATSC). The charter members of the ATSC were the National Association of Broadcasters (NAB), the Electronic Industries Association (EIA), the Institute of Electrical and Electronic Engineers (IEEE), the National Cable Television Association (NCTA), and SMPTE.[1] The ATSC, in other words, represented primarily the interests of the broadcasting and program production communities. Because the EIA was already dominated by foreign consumer electronics producers, and especially by Japanese and European firms, the American electronics firms did not feel that they were adequately represented on the ATSC. So even though the ATSC was supposed to be for HDTV the analog of the NTSC for monochrome and color TV, it could not play that role.

On 13 February 1987, the Association of Maximum Service Telecasters (AMST) and fifty-seven other broadcast organizations and companies filed a joint Petition for Notice of Inquiry with the FCC. This began a prolonged FCC process for studying HDTV issues, which was eventually to lead to a series of important decisions.

The FCC opened a proceeding on HDTV technical and legal issues in July 1987 (MM Docket No. 87–268) and invited public comment on these issues. It established an Advisory Committee on Advanced Television Service (ACATS) in November 1987 (see Table 5.1). Chaired by Washington communications lawyer Richard E. Wiley, the ACATS also included (among others) Robert Hansen of Zenith, Thomas Murphy of

---

[1] Corey Carbonara, "The Evolution of High Definition Television," in *HDTV Proceedings for 1991* (Washington, DC: National Association of Broadcasters, 1991), p. 13.

Table 5.1 *Members of* ACATS

Name	Title	Organizational affiliation	Position in ACATS
Richard Wiley	Attorney		Chairman
Frank Biondi	President and CEO	Viacom	Voting member
Joel Chaseman	Chairman	Chaseman Enterprises International	"
Joseph Collins	Chairman and CEO	American Television and Communications Corp. (Time-Warner)	"
William Connolly		Sony	"
Marin Davis		Wellspring Associates Inc.	"
Irwin Dorros	Director	Bellcore	"
James Dowdle		Tribune Broadcasting Co.	"
Ervin S. Duggan		Public Broadcasting Service	"
Joseph Flaherty	Senior Vice President	CBS Inc.	"
Samuel Fuller		Digital Equipment Corp.	"
Stanley S. Hubbard	President and CEO	Hubbard Broadcasting	"
James Kennedy	Chairman and CEO	Cox Enterprises	"
James C. McKinney	Chairman	Advanced Television Systems Committee	"
Craig Mundie	Vice President	Microsoft Corporation	"
Thomas S. Murphy	Chairman	Capital Cities/ABC Inc.	"
Rupert Murdoch	Chairman	Fox Inc.	"
Jerry K. Pearlman	President and CEO	Zenith Electronics Corp.	"
F. Jack Pluckhahn	President and COO	Quasar (Matsushita)	"
Ward Quall	Founder	Ward L. Quall Co.	"
Richard D. Roberts		TCI	"
Burton Staniar	Chairman and CEO	Westinghouse Broadcasting	"
James Tietjen		SRI International	"
Laurence Tisch	President and CEO	CBS Inc.	"
Robert Wright	President and CEO	NBC	"
Peter Bingham	President	Philips Laboratories	Nonvoting member
Wendell Bailey	Vice President	National Cable Television Association	"

Table 5.1 (*cont.*)

Name	Title	Organizational affiliation	Position in ACATS
Henry L. Baumann	Executive Vice President	National Association of Broadcasters	"
Joseph Donahue	Retired Executive Vice President	Thomson Consumer Electronics	"
Brenda L. Fox	Partner	Dow, Lohnes & Albertson	"
Richard Friedland	Chairman and CEO	General Instrument Corp.	"
Robert Graves		AT&T	"
Larry Irving	Director	NTIA, U.S. Department of Commerce	"
Keiichi Kuboto	Deputy Director, Advanced TV Research	NHK Science and Technical Research Labs	"
Jae Lim	Professor	MIT	"
Vonya B. McCann	Deputy Assistant Secretary	U.S. Department of State	"
George Vradenburg III		Latham & Watkins	"
Margita White	President	Association for Maximum Service Television	"

Sources: J. G. Polic, "HDTV Policy Formation in the United States: The Federal Communication Commission's Advisory Committee on Advanced Television Services 1987–1991," doctoral dissertation, University of Pennsylvania, Philadelphia, 1993, p. 96; Federal Communications Commission, Fact Sheet on *Advanced Television* (Washington, DC: March 1990).

Capital Cities/ABC, Jack Pluckhahn of the Matsushita-owned television firm Quasar, Laurence Tisch and Joseph Flaherty of CBS, Irwin Dorros of Bellcore, and James Tietjen of the David Sarnoff Research Center. Alfred Sikes of NTIA/Commerce, Craig Fields of the Defense Advanced Research Projects Agency (DARPA), Diana Dougan of the Department of State, Greg DePriest of AMST, and John Abel of the National Association of Broadcasters (NAB) were all ex-officio (nonvoting) members. The ACATS had three subcommittees (Planning, Systems, and Implementation) and each subcommittee was allowed to set up working parties and advisory groups to provide legal and technical advice on specific questions.[2] There was substantial overlap in the membership of the various

[2] Richard E. Wiley, *Third Interim Report of the FCC Advisory Committee on Advanced Television Service*, unpublished xerox, Washington, DC, 21 March 1990.

ACATS committees and that of the ATSC. One big difference, however, was the greater representation of US-owned electronics manufacturers, and especially of members of the American Electronic Association.

The first major issues the ACATS handled were those of how to deal with the existing park of NTSC TVs and whether to allocate new spectrum for HDTV over-the-air broadcasts. The Hi-Vision system required more bandwidth (8.1 megahertz) than was available to existing local terrestrial broadcasters (6 megahertz). In addition, the Japanese system was incompatible with the 140–160 million NTSC receivers in the United States. Consumers would have to purchase expensive satellite dishes, satellite tuners, and down converters to receive Hi-Vision signals on their NTSC sets, and would probably receive lower quality pictures as a result. So one of the first FCC rulings on HDTV was to protect the owners of NTSC equipment by requiring on 1 September 1988, that "existing service to viewers utilizing NTSC receivers must be continued . . . at least during a transition period."[3]

If there was to be a transition period between NTSC and HDTV, and if the HDTV signal could not be received on NTSC sets, then there were only two possible ways to deal with the transition: (1) the augmentation approach or (2) the simulcasting approach. In the augmentation approach, the existing 6 megahertz channel would be used to transmit an NTSC-compatible TV signal and an additional 3–6 megahertz channel would be assigned to each broadcaster to transmit "enhancements" to the NTSC-compatible signal to bring the resolution and audio up to HDTV levels. Initially, both Thomson and Philips, the two largest European manufacturers of consumer electronics, favored the augmentation approach. The simulcasting approach involved using one 6 megahertz channel to transmit a regular NTSC signal and another 6 megahertz channel to transmit an NTSC-incompatible HDTV signal simultaneously. NHK and a number of video engineers in the United States favored the simulcasting approach.

The Chairman of the FCC in 1988, Dennis Patrick, stated publicly that he believed it was necessary to make it possible for the local broadcasters (and not just the cable and DBS companies) to compete in delivering HDTV signals to homes, so he asked the Planning Subcommittee of ACATS to explore means for implementing either the augmentation or the simulcasting approach. The FCC expressed a preference, early on, that no new spectrum outside the existing TV spectrum (UHF and VHF) be allocated for television. Strong pressures were coming from the

---

[3] Christopher Sims, "FCC Sets Technical Guidelines for High-Definition TV in 1990s," *New York Times*, 2 September 1988, p. 1.

cellular telephone industry, for example, to allocate unused spectrum in the gigahertz range for their applications, even as TV satellite companies were lobbying to obtain it for TV broadcasts.[4]

The issue moves to a higher level

The HDTV issue rose higher on the national agenda when the new Secretary of Commerce for the Bush Administration, Robert Mosbacher, announced at his nomination hearings in January 1989 that he would make the promotion of HDTV one of his top priorities. This elevation of the issue was to be short-lived. The inner circle of Bush Administration economic advisers – White House Chief of Staff John Sununu, Council of Economic Advisers Chairman Michael Boskin, and OMB Director Richard Darman – instructed Secretary Mosbacher to make HDTV industrial policies a lower priority item in his own agenda, withheld HDTV funds from the Defense Advanced Research Projects Agency, and in April 1990 fired Craig Fields, the acting director of that agency, an important backer of HDTV policies in the Department of Defense.

The ideological concerns of the Bush Administration's inner circle were heightened by the specific tactics of US business groups, and especially the American Electronics Association, in pushing for particular types of HDTV industrial policies. But even more moderate and traditional responses were ruled out at the highest levels by an overwhelming desire to avoid endorsing any form of industrial policy for any purpose whatsoever.

The HDTV issue did not actually die in 1990. Instead, the initiative for HDTV policy-making returned to the FCC. Two FCC decisions had an important impact on the global HDTV debate: to give all US terrestrial broadcasters an additional channel for simultaneously broadcasting (simulcasting) an HDTV signal and to require that proponents of HDTV standards for the United States attempt to use digital rather than analog signals for encoding, transmission, and decoding of HDTV materials. While the simulcasting decision had little impact on how the rest of the world thought about HDTV, the digital signal decision caused key actors in Japan and Europe to rethink their HDTV strategies.

The AEA Task Force for High Definition Television

On 6 June 1988, the American Electronics Association (AEA) convened a meeting on Advanced Television at its headquarters in Santa Clara,

---

[4] Keith Bradsher, "The Elbowing is Becoming Fierce for Space on the Radio Spectrum," *New York Times*, 24 June 1990, p. 1.

California. The 6 June meeting was attended by a number of top executives from American computer, telecommunications, and semiconductor firms. A Department of Commerce study (1988) on future demand for HDTV receivers was presented to the group at this meeting along with several other summaries of the issues. The meeting was followed by two others: one on 1 September in Washington, DC and another on 10 November 1988 in Santa Clara. By the September meeting, the group was calling itself the Task Force for Advanced Television. From the Task Force emerged two reports that had a major influence on the course of the national debate on HDTV.

The AEA is a business association of 3,700 US-owned firms in the electronics industries. It is significant that the AEA convened the meetings in 1988 and not the Electronic Industries Association (EIA).[5] The EIA is also an American business association of firms in electronics, but, whereas the charter of the AEA requires that members be 100 percent US-owned, the EIA has no such requirement. Most of the major Asian and European firms with subsidiaries in the United States, therefore, are members of the EIA but not the AEA. Some US-owned firms, like IBM, AT&T, and Apple Computer, belong to both organizations. Both the AEA and the EIA are active in lobbying activities in Washington. The EIA, however, is based in Washington while the AEA is headquartered in California. The EIA has much larger revenues than the AEA, because they include the profits of two large annual consumer electronics shows (in Las Vegas and Chicago).[6]

One of key movers of the AEA initiative was Richard J. Elkus, Jr., the chairman of a small firm called Prometrix, Inc., that produced testing equipment for semiconductor manufacturing. Elkus's interest in HDTV sprang from his personal involvement in the development of the videocassette recorder while working at Ampex Corporation.[7] Elkus believed the failure of Ampex and other US companies to develop VCR technology was the beginning of a series of blunders that threatened the survival of the US electronics industry. He promulgated the theory that a strong presence in both upstream and downstream industries was required to remain internationally competitive in electronics. The retreat from consumer electronics in the 1960s and 1970s was coming back to haunt the US electronics industry. HDTV – whether from Japan or Europe – would be the knockout blow unless US firms made a concerted effort to

[5] The EIA was later to form its own task force on HDTV.
[6] Stan Prentiss, *HDTV: High Definition Television* (Blue Ridge Summit, PA: TAB Books, 1990), pp. 213–19.
[7] Jeffrey A. Hart, "The Consumer Electronics Industry in the United States: Its Decline and Future Revival," *Business in the Contemporary World*, 3 (Summer 1991), pp. 46–54.

reenter consumer electronics by whatever means available.[8] This theory was already broadly accepted in the electronics community, but Elkus became its chief defender for a while. He pushed strongly for using HDTV industrial policies to promote US-owned firms' reentry into consumer electronics markets.

The AEA Task Force on Advanced Television produced two key reports. The first AEA report, released in November 1988, provided statistical projections of demand for HDTV receivers and related that demand to demand for semiconductors and advanced workstations.[9] Like the earlier report of the Department of Commerce, the AEA report was optimistic in its projections of the demand for HDTV products. In addition, the report argued that the failure of US firms to participate in future markets for HDTV receivers would translate rather directly into the rapid loss of global production shares for both semiconductors and workstations. The report stated that the US semiconductor industry could lose as much as 50 percent of its global share of world production if US firms failed to produce HDTV receivers. It argued further that the United States would have to have at least a 50 percent share of world production of HDTV receivers to maintain its current 70 percent share of world production of advanced workstations.

The issuance of the first AEA report was widely covered in the national press. That coverage created strong pressures in Congress for public policies to address the HDTV technology gap. Congressman Edward J. Markey (D.-Massachusetts), Chairman of the Subcommittee on Telecommunications and Finance of the House Committee on Energy and Commerce, and two other members of that subcommittee, Don Ritter (R.-Pennsylvania) and Mel Levine (D.-California), believed that there needed to be a review of US policies toward HDTV and Markey pushed for hearings on that subject early in 1989 (see below). Ritter and Levine were convinced even before the 1989 hearings that there needed to be special industrial policies to promote domestic HDTV activities. More importantly, Ritter and Levine wanted to use the HDTV issue to push a broader industrial policy agenda and to use the failure to adopt industrial policies for HDTV as a way of criticizing the Bush Administration's approach to problems of competitiveness. In the Senate, Senators

---

[8] Richard J. Elkus, Jr., *Toward a National Strategy: The Strategy of Leverage* (Washington, DC: Economic Strategy Institute, 1991).

[9] Advanced Television Task Force Economic Impact Team, *High Definition Television (HDTV): Economic Analysis of Impact* (Santa Clara, CA: American Electronics Association, November 1988). A full-scale critique of this report can be found in Phillip C. Webre, *The Scope of High-Definition Television Market and its Implications for Competitiveness* (Washington, DC: Congressional Budget Office, July 1989).

Albert Gore (D.-Tennessee) and Ernest "Fritz" Hollings (D.-S. Carolina) were also concerned about HDTV policies and held their own hearings in early 1989.

The new Secretary of Commerce, Robert Mosbacher, also reacted positively to the first AEA report. In January 1989, Mosbacher stated strong support for promoting a US-based HDTV industry.[10] In testimony before Edward Markey's Subcommittee on Telecommunications and Finance of the House Committee on Energy and Commerce in March 1989, Mosbacher said he thought HDTV could be "a major catalyst for technological progress" and favored the removal of antitrust barriers for companies interested in forming joint ventures.[11] He also opposed government sponsorship of foreign HDTV research efforts and stated that US firms should be the primary beneficiaries of any US government support.[12] Similarly, the Deputy Director of the Defense Advanced Research Projects Agency (DARPA), Dr. Craig Fields, firmly supported government assistance for the development of HDTV technologies and discussed the new DARPA competition for grants for research on HDTV display technologies (see below).

The role of DARPA

In November 1988, the Defense Advanced Research Projects Agency (DARPA) announced a new $30 million grant competition for the development of high-definition displays and display processors. The $30 million was to be split equally between display and processor research. Eighty-seven proposals were received prior to the March 1989 deadline. In June 1989, thirteen grants were announced for research on high-definition displays. This strong interest in the competition by a number of small but highly innovative firms was cited by Craig Fields in his testimony before the Markey Committee as evidence of the desirability of government involvement in promoting HDTV technologies. Many in Congress and in the electronics industry agreed with him, but Fields came to find himself more and more at odds with the Bush Administration's inner circle over HDTV and industrial policy.

Some background on DARPA may be useful to understand the central role that DARPA played in 1988–9 in the governmental debates over

[10] Eduardo Lachica, "Commerce Designate Mosbacher Vows Policies to Boost United States Competitiveness," *New York Times*, 25 January 1989, p. A22.

[11] Paul Blustein and Evelyn Richards, "If it Looks Like a Duck and Walks Like a Duck Does that Make it an Industrial Policy?" *Washington Post National Weekly Edition*, 15–21 May 1989, p. 31.

[12] Christopher Sims, "Hearings on High-Definition TV," *New York Times*, 9 March 1989, p. C1.

industrial policy. DARPA was established in 1958 (it was originally called the Advanced Research Projects Agency; the Clinton Administration returned to the original name in 1993) in the wake of the successful launch of the Sputnik satellite by the Soviet Union. DARPA was initially involved primarily in supporting R&D in military space programs, including ballistic missile detection and defense technologies. During the Vietnam War, DARPA turned its attention to a broader set of technologies, including artificial intelligence and other aspects of computer science. In the early 1970s, DARPA research pioneered the development of digital telecommunications networks, including packet switching and the development of new ways of interconnecting different types of computing systems. DARPA funding in the early 1970s was central to the development of the UNIX workstation and reduced instruction set computer (RISC) microprocessors used in workstations. In the late 1970s, DARPA was involved in the development of stealth technologies and new conventional weapons technologies, while at the same time continuing to push out the envelope in military space technologies. In short, DARPA was involved in military and dual-use technology development from the 1970s on.[13]

DARPA had also played a central role in the funding and management of two government–industry R&D projects: the VHSIC (very high-speed integrated circuits) Program and Sematech (Semiconductor Manufacturing).[14] In VHSIC and Sematech, DARPA had learned that solving problems connected with increased competition from the Japanese semiconductor industry required more than the traditional support of military R&D. Staying at the cutting edge of electronics technologies increasingly required the development of process technologies connected with high-volume manufacturing. Most defense contractors did not produce in high enough volumes to develop these technologies. So DARPA found itself working increasingly with predominantly commercially oriented electronics concerns in advancing the state of the art in electronics. That is why DARPA delegated more management authority to the private firms in Sematech than it had done in VHSIC. When the effort to take the results of Sematech into high-volume manufacturing through the creation of US Memories failed, DARPA was forced to reassess its overall strategy.

---

[13] Richard Van Atta, "The Government's Role in Fostering Technology Development," presentation to the EIA 21st Annual Spring RDT&D and Budget Conference, Washington, DC, 7 April 1992; François Bar, Jeffrey A. Hart, and Robert Reed, "The Building of the Internet," *Telecommunications Policy*, 16 (November 1992), pp. 666–89.

[14] Glenn R. Fong, "The Potential for Industrial Policy: Lessons from the Very High Speed Integrated Circuit Program," *Journal of Policy Analysis and Management*, 5 (1986), pp. 264–91.

It was in this context that Craig Fields decided to push for greater government leadership in promoting civilian technologies, starting most visibly with HDTV technologies in the high-definition display project. Fields became a major spokesman for the need for a civilian equivalent to DARPA, since he realized that using DoD agencies for the promotion of purely commercial technologies would not work in the long run. Nevertheless, he felt that DARPA support for the development of HDTV technologies could be justified on the basis of their being "dual-use" technologies (for both military and civilian applications).

Robert Costello, Assistant Secretary of Defense for Acquisition, supported Fields. Both Costello and Fields believed that the government needed to be concerned about the "defense industrial base." A series of studies done by the Defense Science Board in the mid- and late 1980s about US dependency on imported components for military systems strengthened the position of the supporters of defense-related industrial policies in the DoD like Costello.[15]

The AEA proposal for HDTV industrial policies

The second AEA report was made public at a special Congressional hearing on 9 May 1989. The report was based on a study done by the Boston Consulting Group (BCG) and paid for by small contributions from eighteen AEA Task Force members. The BCG was given instructions to produce recommendations for ensuring the successful launch of HDTV industries in the United States under the assumption that US-owned firms would produce most of the technology and equipment. The BCG study group, led by Todd Hixon, examined the state of the US consumer electronics industry and compared it with those in Japan and Western Europe, and then correctly noted that it would take major government subsidies for US firms to catch up with the state of the art in HDTV technologies.

The BCG study made much less optimistic assumptions about the growth in demand for HDTV products and services than the Commerce and first AEA reports, especially in mass consumer markets, and noted the dependence of demand on the availability of HDTV programming. The BCG accordingly recommended major subsidies and loan guarantees to create the necessary preconditions for the revival of US consumer electronics production and for investments in HDTV programming and

---

[15] Interview with Robert Costello at the Hudson Institute, Indianapolis, Indiana, Summer 1993.

transmission equipment. As a result, the second AEA report called for direct subsidies of $350 million and loan guarantees of $1 billion for a total of $1.35 billion in total government allocations.[16]

When the AEA released its second report, the immediate reaction from the Bush Administration, including Secretary Mosbacher, was quite negative. Mosbacher had not been warned ahead of time about the contents of the second report.[17] Pat Hubbard, Vice President of the AEA, released it in a Congressional hearing room at the same time Mosbacher was testifying before the Senate Commerce Committee. When he heard of the funding request he argued that US firms were holding back on HDTV research in hopes that the government would step in. He said: "Frankly, the problem is they're hoping that...Uncle Sugar will fund it. I don't think they should depend on that." Senator Ernest Hollings strongly criticized Mosbacher for his change of heart, arguing that the Bush Administration was doing nothing specific about competitiveness. Mosbacher replied "industry must be the ones who are the primary suppliers of money."[18] By September 1989, Mosbacher had backed even further away from his initial support of special policies for HDTV. Now he favored only broad governmental support for a range of technologies, without a focus on any specific one.[19]

Not only had Mosbacher been blindsided with the announcement of the new AEA study, he was getting blasts of criticism from the inner circle of White House advisers about his earlier support for HDTV industrial policies. George Bush had taken a stand against industrial policy-making in a campaign speech in San Francisco in September 1988 when he said: "I oppose the federal government's picking winners and losers in the private sector. That's known as 'industrial policy.'"[20] Michael J. Boskin, chairman of the Council of Economic Advisers, Richard G. Darman, director of the Office of Management and Budget, and John Sununu, White House Chief of Staff, all subscribed to this same belief. A senior OMB aide (probably Darman) was quoted in *Business Week* in November

---

[16] Testimony of Pat Hill Hubbard, Vice President, American Electronics Association, before the Committee on Commerce, Science, and Transportation, United States Senate, 9 May 1989. This testimony includes the entire text of the BCG report together with a summary written by the staff of the AEA.

[17] The reason for this, apparently, was that the AEA had not reached an internal consensus on what to do with the BCG report until the evening before. I learned this in an interview with Ron Rosensweig, a participant in the AEA HDTV Task Force, in January 1990.

[18] C. T. Hall, "Feds Say Their Funding of HDTV to Be Modest," *San Francisco Chronicle*, 10 May 1989, p. C1.

[19] John Markoff, "Cuts Are Expected for United States Financing in High-Tech Area," *New York Times*, 16 November 1989, p. 1.

[20] Blustein and Richards, "If it Looks Like a Duck."

1989: "We just don't believe in picking specific winners and losers."[21] They were not alone, of course, in holding this view.

The Bush Administration clamps down on DARPA

On 16 November 1989, the Bush Administration announced plans for sharp cuts in Department of Defense programs to support research and development. Included prominently in the list of items to be cut was DARPA's high-definition display technology project. In addition, OMB asked the Department of Defense to put a hold on several of the research contracts already awarded under the project. This decision came only a week after the Administration announced that it was merging the Defense Manufacturing Board into the Defense Science Board, presumably in a related effort to curb DoD industrial policy-making activities.

Apparently the internal debate over the need for "industrial policies" was reaching a new stage. The Bush inner circle was circling the wagons for an all-out battle on this issue. The 16 November announcement occurred just a few days before the publication of the initial proposals of the National Advisory Committee on Semiconductors (NACS). The NACS had been formed under Congressional mandate to deal with declining US competitiveness in the semiconductor industry. It was composed of chief executive officers of the largest computer and semiconductor firms, and headed by Ian Ross, the head of Bell Labs. The NACS reports and recommendations focused squarely on the role of downstream industries like consumer electronics in strengthening US competitiveness, and called for among other things a Consumer Electronics Capital Corporation (CECC) to help lower the cost of capital for US firms wishing to reenter consumer electronics markets.[22] The Bush Administration totally ignored the recommendations of the NACS, and continued to do so after receiving visits from high-level industry delegations and subsequent reports. The inner circle began to talk about the need to refocus DoD efforts away from dual-use technologies toward military sole-use technologies in the post-Cold War environment.

Things came to a head when Craig Fields decided to fund the high-definition research projects out of DARPA's discretionary funds in April 1990 and to continue to speak out aggressively in favor of civilian technology programs. Congress had authorized $20 million for the HDTV

---

[21] J. Carey, "Will the White House Torpedo America, Inc.?" *Business Week*, 27 November 1989, p. 80.
[22] Andrew Pollack, "United States Aid Sought for Electronics," *New York Times*, 30 October 1989, p. 1.

efforts at DARPA, contingent upon receiving a report explaining the need for the funds. DARPA had not been able to supply this report to Congress because the Administration blocked its release.[23] Fields had been tapped to become the Director of DARPA in May 1990. When DARPA decided on 20 April to invest $4 million in Gazelle Microcircuits, a small Silicon Valley firm working on gallium arsenide integrated circuits, under a new Congressional program to support such investments, the Bush inner circle had Fields removed from his position.

The firing of Craig Fields was covered very widely in the national media, and actually raised the salience of the HDTV issue for a short time, but it eventually reduced the visibility of the issue by removing one of its most important defenders and making it costly for his successors to continue along the same lines. Reactions to the firing among the national security elite were surprisingly negative. William Perry, former Undersecretary of Defense, said:

What [Fields] was doing could have been justified in terms of just building the defense technology base... He seems to have been caught in a semantics war of whether it was industrial policy or whether it was doing just well-conceived defense technology programs.[24]

Fields was caught between a Congress and an electronics industry that were enthusiastic about industrial policies – at least for certain parts of high-technology electronics – and an Administration that strongly opposed them. Special policies for HDTV had been hurt by their explicit linkage with a broader debate about the need for industrial policies by industry spokesmen like Richard Elkus and legislators like Mel Levine and Don Ritter. But the Bush Administration had paid a price for its ideological stance – a greater rift between itself and Congress on these and related matters and reduced support for the Bush presidency on the part of business leaders in high-technology electronics.

The FCC standards decisions

After the firing of Craig Fields, the initiative to make policies regarding HDTV returned to the FCC. The FCC had already announced in 1988 that it wanted to assure people with NTSC receivers that they would not have to throw away their sets immediately after the initiation of HDTV

[23] John Markoff, "High-Detail TV Faces Fund Cuts," *New York Times*, 6 April 1990, p. C1.
[24] Evelyn Richards, "Should Uncle Sam Be Technology's Godfather?" *Washington Post National Weekly Edition*, 7–13 May 1990, p. 31.

broadcasts, and that two approaches – the augmentation and simulcasting approaches – should be examined. Either one meant that additional spectrum would have to be allocated to allow each existing licensee to simultaneously broadcast NTSC and HDTV signals. This posed two important problems: (1) since the existing HDTV systems all used more than the 6 megahertz allocated to NTSC channels, was it possible to reduce the bandwidth requirement of HDTV also to 6 megahertz?; and (2) even if HDTV signals could be broadcast in 6 megahertz channels, where would the additional spectrum come from?

One proponent of HDTV systems for the United States, Zenith, announced a system called Spectrum Compatible television in November 1988 which required only 6 megahertz for HDTV broadcasting because part of the HDTV signal was to be transmitted in compressed digital form. In addition, the Zenith system engineers claimed they would be able to use the "taboo" channels that were left empty between existing channels to prevent cross-channel interference without causing interference with neighboring channels. Engineers at Zenith, MIT, and Berkeley were able to convince Alfred Sikes, who became chairman of the FCC in the spring of 1990, that simulcasting would work better than augmentation in the transition from NTSC to HDTV. Accordingly, in March 1990, the FCC directed the ACATS to discontinue its consideration of augmentation systems and to consider only those proposals for US HDTV systems that used a simulcasting approach.[25]

A private, non-profit corporation called the Advanced Television Testing Center (ATTC) was set up in 1989 by Capital Cities/ABC, CBS, NBC, PBS, the EIA, the Association of Independent Television Stations (INTV), AMST, and the National Association of Broadcasters (NAB) with a combined contribution of $3.5 million.[26] The ATTC was designed to test the ability of the proposed system to accurately encode, transmit over the air, and decode a variety of HDTV images. The ATTC had a cooperative agreement with the Advanced Broadcast Systems of Canada to do "subjective" testing of HDTV images. In subjective tests, average consumers rather than engineers judge the quality of the images. A separate facility at the Cable Television Laboratories (operated and financed by the National Cable Television Association) was used to test cable delivery of HDTV signals. The ATTC and the Cable Labs began testing proposed HDTV systems in the summer of 1991. The testing process would be completed by fall 1992. The FCC would base its final decisions

[25] Richard E. Wiley, "HDTV: The Video Future," in John Rice (ed.), *HDTV: The Politics, Policies and Economics of Tomorrow's Television* (1990), pp. 9–16.
[26] Prentiss, *HDTV*, pp. 132–3.

on HDTV standards in mid-1993 at least partly on the reported results of the ATTC and Cable Labs testing process.

Seven systems were proposed by the June 1990 deadline for testing. Several smaller firms and labs who had said they would submit proposals had already dropped out of the running by that time. Two days before the deadline, General Instrument announced that it was submitting a proposal based on a new method of compressing digitized HDTV video signals into a 6 megahertz bandwidth. As a result of this unexpected development, FCC chairman Sikes expressed a strong preference for all-digital systems.

By summer 1991 when the ATTC testing was to begin, there were only five major proposed systems left from the original seven: (1) the Advanced Digital Television (ADTV) system proposed by the Advanced Television Research Consortium made up of the North American Philips Corporation, Thomson Consumer Electronics, NBC, Compression Labs, Inc., and the David Sarnoff Research Center in Princeton, New Jersey; (2) the Spectrum Compatible (SC) system proposed by Zenith and AT&T with support from Scientific-Atlanta; (3) the Narrow MUSE system proposed by NHK; and (4) two all-digital systems proposed by the American Television Alliance (MIT and General Instrument).

MIT and General Instrument formed the American Television Alliance as a joint venture in April 1991, the Zenith–AT&T partnership followed closely on its heels. The Advanced Television Research Consortium added the Compression Labs as a partner when it felt it needed more help with creating an all-digital system. Scientific-Atlanta joined the Zenith–AT&T team to help them develop a workable HDTV cable system.[27] When it was absolutely clear that the FCC would not choose an analog system – and just before it was NHK's turn to test its narrow MUSE entry – NHK withdrew from the competition. That left three teams with four systems in the race.[28]

The FCC would make its final decisions on HDTV standards based on the recommendation of ACATS. The recommendations from ACATS would depend at least partly on the reported results of the ATTC and Cable Labs testing process. On 16 February 1993, Richard Wiley of ACATS reported that the tests had yielded "no superior system," that all of the proposed systems were quite similar but flawed in some respect. Accordingly, the ACATS recommended to the FCC two alternative courses of

---

[27] W. Sweet, "Future of Electronics Companies at Stake in Development of New TV Systems," *Physics Today*, March 1991, p. 57.

[28] The American Television Alliance – MIT and General Instrument – entered two slightly different systems in the competition: a joint entry with an 1125/60 interlaced production format and an MIT-only system with a progressive scanning.

action: (1) ask the three teams to merge into a superteam that would solve the remaining technical problems to the satisfaction of ACATS and the FCC; or (2) allow the teams more time to perfect their systems and then have a second round of tests. The first course of action was preferred because it would save the time and expense of a new round of tests and would eliminate the possibility that a losing team would initiate litigation over the fairness of the competition.[29] On 24 May 1993, the three teams announced their decision to merge.

The American system, therefore, would be a digital system. The Japanese Hi-Vision and European HD-MAC systems were both based on the delivery of analog signals by DBS satellites. There was still some uncertainty whether it would be possible to devise practical means for delivering digital HDTV via terrestrial antennas, especially in noisy urban markets, but chairman Sikes leaned strongly in this direction in hopes that an all-digital HDTV will be something the US electronics firms could do better than the Japanese and the European firms. The Japanese and European firms would still be major suppliers of HDTV components and systems for the American market, no matter what standard was selected, because of the R&D work they had already done and because the US market was likely to remain open to imports and inflows of direct investment.

Conclusions

After a concerted effort on the part of industrialists and allied members of Congress from 1988 to 1990 to link the issue of HDTV to broader industrial policy concerns, the US government ended up with a policy on HDTV that was defined by the FCC process. The FCC protected the interests of NTSC set owners (in the phase-out period decision), local terrestrial broadcasters (in the simulcasting decision), and the US electronics industry (in the preference of the FCC for digital systems). To be a bit more specific, the combination of "go-slow" forces (consumers and local broadcasters) and "go-digital" forces (the US semiconductor and electronics manufacturers) was crucial in the US decision to go its own separate way in the adoption of HDTV standards.

It is not surprising that broadcasters strongly influenced the FCC process. This was to be expected from an established agency with a well-defined bureaucratic clientele. It was also not too surprising that consumer interests would be represented in FCC decisions, given the

[29] M. L. Carnevale, "FCC Panel Urges New Set of HDTV Tests," *Wall Street Journal*, 6 February 1993, p. B7.

legislative mandate for that agency. The novel element here was the effort made to reconcile the interests of consumers and broadcasters, on the one hand, with those of the electronics industry on the other. The United States was in a much more vulnerable position in the global competition for electronics markets than it had been since the beginning of that industry. The recognition of that fact played a very important role in US policies toward HDTV.

6   HDTV in Europe

Introduction

The international HDTV standard-setting effort became especially politicized due to competitive imbalances between the three major poles of industrial activity: Japan, Europe, and the United States. The significance of these imbalances was magnified by certain structural weaknesses of the European Commission, which led to an especially complicated interaction among the regions, and which ultimately defeated hopes for a unified world standard.

After NHK initially gained the upper hand in Japanese policy circles it tried to consolidate its position through ties to American users of the new technology whose behavior would affect the attractiveness of the MUSE/Hi-Vision standard internationally. NHK then tried to use that transnational coalition to globalize its standard in the CCIR, which would have further strengthened its position at home. Compromises made in order to secure American collaboration backfired, however, as they alerted key European consumer electronics firms and the European Commission to the potential threat to European competitiveness. As the guardian of the "Community interest," the Commission played up the potential harmful consequences of global adoption of a Japanese standard for the market position of European electronics and audiovisual producers. The Commission then forged a blocking coalition with producers and PTTs that enabled Europe to forestall a choice on global standards. The European delay activated American interests which had hitherto been passive about the issue, sparking debate in America with respect to the technology's consumer and strategic implications and rekindling a competitive standards-setting process in the US.[1]

---

[1] The most important of these were consumers, local broadcasters, and electronics manufacturers.

The EC blocks adoption of a modified Japanese global standard

In international standards forums, the Japanese government adopted a stance of global leadership, arguing for the need to replace the divisive multiple standards of the contemporary color TV world (NTSC, PAL, and SECAM) with a new unified global standard based on Hi-Vision. Although important allies in the US backed the proposal, other influential groups in Europe and the United States perceived the Japanese proposal to be part of a general effort to consolidate Japan's dominance in consumer electronics and therefore proceeded to block the NHK initiative. Nevertheless, the rapid rise of Japan to dominance in the consumer electronics industry recast perceptions of the issue of global standards, particularly for Europe.

At the CCIR meeting in Dubrovnik, the Europeans strongly opposed acceptance of Hi-Vision as a global standard. The reasons for this are complex, but in essence, they sprang from European concerns that their consumer electronics, film, and television production firms would lose out to US and Japanese producers by the acceptance of a Japanese production standard for HDTV.

The Europeans believed that even though the CCIR was being asked only to endorse the Hi-Vision production standard, such a decision would eventually translate into a general adoption of Japanese HDTV transmission and reception standards. Their own earlier strategy of survival in consumer electronics had depended on maintaining incompatible regional color TV standards (PAL and SECAM).[2] Consistent with its focus on the single market, the Commission was trying to get beyond multiple standards within Europe by migrating away from both PAL and SECAM to a new set of standards based on the idea of multiplexed analog components (MAC). The MAC standards were well suited to signal delivery via direct broadcast satellites – the preferred method for both France and Britain – and they could be upgraded easily to produce higher resolution and widescreen images. But the MAC standards were incompatible with Hi-Vision, because they were based on multiples of 625 scanning lines and a refresh rate of 50 fields per second, as opposed to NHK's respective parameters of 1,125 and 60.[3]

Beyond the technical costs was an overriding political concern: it would be difficult to continue the strategy of harmonization of broadcasting

[2] On this topic, see Rhonda J. Crane, *The Politics of International Standards: France and the Color TV War* (Norwood, NJ: Ablex, 1979).
[3] Initially Europeans doubted the possibility of down conversion, but having seen the success of the Japanese prototype they claimed instead that its cost was prohibitive.

within the region while excluding foreign TV manufacturers if the EC went on record as supporting Hi-Vision as a global production standard. The European manufacturers did not want to make things easier for their Japanese competitors in consumer electronics. Notably, though, it was not the manufacturers but rather officials from the European Commission who flagged the CCIR discussions of HDTV standards as an important issue for the Community.[4]

The European approach to HDTV

The Europeans were concerned that adoption of 1125/60 as a world production standard would damage their chances of participating in HDTV equipment markets. The largest European consumer electronics producers – especially Philips, Bosch, and Thomson – therefore supported a European response to the Japanese HDTV initiative. There were two main thrusts to this response: (1) negotiation of an agreement to do away with the multiple television standards within Europe, and (2) new funds for collaborative R&D in high definition technologies.

As of the mid-1960s, Europe had two main color TV standards – SECAM (séquential couleur à mémoire) and PAL (phase alternation by line). SECAM was invented in France, PAL in Germany. While both PAL and SECAM have the same number of scanning lines (625), the two standards are incompatible at the signal level. Most of Western Europe adopted the PAL standard, while France and the Soviet bloc adopted SECAM.[5]

When new standards were developed for satellite transmission, the attempt to improve upon the old technologies inherent to PAL and SECAM resulted in a further proliferation of incompatible standards in Europe. By the early 1980s, renewed momentum behind a single market meant that there would be support for negotiating unified European television standards for the various delivery media. An additional factor was the expiration of the patents for PAL and SECAM technologies and the subsequent entry of Asian electronics firms into European markets for color televisions. Efforts to create a genuinely European market for television equipment and services without making it easier for Asian firms to dominate equipment markets had a major impact on strategies for HDTV. To understand how this happened, we need to go back to the standards originally developed for satellite transmission, the MAC standards. We also

[4] See p. 99, text and note 26.
[5] See Crane, *The Politics of International Standards*; Eli Noam, *Television in Europe* (New York: Oxford University Press, 1991), pp. 294–6.

need to place the standards question in the context of the Community's move toward use of the single market as the cornerstone of industrial policy.

The origins of MAC

The Independent Broadcast Authority (IBA) in England developed the MAC (multiplexed analog components) standards.[6] MAC signals were suited to satellite delivery because they were analog and fit within the bandwidth limits of existing satellite transponders (27 megahertz). One could not receive MAC signals on existing PAL and SECAM sets, however, and direct reception in homes was impossible without the use of higher power satellites at the transmission end, and of a satellite dish and decoder at the reception end.

MAC was designed to be consistent with an international standard, CCIR 601, negotiated in 1982 at the CCIR plenary. One version of MAC, C-MAC/Packet, was adopted as a European standard by the European Broadcasting Union (EBU) in 1982. While Britain adopted C-MAC, France and Germany balked at the cost of C-MAC receivers and adopted a D-MAC standard deliverable by cable. The French and the Germans then developed yet another type of MAC, D2-MAC, which like D-MAC could be delivered either by cable or by satellite, but which could be easily upgraded to higher levels of picture resolution. D2-MAC/Packet was adopted as an EBU standard in April 1985. Distinctive variants of the MAC standard (B-MAC, C-MAC, D-MAC, and D2-MAC) were adopted for use by public broadcasters in Britain, France, Germany, and the Netherlands, but few MAC receivers were sold initially and there were problems with the launching and/or operation of new DBS satellites. Nevertheless, unlike PAL and SECAM, MAC was designed in such a way as to make it relatively easy to upgrade signals to higher resolutions without losing backward compatibility. This made it possible for Europeans to envision a gradual evolution from PAL and SECAM, to MAC, to enhanced MAC (with widescreen capability and better sound), and finally to HD-MAC.[7]

---

[6] The IBA was privatized in October 1991 and renamed National Telecommunications Ltd. (NTL).

[7] Ronald K. Jurgen, "Chasing Japan in the HDTV Race," *IEEE Spectrum*, October 1991, p. 28; Adam Watson-Brown, "The Campaign for High Definition Television: A Case Study in Triad Power," *Euro-Asia Business Review*, 6 (April 1987), pp. 3–11; Adam Watson-Brown, "Towards the Triumph of the Matt Black Box," *Intermedia*, 16 (January 1988), pp. 21–4; and "How Soon the Super Telly," *Economist* (30 January 1988), p. 70.

EC policies for technological competitiveness: frameworks for an HDTV response?

Although analyses of the Single European Act sometimes point to the importance of the "new approach," moving from mandatory harmonization to mutual recognition of national regulations, it is important to recognize that the number of common standards has grown significantly as part of the creation of a single market.[8] Since standards help define markets for producers and consumers they are particularly important where the incentive to invest in expensive new technologies would be severely dampened without the prospects of exploiting scale economies in a genuinely single European market. In addition, severe limits on the Commission's fiscal resources made regulatory policies such as setting regional standards particularly attractive.

The Commission's formal powers in industrial policy had been limited since the origins of the Community. The Treaty of Rome reflected the German interest in free markets and the French interest in retaining planning instruments at national levels only. The most notable power delegated to the Commission was its ability to negotiate common external tariff levels, although it was also empowered to monitor and correct restrictive or monopolistic business practices and state aids to industry.[9] The Commission's relatively small staff and untidy overlap of internal mandates posed another challenge, which was well illustrated in the area of industrial policy. Core components of industrial policy-making were distributed between Directorate General III (Internal Market and Industrial Affairs) and Directorate General XIII (Information Technology), but at least three other departments had some say.[10]

Given these administrative properties, it is not surprising that the Commission "developed an elaborate machinery for consultation in the policy formulation phase and for political management when general ideas are translated into firm proposals." The Commission was fairly careful

---

[8] Commission of the European Union, "European Industrial Policy for the 1990s," *Bulletin of the European Communities Supplement No. 3* (1991), pp. 15–16; see also Wayne Sandholtz, "Institutions and Collective Action: The New Telecommunications in Western Europe," *World Politics*, 45 (January 1993), pp. 242–70.

[9] Loukas Tsoukalis and Antonio de Silva Ferreira, "Management of Industrial Surplus Capacity in the European Community," *International Organization*, 34 (Summer 1980), pp. 357–8. Despite the inclusion in the Maastricht Treaty on European Union of a specific title on industry, the Commission's ability to devote new resources to "competitiveness" projects remains at the mercy of a single national veto in the Council. See Pierre Buigues and Andre Sapir, "Community Industrial Policies," paper presented at the Workshop on Industrial Policy: Challenge for the Nineties, Maastricht, 30–31 March 1992.

[10] These include DG IV Competition, DG XII Research and Development, DG II Economic and Financial Affairs, and perhaps DG I External Affairs.

not to overstep its legal bounds, and its "effectiveness is immensely enhanced in a function-oriented Community... [where] the commitments of the member states to specific policy ends are precisely spelled out."[11] The Commission learned from the case of completing the single market that policy successes stemmed from specific enumeration of tasks and by establishing a firm calendar of action. Under these circumstances the Commission managed to "anticipate spillover" and exercise its powers of initiative more fully.[12] In research and development, the Commission was careful to situate its narrow role of facilitating inter-firm collaboration in the broader context of a "Community interest" in international economic competitiveness.[13]

The first suggestion of Commission leadership for inter-firm collaboration on new product technologies could be traced to a 1970 Commission communication on industrial policy by Internal Market and Industrial Affairs Commissioner Guido Colonna. In subsequent years a legal basis for Commission involvement emerged, but the crucial political entrepreneurship was orchestrated by Viscount Etienne Davignon. Davignon's direct contacts with firms in the steel industry in the early 1980s allowed him to obtain a consensus among industrialists and thus helped to head off problems at the level of the Council, because he was able to counter objections from government ministers with direct support from national industrialists.[14]

Davignon's belief that direct talks with industry representatives were helpful influenced the decision of the Commission to formalize its commitment to consultation in subsequent statements regarding industrial policy in general and HDTV in particular. In 1979, Davignon initiated "round table" talks directly with twelve leading European firms in information technology (IT). This consultative grouping took on more explicit policy-making or "public" status after the Council of Ministers approved funding for the pilot phase of the European Strategic

---

[11] Peter Ludlow, "The Commission," in Stanley Hoffman and Robert Keohane (eds.), *The New European Community* (Boulder, CO: Westview, 1991), pp. 102, 118.

[12] *Ibid.*, p. 118.

[13] It was Davignon who, recognizing that the Commission's credibility was being undermined by apparent support for "lame duck" industries during the 1970s, linked up with key European firms to lobby for comprehensive structural adjustment policies that would "[aim] at either promoting research and development in high technology sectors or restructuring weak sectors of the economy." Margaret Sharp, "The Community and New Technologies," in Juliet Lodge (ed.), *The European Community and the Challenge of the Future* (New York: St. Martin's Press, 1993), p. 205; Tsoukalis and Ferreira, "Management of Industrial Surplus Capacity," pp. 375–6. See also Wayne Sandholtz, *High-Tech Europe* (Berkeley: University of California Press, 1992).

[14] Author interview with Etienne Davignon, Cambridge, Massachusetts, Fall 1982.

Programme for Research and Development in Information Technology (ESPRIT).[15]

ESPRIT was important for both organizational and economic reasons. It provided something of a prototype for later collaborative R&D and technological diffusion frameworks, including RACE (Research and Development for Advanced Communications Technology in Europe), BRITE (Basic Research in Industrial Technologies for Europe), and Eureka (European Research Coordination Agency). A new element was the emphasis on "demand-led" rather than top-down projects, monitored by small task forces incorporating Commission officials, industrialists, and research institute personnel. ESPRIT was important as a "channel for cooperation" between European firms that facilitated self-fulfilling "convergent expectations about the future." By facilitating greater coordination of responses to external competition, ESPRIT also helped mobilize a powerful constituency in favor of a single market unified by single standards.[16]

One factor facilitating Commission leadership was the severe competitive weakness of European information technology companies. The Community's overall trade balance in information technologies was positive in 1975; by 1980 it had a deficit of $5 billion, and this grew to nearly $22 billion by 1987.[17] Competitiveness was clearly perceived as a problem as early as 1982, when the Commission published a dossier on the subject calling for "positive actions" to promote productive investment and innovation by European firms. Even before the Single European Act relaunched progress on a single market, the Commission asserted the need for pan-European efforts: "In view of the pressure of international competition through innovation, the Community must ensure that industrial R&D is underpinned and enhanced by exploiting the advantages offered by the European dimension – advantages in economic scale (markets), industrial application (innovation) and the breadth of legislative provisions (standards etc.)."[18] The Commission consistently argued that "the European dimension" required a larger core of common European standards in emerging product markets.[19] More recently,

---

[15] Sharp, "The Community and New Technologies," p. 209.
[16] Margaret Sharp, "European Technology – Does 1992 Matter?" *Papers in Science, Technology and Public Policy*, No. 19 (Science Policy Research Unit, University of Sussex, 1989), pp. 8–10.
[17] Commission, *Review of ESPRIT* (Brussels, 1989), p. 11.
[18] Commission, *Competitiveness of EC Industry* (Brussels, 1982), p. 99.
[19] *Ibid.*, pp. 23–4.

in its important communication on industrial policy in the 1990s (the so-called "Bangemann paper"), it acknowledged that common standards "are also becoming a key item for the promotion of industrial competitiveness."[20]

The main problem with harmonizing standards stemmed from the costs of changing products and services to accord with new rules. The distribution of these costs affected negotiations over the appropriate rule to adopt and also influenced the likelihood of Community-wide compliance. One way to prevent distributional issues from derailing common standards was to incorporate as many affected actors as possible in negotiations. Indeed, the 1990 Bangemann paper on industrial policy called for consultation with business and other "interested parties." The Commission stated that coherent industrial policy necessarily stemmed from "active partnership between all the interested parties (firms, social partners, scientific bodies, local, regional, national and Community authorities)."[21] The commitment to a wide-ranging and inclusive network did not, however, amount to equal time for all: "In developing policies and guidelines, it is particularly important that the representatives of industry be fully consulted at the earliest possible stage" contrasted with "employee representatives must be given sufficient opportunities to make comments."[22] The main problem in HDTV was reconciling divisions within business, between public broadcasters, national manufacturing champions, and other users and producers of HDTV equipment and services.

The commitment to consultation reflected the Commission's political-administrative needs for expert information and help in securing implementation. Though wider consultation generated more information as well as consensual legitimacy, its price was slowness and substantial variation in the ability of "partners" to deliver the goods, increasing the level of policy uncertainty.[23] In the case of HDTV standards, as time passed and the number of parties grew, it became increasingly difficult for the Commission to exercise the "tight coordination of the strategy and tactics ... [of] the European parties."[24]

---

[20] *Ibid.*, pp. 15–16.
[21] *Ibid.*, p. 7.
[22] *Ibid.*, p. 21.
[23] Sonia Mazey and Jeremy Richardson, "Interest Groups and European Integration," paper presented at the Political Studies Association Annual Conference, Belfast, 7–9 April 1992, pp. 23–6, 29.
[24] Commission, *EC Policy in the Audivisual Field* (Brussels, 1990), p. 60.

The Eureka EU95 program

Intergovernmental bargains underwrote some of the early phases of the joint HDTV effort. In June 1986, the Eureka EU95 program was inaugurated at the first ministerial conference of Eureka in London, at the initiative of French President François Mitterrand. EU95 was one of the first research programs announced under the Eureka rubric.[25] The heads of state of the members of the European Community decided at their summit conference in Rhodes in December 1988 to make EU95 and HDTV a high priority isssue in Europe. German Chancellor Helmut Kohl and President Mitterrand had their own bilateral agreement to push for a European answer to the Japanese HDTV challenge. In April 1989, the EC Council of Ministers adopted a Decision on HDTV, which outlined a comprehensive strategy for the launch of HDTV service in Europe starting in 1992.[26] EU95 itself was renewed and expanded in 1990 when its first phase ended.

The funding for the program was to have been 190 million ECUs for the first four years, from a mixture of public and private sources. The actual expenditure for the first phase of the program, ending in December 1989 was 270 million ECUs (approximately $350 million). The second phase began in 1990 and was budgeted at 350 million ECUs (around $500 million) for three years. The total estimated spending for HDTV in Eureka between 1986 and 1993 was 635 million ECUs. This figure does not include money spent by individual firms to develop HDTV

---

[25] Alan Cawson, Kevin Morgan, Douglas Webber, Peter Holmes, and Anne Stevens, *Hostile Brothers: Competition and Closure in the European Electronics Industry* (Oxford: Clarendon Press, 1990), p. 335. Eureka began in July 1985 with the membership of nineteen European nations as a way of pooling research efforts across Europe. Eureka was seen as a less bureaucratic alternative to the mechanisms established by the European Commission to conduct joint European research in high technology. The larger EC countries liked Eureka because they were not required in Eureka programs, as they were in official EC programs, to take into account the needs and desires of the smaller and less technically able EC member states. Eureka was also, to some degree, a response to inducements from the Reagan Administration to involve Europeans in research for the Strategic Defense Initiative.

[26] This decision is labeled 89/337/EEC in European Community documentation. It states five objectives: (1) making sure that European industry develops all the technology needed for HDTV services; (2) promoting the adoption of 1250/50 as a global standard; (3) promoting the widespread use of 1250/50 globally; (4) promoting the introduction of HDTV services in Europe as soon as possible after 1992; and (5) making every effort to ensure that the European film and production industry occupy a competitive position in the HDTV world market. For commentary, see Adam Watson-Brown, "Hype, Hope & Clarity," *Television: Journal of the Royal Television Society*, November/December 1989, pp. 312–15.

technologies. Philips, for example, spent between 350 and 400 million guilders ($194–222 million) between 1986 and the end of 1992 on HDTV technologies.[27] Total European spending for HDTV development during that period was estimated to be around $1.4 billion.[28]

The most important participants from the beginning were Thomson, Philips, and BTS (a joint venture for the development of advanced television technology created by Bosch and Philips in 1986). Piet Bögels of Philips was named the head of the EU95 HDTV Directorate in Brighton, England in 1986 and remained its director through 1993. Philips directed the program's activities in the Netherlands, Thomson in France, BTS in Germany. Nokia, a Finnish electronics firm with extensive holdings in Europe, was added to the inner circle of program directors in October 1989.[29]

The purpose of EU95 was to develop technologies and prototype equipment for the processing of high-definition video images and stereo sound. From the very beginning, EU95 focused on the development of HD-MAC. HD-MAC video images had 1,250 lines per frame (double the 625 lines of PAL and SECAM, the current standards in Europe), an aspect or width-to-height ratio of 16:9 (the aspect ratio of PAL and SECAM is 4:3), and scanning was progressive or noninterlaced (the current standards are interlaced) at 50 frames per second.[30] HD-MAC

---

[27] "Philips Postpones HDTV Launch," *The Reuter European Community Report*, 30 January 1993.

[28] This is the author's estimate based on the following sources: Andrew Hill, "Europe Will Follow US Lead Over High-Definition TV," *Financial Times*, 19 February 1993, p. 16; and "Philips Postpones HDTV Launch." The former states that total public spending on HDTV was 625 million ECUs or about $700 million. The latter states that total spending by Philips was 350 to 400 million guilders, approximately $200 million. The total in the text includes an expenditure by Thomson of some $400 million, which includes investments in new plants to produce widescreen picture tubes. All other firms connected with the HD-MAC project spent approximately $100 million.

[29] Philips planned to invest 11 billion francs, Thomson 9 billion. See Office of Technology Assessment, *The Big Picture: HDTV and High-Resolution Systems* (Washington, DC: US Government Printing Office, June 1990), pp. 32–4; Patrick Samuel, "High-Definition Television: A Major Stake for Europe," in John F. Rice (ed.), *HDTV: The Politics, Policies, and Economics of Tomorrow's Television* (New York: Union Square Press, 1990); and William Sweet, "Future of Electronics Companies at Stake in Development of New TV Systems," *Physics Today*, 44 (March 1991), pp. 57–61.

[30] "HD-MAC" is frequently used synonymously with "1250/50" in discussion of the European HDTV standard, because HD-MAC, which is a transmission and reception standard, requires a studio or production format of 1,250 lines per frame and 50 frames per second. To be more accurate, however, one should note that the 1250/50 production format may produce digital signals that have not been encoded by HD-MAC encoding methods.

signals were backward compatible with MAC receivers, so people who purchased MAC sets would still be able to view images produced for HD-MAC receivers. They would, however, have to purchase new decoders to receive HD quality images on their MAC sets.

The European HDTV research effort, handled primarily in the Eureka EU95 program, became linked to the European semiconductor research effort in 1987–8 through JESSI (the Joint European Semiconductor Silicon Initiative). Like Sematech, JESSI was focused initially on creating leading-edge semiconductor process technologies. But to demonstrate their power, they had to be applied to high-volume manufacturing of real circuits. No semiconductor manufacturer wanted to invest in the expensive new process technologies unless there was a fairly certain market for the final products. Thus was born the idea, similar to US Memories in the United States, to manufacture HD-MAC chips using JESSI technologies in a new Eureka project called Europroject HDTV. In Europroject HDTV, JESSI 35-micron line-width production technologies would be applied to the production of HD-MAC chip sets. The chip sets would be available for use in low-cost HD-MAC receivers by 1995, the final year of Europroject HDTV.[31]

The participants in the Eureka EU95 program had already agreed to pool the patents they received from work done on HD-MAC, including the patents on circuit technology. So it was natural for there to spring up a connection between the Eureka EU95 program and JESSI for the construction of HD-MAC circuits. In this way, the consumer electronics manufacturers, especially Philips and Thomson, gained further support for their position on HD-MAC in the European Community from the major semiconductor manufacturers and semiconductor manufacturing equipment makers and became more deeply embedded in the highly visible Eureka R&D cooperation efforts.[32]

The EC directive of 1986

All users of high-powered direct broadcast satellites were required to broadcast in packetized MAC formats under the European Council

[31] J. Robert Lineback and Elizabeth De Bony, "Europe's Wide Screen TV Shift: Big MAC Trouble; High Definition Television, Europe's Multiplexed Analog Component Standard," *Electronic News*, 30 November 1992, p. 16. For background on the Mega Project and JESSI, see Jeffrey Hart, *Rival Capitalists* (Ithaca, NY: Cornell University Press, 1992), pp. 214–17.

[32] See John Peterson and Margaret Sharp, *Technology Policy in the European Union* (New York: St. Martin's Press, 1998).

directive on 3 November 1986.[33] This directive was brought to the European Council by the EBU with the intention of committing all European broadcasters to the idea of gradually upgrading DBS transmissions to high definition via MAC (the MAC to D2-MAC to HD-MAC path). The EBU's proposal was for a Council directive to apply to DBS signals for both FSS (Fixed Satellite Services) and BSS (Broadcast Satellite Services) satellites, but the representatives of Britain and Luxembourg vetoed the inclusion of FSS satellites, and so the 1986 directive applied only to BSS satellites.

BSS satellites broadcast at higher power levels (230 watts) than FSS satellites (130 watts) and therefore required slightly smaller dishes for reception of TV signals (30cm instead of 60cm). They had national "footprints" (mandated under World Administrative Radio Conference [WARC] '77 regulations), whereas some FSS satellites had footprints that were not so respectful of national boundaries. When the 1986 directive was issued, it was not possible to broadcast TV signals from FSS satellites.

The supporting coalition behind the 1986 directive had included the national governments, their PTTs, the major consumer electronics firms, and the public broadcasters. This coalition agreed to jointly finance the BSS satellites and related infrastructure. The governments and the PTTs paid for the building and launching of the satellites. The consumer electronics firms committed themselves to produce TV receivers for MAC signals. The broadcasters committed themselves to pay for new transmission equipment (which was not very expensive, as it turned out).

The governments supported the 1986 directive in order to protect the European consumer electronics industry and to promote the nascent satellite launcher industry. The governments wanted also to preempt the use of American launchers and satellites for TV broadcasting in Europe and to preserve their control over national cultures that they associated with the continued dominance of public broadcasting. The governments of the smaller European countries had less to gain here than those of the larger countries, although the Netherlands was a key supporter because one of the consumer electronics champions, Philips, was a Dutch concern.

The PTTs supported satellite delivery of TV because they wanted to reserve their terrestrial facilities for telephone and data traffic. It was logical to use satellites this way because of the inherently one-way nature of TV broadcasting, the great bandwidth required for TV, and the heavy

---

[33] 86/529/EEC published in the *Official Journal of the European Communities*, No. L311, 6 November 1986, pp. 28ff.

expense of building and maintaining terrestrial broadcasting antennas, especially in rural areas. Cable TV had not gained much of a foothold in Europe outside the Benelux countries, and consumers had not yet been presented with the choice of more variety in programming via more channels vs. higher quality of signals and programs.

The public broadcasters went along with the 1986 directive on the assumption that by doing so they would steal a march on private broadcasters and cable operators by offering an improved quality of signals to households while simultaneously reducing their own costs of transmission. In addition, the 1986 directive called for the encryption of MAC signals using a standard called "Eurocrypt" which would make it impossible for viewers to decode the signal unless they paid their satellite subscription fees. Unfortunately for them all, this strategy proved to be a disaster.

Failures of the BSS satellites

Problems with the launching and successful operation of BSS satellites and innovations in FSS satellite systems permitted several major private broadcasters to deliver television signals directly to European households in PAL and SECAM formats, while the public broadcasters had been committed by their governments to use the BSS satellites and had to broadcast in the MAC formats, which required the consumer to purchase a new TV set. In addition, the private broadcasters were able to offer more channels to their satellite customers than the public broadcasters.[34] It is not surprising, therefore, that the private broadcasters were greatly strengthened in their efforts to compete – precisely the opposite of the result desired by the public broadcasters.

The first German DBS satellite, TV-SAT1, was launched in November 1987 (see Table 6.1). It failed shortly after a successful launch, because the solar panels that provide power to the satellite failed to unfold. The second German DBS satellite, TV-SAT2, was launched in 1989. It also experienced a series of technical difficulties. The German public broadcasters became understandably nervous about staking their futures on DBS delivery over the BSS satellites. In 1988, ARD and ZDF began to explore the possibility of implementing the Japanese HDTV system in Europe. Like the private broadcasters in Germany, they argued for the continued use of PAL formats in all major delivery media and supported

---

[34] The Astra satellite, for example, carried sixteen channels, while the BSS satellites only offered five channels at the most. See below for further information on DBS satellites.

Table 6.1 *European DBS Satellites*

Name	Date of launch	Type of satellite	Operator
TDF-1	Oct 1988	BSS	France Télécom
TDF-2	Aug 1989	”	”
TVSAT 1	Nov 1987	”	Deutsche Bundespost
TVSAT 2	May 1989	”	”
Tele-X	Apr 1989	”	Nordsat
Astra 1A	Dec 1988	FSS	SES
Marcopolo I	Dec 1989	”	BSB, later BSkyB
Marcopolo II	Jun 1990	”	”
Astra 1B	Mar 1991	”	SES
Olympus	Apr 1988	”	Italo-European Consortium
DFS Kopernikus F1	May 1989	”	German group
DFS Kopernikus F2	Nov 1989	”	”
Eutelsat I-F4	Sep 1987	”	Eutelsat
Eutelsat I-F5	Jul 1988	”	”
Eutelsat II-F1	Dec 1990	”	”
Eutelsat II-F2	Dec 1990	”	”
Eutelsat II-F3	Dec 1990	”	”

Sources: Mark Long, *World Satellite Almanac*, 2nd edition (Indianapolis: Sams, 1987); David Rees, *Satellite Communications* (New York: Wiley, 1990), Appendix C.

the upgrading of PAL by working on improved definition and widescreen versions of that standard.

The first French DBS satellite, TDF-1, was launched in October 1988. The French government subsidized this launch at a cost of around $400 million.[35] TDF-1 was supposed to permit the transmission of five TV channels, but several of the transponders failed early in the life of the satellite. TDF-2 was launched shortly after, and it also experienced problems with transponders. Out of the total of ten transponders on TDF-1 and TDF-2, only six were working in 1990.

Much more important than the technical problems with the French satellites was the requirement that TV signals be broadcast in MAC formats. Since there were very few MAC receivers in French homes, the broadcasters, including the public ones, were not interested in broadcasting in MAC formats. Programmers did not want to create programs in MAC formats for the same reason. Thus, the French government was obliged to coerce its broadcasters to live up to the 1986 directive.

---

[35] *Satellite and Cable Report*, 1, 1990, p. 15, as cited in Paul Slaa, "High Definition Television in Europe: The Risk of Picking a Loser," paper prepared for delivery at the annual meeting of the International Communications Association, Miami, May 1992.

The French government twisted the arm of Canal Plus to put its pay-TV services on TDF-1 (the CEO of Canal Plus – André Rousselet – was a close friend and political adviser of François Mitterrand), but in doing so, had to agree to permit Canal Plus to simulcast its programs in SECAM format. Canal Plus was also permitted to encrypt its signals using a proprietary technology so that the company would be able to pay for its MAC conversions partly by charging its satellite customers not just for the satellite programming but also for the satellite decryption devices that were necessary to decode their pay-TV signals.[36]

The successes of Astra and the FSS satellites

MAC was challenged by a group of private broadcasters who committed themselves to prolonging the life of the PAL standard by moving to enhanced versions of PAL – PALplus and widePAL.[37] Rupert Murdoch's Sky Television, for example, was able to win important increases in European audience shares by directly delivering PAL signals to homes and cable operators via privately owned medium-power communications satellites owned by British Satellite Broadcasting (BSB) and the Société Européenne des Satellites (SES), as opposed to the high-power communications satellites owned and operated by the public telecommunications agencies of Europe.

Not only did Murdoch steal a march on the PTTs and the public broadcasters by broadcasting in PAL, he also provided more international programming to Europeans, mainly from Britain and the United States, than the public broadcasters. Thus, many Europeans bought satellite dishes or subscribed to cable services offered by BSB and SES in order to get a greater variety of programs.[38]

When Sky Television merged with British Satellite Broadcasting (BSB) at the end of 1990 (both were losing money at the time), the new company, British Sky Broadcasting (BSkyB), announced that it would continue to

---

[36] Paul Lewis, "France in Uproar Over TV Licensing: Luxembourg Joins Dispute," *New York Times*, 10 February 1986, p. D21.

[37] PALplus is an improved definition version of PAL that makes the image clearer by correcting errors introduced in transmission of PAL signals. WidePAL is an enhanced definition version of PAL that makes the image wider by moving from the current 4:3 aspect ratio to the 16:9 aspect ratio of HDTV but without great increases in picture resolution.

[38] I am indebted to Adam Watson-Brown and Hans Kleinsteuber for explaining these details to me. See also Alan Cawson, "The Politics of Consumer Electronics: The British and European Industry in the 1970s and 1980s," rough draft of a unit produced for the Open University Social Sciences course Running the Country, University of Sussex, September 1990; William Shawcross, *Murdoch* (New York: Simon and Schuster, 1992), pp. 340–51.

broadcast in PAL and would drop BSB's former plans to convert its signals to MAC. From then on, Murdoch, together with his European allies, argued against EC efforts to require all high-powered satellite broadcasters to adopt the MAC standard, despite the counterargument of MAC supporters that PAL was incapable of being upgraded to high definition, and that failure to enforce uniformity of broadcast standards would confuse consumers and disrupt the future market for HD-MAC products. In essence, the argument concerned whether the already rather large investments in developing HD-MAC technologies should be written off, with a predictable cleavage between those who had invested already and those who had not.

Choosing a successor to the 1986 directive

The main result of this division was to severely complicate the Commission's task in preparing a successor to the 1986 directive, which expired at the end of 1991. Community officials began in 1990 to examine the Community's options for salvaging the key elements of the deal worked out in 1986 in light of the disastrous failure of the DBS-MAC strategy. There was still a strong desire to promote a unified European standard for advanced television, to avoid dependence on non-European TV programs and technology, and therefore to protect European electronics manufacturers and program producers who would engage in risky advanced television activities. Since the Eureka EU95 program had focused on developing HD-MAC technologies, there was a strong desire among participants in that program to stay with MAC, despite the DBS failures. It was still possible that the United States would opt for the European approach to HDTV (although that possibility grew dimmer and dimmer over time), so planning for the replacement for the 1986 directive focused on new methods for promoting the approach of gradually upgrading to HD-MAC via an intermediate MAC standard, D2-MAC.

D2-MAC permitted the display of widescreen images with an aspect (width-to-height) ratio of 16:9. Unlike HD-MAC, D2-MAC pictures would not be higher in resolution than PAL or SECAM, but D2-MAC receivers would include some new circuitry to reduce visual artifacts and thus could deliver somewhat crisper pictures. In addition, the D2-MAC sets would use displays that were progressively scanned. Progressively scanned displays could be used for computer monitors as well as televisions. As before, the strategy was to use the EC's control over satellite and cable delivery standards to get the various parties committed to a unified European approach.

The European Council decision on 27 April 1989 on high definition television called for a single world standard for HDTV based on the European system. The decision did not mention HD-MAC specifically but focused instead on the 1250/50 production standard. This document highlighted the Council's concern for the continued health of the European consumer electronics and programming industries. It called for an "action plan" for the success of HDTV in Europe. The fourth objective stated in the plan was particularly noteworthy: "To promote the introduction, as soon as possible – and in accordance with a suitable timetable from 1992 – of HDTV services in Europe."[39]

In 1990, Commissioner Filippo Maria Pandolfi, who was at that time Vice President of the Commission and head of the Directorate General for Information Technology (DG XIII), initiated discussions for the follow-on strategy for the 1986 directive, partly in response to urgings from Philips and Thomson. Pandolfi widened the bases of consultation somewhat in an effort to arrive at a consensus on how to replace the 1986 directive. Pandolfi conferred directly with manufacturers, broadcasters, and satellite and cable operators in plenary meetings on 28 February and 27 March 1991, and subsequently in smaller subgroups, as part of the overall consultation effort.

The Commission's use of direct industry consultation for HDTV policies resulted in a more inclusive mechanism for deciding what to do next than was available to the Commission before the 1986 directive. It gave the private broacasters much more say than they had had earlier, and as a result diluted the power of the consumer electronics manufacturers. The manufacturers, having invested considerable sums of their own money in HD-MAC development, wanted the HDTV decision-making process to proceed as quickly as possible and with minimal changes from the earlier decision to back HD-MAC. The broadcasters, especially the private ones, wanted to slow down the process and to reexamine the choice of HD-MAC as the favored transmission and reception standard. They were particularly concerned about the reliance on DBS satellites to make the transition to HD-MAC, given the problems with the BSS satellites.

The private broadcasters began to argue for the idea of transmitting HDTV signals digitally, especially after the FCC began to tilt toward an all-digital HDTV for the United States, partly because they thought that the analog/digital hybrids like HD-MAC would quickly become obsolete but mainly because they wanted to delay their own expenditures on HDTV equipment. They did not like the fact that HD-MAC signals

---

[39] 89/337/EEC, published in the *Official Journal of the European Communities*, No. L 142, 25 May 1989, p. 1.

could not be delivered via terrestrial antennas, but only via DBS satellites and cable. They argued that digital TV could be delivered by all three methods and that it was more likely than hybrid HDTV to generate adequate revenue streams. The private broadcasters and some of the public broadcasters, including the ZDF in Germany, argued for improving existing color TV standards like PAL and SECAM before going to digital HDTV.

The manufacturers argued that delays in moving to D2-MAC would result in delays in upgrading to HD-MAC and would confuse consumers. They also believed that it would be quite a long time before all-digital TV could be developed and thought there was a reasonably large window of opportunity for a hybrid HDTV system like HD-MAC. Finally, they argued that it was too late to retreat from the MAC strategy, since so much time and money had already been invested in HD-MAC technology.

Pandolfi's strategy was to insist upon consensus and to avoid majority voting in the Council. A variety of draft directives was circulated and revised. On 3 June 1991, Pandolfi presented a draft directive that reflected his attempt to extract a consensus from the industry consultations. On 26 June, the Commission sent a draft proposal for a directive to the Council and the European Parliament. This was a much more qualified document than the June draft directive, with over 200 amendments appended. The draft required all new satellite transmissions to be in D2-MAC format by January 1992. It also stated "all set-top satellite receivers must incorporate D2-MAC circuitry, either on its own or with additional PAL circuitry." All PAL and SECAM transmissions would be phased out by 1994 except in Britain where the phase-out date was extended to 1996. During the interim, all broadcasters using PAL and SECAM would be required to "simulcast" in D2-MAC. To help the broadcasters pay the costs of simulcasting, the EC was prepared to pay up to 100 million ECUs in subsidies.[40]

On 24 July, the Commission sent both the Council and the European Parliament a memorandum setting out its analysis of the issue. In that document, the Commission provided information it gained from further consultations with the television program-producing industry. The latter asked that arrangements for making the transition to HDTV take into account the cost of converting library material to HDTV formats, the need to gradually phase in production of material in HDTV formats that are only to be viewed once (like news programs), and the desirability of

---

[40] Barry Fox, "Broadcasters Clash Over Satellite Rules," *New Scientist*, 9 March 1991, p. 14; Barry Fox, "Britain Left Behind by High-Definition Television," *New Scientist*, 15 June 1991, p. 26; and "High Definition Tunnel Vision," *The Economist*, 9 November 1991, p. 17.

encouraging experimentation in multimedia technologies (which combine television and computer technologies).[41]

The Memorandum of Understanding

In the meantime, Pandolfi found that it was necessary to go beyond the directive to maintain a supporting coalition for HDTV. Not all the required elements of an HDTV launch could be contained in the directive, which after all was a public document legally binding only on the member states of the EC. To get the cooperation of the growing variety of HDTV private interest groups in the EC's plan, Pandolfi discovered it was necessary to supplement the directive with less public and more informal undertakings. Thus arose the idea of a "Memorandum of Understanding" (MOU) to be signed by the enterprises (public and private) connected with the various HDTV launch activities. The MOU laid out explicit expectations of the broadcasters, cable operators, and equipment manufacturers, specifying dates by which broadcasts and receivers would be available in D2-MAC format. It also affirmed that HD-MAC would be the sole European standard (within ten to fifteen years). Agreement on these specific goals would be facilitated by subsidies to the players amounting to 500 million ECUs over the next five years.[42]

Essentially the draft Memorandum of Understanding was a payoff to the private broadcasters and the program producers to go along with the earlier agreement among the governments, the PTTs, the public broadcasters, and the electronics firms to adopt HD-MAC as the European HDTV standard. Some concessions were made on timing and on the continued use of PAL and SECAM for smaller TVs, but the basic idea was to make it worth everyone's while to go along with the original program. Unfortunately, it was this payoff element of the revised deal that was eventually to be its undoing.

The third pillar of the HDTV bargain: the Action Plan

The Memorandum of Understanding (MOU) was a private document and was a "declaration of intent," not legally binding on the signatories.

---

[41] Jean Dondelinger, "High-definition Television: A Technological and Cultural Challenge for Europe," *Target*, 92, January 1992, p. 1. Dondelinger was the Commissioner in charge of the Directorate General for Audiovisual Information, Communications, and Culture (DG X). Dondelinger and Pandolfi were the two Commissioners primarily responsible for HDTV policies.

[42] Jörg Meyer-Stamer, "European Technology and Industry Policy: The Case of HD-MAC," revised version of paper delivered at the annual meeting of the American Political Science Association, Chicago, 3–6 September 1992, p. 9.

SES and the German satellite operators had insisted on this in order not to get locked into broadcasting in MAC formats. However, acceptance of both the directive and the Action Plan by the Council and the Parliament were made conditional on the acceptance of the Memorandum of Understanding by its signatories. Thus, there was no way to avoid the MOU itself. In addition, the Commission could not authorize the subsidies mentioned in the Memorandum without formal approval by the Council and the Parliament. So was born a third document called the Action Plan. Thus, Europe's HDTV strategy was to be built on "three pillars," the directive, the MOU, and the Action Plan.

The private broadcasters continued to resist the program because of the uncertainties about consumer acceptance of D2-MAC and HD-MAC equipment, a key factor in the success of the launch. The Commission, as a result, asked two consultant groups to conduct studies on the impact of the proposed Action Plan on future markets for HDTV receivers and HDTV programs. The results of these studies showed much slower development of the markets in the absence of an ambitious action plan. These two studies convinced Pandolfi and the Commission to push hard for subsidies totaling 850 million ECUs, 350 million ECUs higher than the 500 million ECUs mentioned in the earlier draft of the Action Plan.[43]

In May 1992, the Council adopted a new directive on television standards stipulating that

only HD-MAC may be used for HDTV transmissions that are not fully digital; new programs and satellites launched after 1995 will be required to use D2-MAC (a transitional standard), in certain cases in simulcast with current standards (PAL/SECAM); [and] existing operators (television channels, producers, cable and satellite operators) will encourage the use of D2-MAC with the Commission's financial support.[44]

The importance of the second provision was that it backed off the earlier demand for all satellite broadcasters to simulcast in D2-MAC, instead requiring it only under certain circumstances. Financial support to enable compliance in those cases would come from subsidies to be provided in the Action Plan, which was not yet approved. New drafts of the Memorandum of Understanding and the Action Plan accompanied the new directive. The revised version of the MOU affirmed the "strategic importance" of HDTV for Europe's consumer electronics and

---

[43] For information on the content of the two studies, see "HDTV: Without an Action Plan, the Outlook is Bleak," *Tech Europe*, 3 December 1992.
[44] 92/38/EEC.

audiovisual producers and also cited the virtues of satellite delivery. It made a distinctly weaker case for adoption of the D2-MAC standard, however:

> Rapid implementation of common technical specifications [namely the 16:9 aspect ratio] simplifies the broadcasting of television programs in all countries of the European Community (the "EC") and makes a significant contribution to the development of a true European audiovisual market. In this context, the D2-MAC standard is available and offers an immediate means, compatible with the Directive, to implement 16:9 aspect ratio transmissions by satellite and cable.[45]

Accompanying the statement of principles were guidelines on the tasks facing each of the players (or "entities") involved in creating the market for the new technologies. Additional paragraphs detailed the role of the Commission, the broadcasters, the industrial manufacturing companies, the satellite operators, and the cable network operators. The interaction among these players would be guided by the notion that the directive's goals could be achieved "only through the overall synchronization of the activities of the Entities, facilitated by the Commission." The main goal of EC-level activity outlined in the MOU would be "to create minimum market conditions enabling the major investments which are implied by this cooperative action and the Directive." The signatories of the Memorandum agreed to become members of a consortium to promote the general principles stated above. The Memorandum would remain in force "as long as EC financial support is made available according to the Action Plan."[46]

The "existing operators" signed the Memorandum of Understanding in Brussels on 15 June 1992, even though initial consideration of the Action Plan in May had resulted in deadlock. Signatories included the three major consumer electronics firms (Thomson, Philips, and Nokia), major broadcasters (BBC, MTV Europe, Super Channel, BSkyB, ARD, ZDF, RAI, A2, TV3, Canal Plus, etc.), and major satellite operators (SES, France Télécom, and Deutsche Bundespost Telekom) (see Table 6.2 for the complete list). Commissioner Pandolfi said that the MOU "will lead to enormous benefits for operators, manufacturers and consumers."[47]

---

[45] Final Draft of the Memorandum of Understanding, signed in Brussels on 15 June 1992. The text was obtained via the NEXIS online database.

[46] Final draft of the Memorandum of Understanding.

[47] "EC TV Broadcasters, Programmers, Makers Agree on Moving to Single TV Standard," *International Trade Reporter* (Bureau of National Affairs), 24 June 1992, text obtained via NEXIS online database.

Table 6.2 *List of organizations represented at the meeting on the Memorandum of Understanding in Brussels, 15 June 1992*

Broadcasters	Satellite operators
BSkyB	Eutelsat
A2	SES
Canal Plus	Deutsche Bundespost Telekom
NOS	France Télécom
TV Plus	Hispasat
CLT	
Premiere	**Cable operators**
RTP Plus	Lyonnaise
ZDF	KTAS Kabel-TV
ARD	Tele Denmark
RAI	Cie. Gén. de Videocommunication
Super Channel	
Filmnet	**Equipment manufacturers**
ETN	Philips
Lyonnaise	Thomson
RTI/FININVEST	Nokia
Ellipse Cable	
VOX/Westschienenkanal	
TV3 Broadcasting, Ltd.	
MTV Europe	
BBC World Service Television	
PTT Telecom NL	
Thames Television	
EBU	
Pro 7/Der Kabelkanal	
VPRT	

Source: Memorandum of Understanding.

The meeting of the Telecommunications Council in Luxembourg

The next hurdle was to be a discussion of the Action Plan at a meeting of EC telecommunications ministers in Luxembourg on 19 November 1992. The objectives stated in the draft of the Action Plan presented at that meeting were to achieve, before the end of 1996:

A critical mass of satellite television services in D2-MAC in 16:9 format, or in HD-MAC; a significant and constant increase in the number of cable television networks providing high-quality D2-MAC programs in 16:9 format to their subscribers; [and] adequate and growing production of programs in 16:9 format and of high technical quality, in terms of both image and sound.

This draft of the Action Plan included a package of incentives totaling 850 million ECUs. Prior to the meeting, the ministers had agreed that the funds should be divided roughly as follows: 5–15 percent would go for distribution of programs by cable, 30–50 percent for satellite broadcasts, 5–15 for adaptation of studios, and 30–40 percent for production and conversion of programs.

Approval of the expenditures was clouded, however, by member state reservations. The governments of Italy, Greece, and Spain opposed any reference to financing in the Action Plan until more was known about changes in the overall EC budget, and particularly what would be in the "second Delors package." Portugal also expressed concern. Ireland and Denmark wanted to reduce the proposed funding by half; Britain preferred no funding at all. The Germans wanted subsidies to go not just for D2-MAC and HD-MAC programs but also for the PALplus programs they intended to broadcast via terrestrial antennas. The Germans wanted the Action Plan to be flexible enough to accommodate any system that presented images in a 16:9 format.

Edward Leigh, the Minister of Telecommunications in the British Ministry of Trade and Industry, chaired the meeting. At the meeting on 19 November, Britain and Denmark both opposed funding of the Action Plan, even on a conditional basis. Because the vote had to be unanimous, British and Danish opposition effectively blocked approval of the Action Plan. Leigh went further to oppose the convening of a special meeting of the telecommunications ministers to follow the EC summit in Edinburgh in December.

Pandolfi was furious. He blamed the British for holding up the process. He noted that "Everything is ready for an agreement, except the financial position." The Dutch Minister of Telecommunications, Hanja Maij-Weggen, criticized Leigh for "sabotaging the Council" by blocking the special meeting in December. The French and the Dutch representatives accused Leigh of conducting the meeting on the basis of national interests and failing to respect his commitment as chairman of the meeting to act in the interests of the Community.[48]

The British claimed that six other member states supported their position, even if they had not openly voiced their opposition to the proposed funding of the Action Plan. It is quite likely, in fact, that the representatives of Italy, Ireland, Spain, Portugal, and Greece were not as

---

[48] It appears that Leigh had gone beyond his legal mandate in attempting to bar the special meeting, as such a request had to be honored under Article 1 of the Council's Regulation, and as a special meeting of the Telecommunications Council was scheduled, as requested, for December 15.

enthusiastic as Belgium, France, Germany, and the Netherlands about the Action Plan because they had less to gain in either electronics or television programming. They were probably holding out for some special compensation, such as additional regional aids, prior to granting their approval for the plan. In the following weeks, however, the collective fury of the HD-MAC supporting coalition was focused on the British government.[49]

The EC summit in Edinburgh

At the EC summit meeting in Edinburgh, on 12 December, Pandolfi circulated a "compromise" for the Action Plan that had been suggested to him by Tim Sainsbury, the new British Minister of Telecommunications. Pandolfi also presented the proposal at the special meeting of the Telecommunications Council in Brussels on 15 December. Under Sainsbury's proposal, funding would be limited to 80 million ECUs for 1993, the Commission would have a study done of the technical feasibility of all-digital HDTV prior to February 1993, after which the Action Plan could be revised, and the discussion of the funding of the Action Plan after 1993 would be postponed until a meeting of the Telecommunications Council in May 1993.

Accounts differ on what actually took place at this meeting: several participants seemed to get the impression that the British compromise proposal was serious and that progress had been made, while others considered the proposal to be a sham. It does appear that a better climate for cooperation was created by the replacement of Leigh with Sainsbury. In addition, the British government seemed to be willing to let the proposed study on digital TV determine whether the Action Plan was worth the proposed expenditure. This did not prevent others from believing that the British government was simply "stonewalling" the Action Plan.

The HD-MAC issue aspired to the nether reaches of high politics on 16 December when Jacques Delors and John Major were interviewed while both were en route to a summit meeting with Canadian Prime Minister Brian Mulroney. Delors, in an unscheduled interview with Peter Bale of the Reuters News Service, claimed that Major had agreed to approve the Action Plan in Edinburgh late on Saturday night, 12 December, in exchange for an agreement by the Dutch Prime Minister, Ruud Lubbers, to put aside his objections to EC institutions being divided up between France, Belgium, and Luxembourg. Delors said: "My understanding is that Mr. Major gave his agreement to HDTV as a

---

[49] "HDTV: UK Presidency Accused of 'Sabotage,'" *Tech Europe*, 3 December 1992.

Community consideration in the research programs of the EC . . . For me it is part of the global agreement [reached at the Edinburgh summit]."

The British government quickly denied that any such agreement had occurred. Major himself said that he did not agree to accept the Action Plan, despite attempts by Mitterrand and Lubbers to persuade him, brushing it off as "detail." He admitted to giving the impression of flexibility by saying the issue should be discussed further at the 15 December special meeting of the Telecommunications Ministers in Brussels, but nothing more. Tim Sainsbury said that Major had never suggested that Britain would support an agreement regardless of its content. A senior British official said that the British government could not justify spending taxpayers' money on a technology that may become obsolete in only a few years' time. In short, the British reiterated the sentiments that were implicit in Sainbury's compromise proposal of 12 December.[50]

Europe reacts to the British veto

French and Dutch officials, whose manufacturing giants had so much at stake, continued to complain about Britain's delaying tactics. In the meantime, however, an important change within the Commission helped revive movement toward closure. This change was the installation of Martin Bangemann of Germany as Commissioner with portfolio for information technology (replacing Pandolfi) and João de Deus Pinheiro of Portugal as Commissioner in charge of audiovisual and cultural affairs (replacing Jean Dondelinger) in January 1993.

Bangemann was much more willing than Pandolfi to accept the British arguments about the limited potential lifespan of the hybrid HD-MAC system and of the desirability of seeking an all-digital HDTV. For example, on 2 February, Bangemann said: "At this stage, we don't see any signs of the UK showing more flexibility . . . In those circumstances, the Commission might have to revise its strategy, taking into account that digital technology could become a feasible alternative to HD-MAC within three to four years." Bangemann also suggested that a revised Action Plan might concentrate funds on the development of widescreen

---

[50] Suzanne Perry, "Britain Blocks HDTV Accord, Accused of Violating Summit Spirit," *The Reuter European Community Report*, 15 December 1992; Lionel Barber, "Major 'Misled EC Partners over HDTV,'" *Financial Times*, 17 December 1992, p. 2; Peter Bale, "Delors Says Major Agreed to HDTV Deal at EC Summit," *The Reuter European Community Report*, 18 December 1992; and "EC Ministers Fail to Approve Strategy for Development, Financing of TV Services," *International Trade Reporter*, 23 December 1992.

TV equipment, liquid crystal displays (LCDs), and the production and conversion of programs in widescreen formats.[51]

In short, Bangemann's strategy was to reduce the costs for the HD-MAC coalition of making a shift toward a digital approach by pushing for widescreen television standards without mandating that widescreen TVs or programs be in the D2-MAC format. The total subsidies package was reduced from 850 million ECUs to 500 million.

Philips had announced suspension of its plans to mass produce HD-MAC receivers at the end of 1992 because of the British veto of the Action Plan. Both Philips and Thomson made it clear, however, that they would continue their plans to market widescreen television equipment, but would probably not be able to produce any receivers with MAC decoders until the Action Plan was approved.[52] Both firms expressed regrets about the shift away from MAC standards, but also clearly signaled their intent to market a new generation of widescreen equipment. Thus, Bangemann's strategy fit quite well with the plans of the two largest consumer electronics firms.

Britain remained opposed to the size of the subsidy package, even after it was reduced to 500 million ECUs. A very negative report on future HD-MAC markets was published in Britain in December 1992 by a group of researchers at National Economic Research Associates (NERA) and at Brunel University. This report highlighted the problems of consumer acceptance of HDTV by focusing on the high initial costs of receivers, problems of developing large, but also inexpensive and compact, high-resolution displays, and of developing systems for terrestrial over-the-air delivery of HDTV signals to complement satellite and cable delivery systems. The NERA/Brunel study was very optimistic about the prospects of developing an all-digital HDTV system for Europe, pointing to the US HDTV competition and the Swedish prototype system called HD-Divine (digital video narrow-band emission). The NERA/Brunel study suggested that Europe should seriously consider adopting the US all-digital approach rather than pursue further the HD-MAC strategy.[53]

[51] Andrew Hill, "New Devices Ruffle TV Plan," *Financial Times*, 4 February 1993, p. 2; and Andrew Hill, "Flagship on the Rocks: The EC's HDTV Strategy is Failing," *Financial Times*, 9 February 1993.

[52] A consumer survey conducted by BIS Strategic Decisions showed that consumers preferred widescreen TV to conventional TV by a margin of 56 percent to 40 percent. This was particularly true of French and British consumers; German consumers appeared to be somewhat more satisfied with their current sets. Those favoring widescreen sets felt that they would be better for viewing films than their current sets. The survey is discussed in Andrew Hill and Andrew Adonis, "Turn On to the Bigger Picture," *Financial Times*, 16 June 1993, p. 19.

[53] Della Bradshaw, Louise Kehoe, and Michiyo Nakamoto, "Searching for a Clearer Picture of the Future: After European HDTV's Expensive Crash," *Financial Times*, 11 February

Bangemann seemed to be leaving this option open when on 19 February he said, "A digital standard doesn't need to be set [by the EC]. Global standards are always the best solution." This position got a considerable boost when the Advisory Committee on Advanced Television Standards (ACATS) to the US Federal Communications Commission (FCC) said that it could not choose among the proposals for an American HDTV system, and entertained the possibility of a "grand alliance" of proponents to solve the remaining problems with the all-digital approach. The successful negotiation of just such an alliance, announced on 25 May, meant that Philips and Thomson would definitely play a central role in the development of the US HDTV system. Knowing that they would eventually receive considerable revenues from their US HDTV operations, the two European firms became more willing to renegotiate the bargain they had struck in Europe.[54]

Endgame in Europe

On 1 April, Bangemann and de Deus Pinheiro published a communiqué stating that adoption of the HDTV Action Plan was essential to the future of the European television industry. The communiqué suggested that funding be directed toward encoding techniques, digital compression, modulation techniques, and LCD technology. It left open the possibility of adopting the standards of other regions, or of using at least some of the same technologies and standards. In a press conference, Bangemann said: "The intention to introduce the D2-MAC or HD-MAC as the obligatory standard for HDTV in Europe would be a mistake to my mind – and more or less everybody is now acknowledging it would be a mistake."[55] The new Danish President of the Council continued to talk with representatives of the member states about the Action Plan, with the hope of settling the remaining disputes before the 10 May meeting of the Council.

1993. It seems quite likely that British authorities had a copy of this report prior to the 12 December EC summit and that its contents had played an important role in their position at the summit and the Telecommunications Council meeting of 15 December. Also, it seems likely that the report itself was shown to the press and to Martin Bangemann in early 1993.

[54] Edmund L. Andrews, "Top Rivals Agree on Unified System for Advance TV," *New York Times*, 25 May 1993.

[55] There were news stories at this time about efforts of Philips and Thomson to arrive at common standards with Japanese firms for HD-VCRs. At the press conference on 1 April, Bangemann suggested that the EC and Japan should work together to produce a standard global digital format for HDTV "that would be acceptable to the United States." See "Bangemann Calls for Standard HDTV Format," *Agence France Presse*, 2 April 1993.

At the 10 May meeting, a new version of the Action Plan was presented. It proposed the abandonment of D2-MAC and HD-MAC as obligatory standards and the funding of research on digital HDTV technologies. As suggested by Bangemann earlier, it focused on the promotion of widescreen TV equipment and programming in the short term and digital HDTV in the long term. The proposed funding level had shrunk from Bangemann's 500 million ECUs to 60–80 million ECUs per year for four years. The reduced funding was intended to win British support for the Action Plan. No action was taken at the 10 May meeting because Britain firmly opposed spending more than 150 million ECUs. The decision was to be delayed at least until the next meeting of the Telecommunications Council on 16 June.[56]

On 26 May 1993, Armin Silberhorn, German Minister of Posts and Telecommunications, said that a group of European broadcasters, satellite operators, manufacturers, and public officials would soon announce the formation of a new organization called the European Launching Group for Digital Video Broadcasting. The group included representatives of the European Commission, the British Department of Trade and Industry, Philips, Thomson, ARD, and SES. An unidentified participant said that the group had been meeting on an ad hoc basis for over a year, and that it would focus its efforts on terrestrial delivery of digital HDTV. Silberhorn said that the group hoped to sign a memorandum of understanding on 2 June.[57]

Yet another draft of the Action Plan was circulated before the 16 June meeting of the Telecommunications Council. The subsidy package had now been trimmed to 228 million ECUs, again in an attempt to win British support. The British government reiterated its view that it wanted no more than 150 million ECUs in the package. But pressure from the British programming industry to accept the Action Plan shifted governmental criticisms away from the size of the subsidy package to the question of the availability of funding for non-European firms. The British government now wanted the Japanese consumer electronics companies which had established manufacturing facilities in Britain to be qualified for HDTV funding. Sony, for example, had a television assembly plant in Wales.[58]

---

[56] "Final Showdown over HDTV," *European Report of the European Information Service*, 15 May 1993.

[57] Suzanne Perry, "European Group to Announce Digital HDTV Strategy," *The Reuter Business Report*, 26 May 1993.

[58] Suzanne Perry, "EC to Make Last-Ditch Effort to Salvage HDTV Plan," *The Reuter European Business Report*, 15 June 1993; Hill and Adonis, "Turn On to the Bigger Picture," p. 19; May Fagan, "Fresh Row Looms Over HDTV: Britain Asks for Research to be Made Available to Japanese Firms," *The Independent*, 16 June 1993, p. 26.

At the 16 June meeting of the Telecommunications Council in Luxembourg, an Action Plan was finally approved. The subsidies package was set at 228 million ECUs, Japanese firms were permitted to apply for funding, and the idea of pursuing widescreen equipment in the near term and digital HDTV in the longer term was endorsed. Many commentators believed that Europe would be likely, as a result, to copy many aspects of the US digital HDTV approach. The French and Dutch consumer electronics firms were miffed about the last-minute inclusion of Japanese firms in the deal. An unnamed official at Philips said: "We are utterly amazed. How many European companies have access to Japanese research programs?"[59] The general mood, however, was one of relief that an agreement had finally been reached.

Discussion: EC policy networks and international competition

The EC HDTV standard-setting process resulted in an outcome closest to the preferences of private broadcasters and rather remote from those of the original HD-MAC coalition of the Commission, consumer electronics producers, and PTTs. In this concluding section I discuss what this outcome illustrates about the effectiveness of the EC policy process in facilitating cooperation between competing interests and the way global economic rivalry among Europe, America, and Japan links into the politics of industrial policy in each locale.

The evolution of the HDTV standards policy demonstrates the limits inherent in the Commission's organizational and political relationship with member states and private groups. Faced with the task of securing harmonization and building consensus, the Commission initially focused its energies on direct consultations with a few large producers of equipment and services, but eventually was obliged to enlarge the scope of discussions as it learned that technological change had broadened the range of private actors whose behavior would affect the shape of the HDTV market and that political legitimacy required their inclusion in negotiations of European rules. In the end the Commission lacked the fiscal and ideological resources to win acquiescence by those parties who had least to gain from adoption of a common MAC standard.

The Commission's manifest inability to overcome the resistance of private broadcasters and skeptical governments can be cited as evidence

---

[59] Nick Nuttall, "Europe Lets Japanese See Electronic Secrets," *The Times*, 17 June 1993; Cynthia Johnson, "EC HDTV Plan Seen as Morale Boost for Embattled Industry," *The Reuter European Business Report*, 17 June 1993.

for the view that it remains essentially the instrument of member states and/or transnational capital.[60] It is true that the Commission's reliance on firms and governments for implementation confers substantial influence on them throughout the policy process. But it is also true that national governments and transnational firms require the Commission to play a "facilitating" role, particularly when there are differences among them about how to improve on a threatening status quo, as it has been for the European electronics and audiovisual industries. International competitive pressures heighten the strategic interdependence between firms, member states, and the Commission, and when none of these actors can realize its interests without some cooperation from the others the Commission's calls for "synchronized" pursuit of Community interests carry greater weight.

Around what position are these interests to be "synchronized"? Is the "Community interest" merely a reflection of the preferences of powerful states?[61] Such a conclusion is problematic in the case of HDTV; it would imply that Britain "won" the bargain, which is surprising considering that none of the principal industry players was British. In other words, the outcome appears strangely skewed toward a state with relatively small material interests at stake. In fact, France, Germany, and the Netherlands appear to have had internally contradictory pressures at play with respect to the broadcast and manufacturing rules.

The fact that the Commission's original (and privileged) partners (state-backed PTTs and national champion manufacturers) failed to secure their preferred outcome reflects both the Commission's capacity for an autonomous vision and its structural weaknesses. The particularistic motives of these "European" parties – to maintain barriers to competition from private broadcasters and foreign manufacturers – were commensurable with the Commission's view that the Community's competitiveness would be further threatened by the globalization of NHK's Hi-Vision standard. Thus the Commission welcomed their participation in a relatively closed industrial policy network. However, as EC efforts to secure a common European standard raised the stakes for private broadcasters and consumers, incorporating these interests became important for bolstering both the technical and political foundation for a

---

[60] See, for instance, Geoffrey Garrett, "International Cooperation and Institutional Choice," *International Organization*, 46 (1992), pp. 533–60; and Wolfgang Streeck and Phililppe Schmitter, "From National Corporatism to Transnational Pluralism," *Politics and Society*, 19 (1991), pp. 133–64.

[61] Stephen Krasner, "Global Communications and National Power: Life on the Pareto Frontier," *World Politics*, 43 (1991), pp. 336–66; and Garrett, "International Cooperation and Institutional Choice."

common standard. Although widening the number of participants frustrated the Commission's ability to ensure coordination around a single proposal, it also effectively prevented its clientelistic capture.

Although wider-ranging "consultation" both reflected and compounded the Commission's inability to secure early and final agreement, it also promoted greater openness to signals coming from the market. Although manufacturers and broadcasters whose investments were tailored to anticipation of an HD-MAC world suffered some losses, it could have been worse. The ability to block global adoption of Japan's standard staved off further decay of a European manufacturing presence in consumer electronics, which was perceived to be at a critical state. The inability to zero in on a MAC standard spared EC producers' exclusion from American (and possibly global) markets that eventually turned toward a digital standard. Japan's "misfortune" illustrates the fact that market evolution is conditioned by the standards adopted to guide investment and consumption; Europe's insistence on rethinking standards changed the fortunes of NHK's HDTV gamble.

The "irony of state strength" applies well to the Commission's experience with HDTV: the quality of a policy network rests not only on the capacity of public actors to intervene in the market but on their ability to adapt to market signals and negotiate retreat from planned interventions.[62] Had the EC remained locked into the HD-MAC bargain it may not have faced the disaster some British opponents predicted, but it is clear that the HD-MAC bargain inherited the same vulnerabilities to technological change as earlier agreements, such as the 1986 Directive on using MAC for satellite transmissions. It is quite likely that the Europeans would have pursued the same near-term strategy of deploying widescreen technology before high-definition technology, and that there would have continued to be a mix of MAC and non-MAC standards. Thus the shift toward digital HDTV represented by the May 1993 Action Plan actually represents a timelier adjustment to the changing technological and political environment than one might have expected.

The losses to major electronics firms like Philips and Thomson were lessened by the fact that HD-MAC technologies were largely digital to begin with and they could use many of them in the transition to digital television. Europe has some important advantages in the delivery of digital signals via terrestrial antennas, which they may put to good use in solving both their HDTV delivery problems and those of the United

---

[62] G. John Ikenberry, "The Irony of State Strength," *International Organization*, 40 (1986), pp. 105–37. See also Ikenberry's "Market Solutions for State Problems," *International Organization*, 42 (1988), pp. 151–77.

States. Finally, the central role that Philips and Thomson would play in the HDTV grand alliance in the United States gave them some additional options in future competition with the Japanese consumer electronics giants.

Chapter 8 deals with the European pursuit of digital television largely via the negotiation of DVB (digital video broadcasting) standards with the global electronics companies. The DVB effort was a direct outgrowth of the retrenchment that followed the collapse of the HD-MAC solution. Chapter 7 extends the discussion of chapter 5 regarding the role that would be played by Thomson and Philips within the US grand alliance and in the introduction of digital television (DTV) in America.

7   Digital television in the United States

Introduction

Chapter 5 provided a history of the US debate over HDTV standards up to the decision on 23 May 1993 to merge the competing electronics firms into a "grand alliance" for a digital high-definition television system. This chapter starts from that point and brings the history up to and bit beyond 3 April 1997, when the Federal Communications Commission formally adopted a standard for digital television (DTV) in the United States. During this period, there was a change in the attitude of the members of the National Association of Broadcasters toward HDTV: they began to see it as an answer to the problem of declining audience shares. There were also continuous but only partially successful lobbying efforts on the part of major computer firms to have the HDTV standards modified to accommodate their perceived interests. The most important change was brought about by the victory of William Jefferson Clinton in the 1992 presidential elections. Clinton's Vice President, Albert Gore, was a strong exponent of governmental support for the building of an "Information Superhighway." Clinton, Gore, and their appointed head of the Federal Communications Commission, Reed Hundt, came to believe in the idea of "digital convergence" and had strong views on the role that television should play in that larger project.

Interlace vs. progressive-scan: round one

There was furious bargaining within the grand alliance prior to the announcement of its formation on 24 May 1993 to reconcile the differences in the four digital systems. Most contentious was the question of whether the merged system should be capable of processing progressively scanned or interlaced images, or both. Another important issue related to scanning was the number of horizontal scanning lines. As is evident in Table 7.1, the ATRC and GI proposed interlaced systems, while AT&T/Zenith and MIT had proposed progressive scanning. The AT&T/Zenith and MIT systems had fewer horizontal scanning lines (720) than the interlaced

150

Table 7.1 *Digital systems tested by the ATTC prior to formation of the grand alliance*

System features	GI	AT&T/Zenith	ATRC	MIT
Modulation method	16-QAM	2-VSB	16-QAM	16-QAM
	32-QAM	4-VSB	32-QAM	32-QAM
No. of horizontal scanning lines	960	720	960	720
Vertical resolution	1,408	1,280	1,440	1,280
Frame rate, p/s	30	60	30,60	60
Interlaced?	yes	no	both	no
Pixel rate, Msmpls/s adaptive selection	40.6	55.3	41.5	55.3
Coding method	MPEG	Vector	MPEG	Vector
Audio system	Dolby AC2	Dolby AC2	Musicam	MIT-AC

Source: William Schreiber, Appendix to *Development of High-Definition Television in Japan, Europe, and the United States* (New York: Springer-Verlag, 1992).

systems because one could obtain higher picture resolution (both static and dynamic) with fewer scanning lines in progressively scanned systems.

A rather heated debate on the virtues of progressive scanning ensued. Michael Liebhold of Apple Computer argued very forcefully at the February 1993 special panel meeting of the ACATS that progressive scanning was the most desirable route because of the difficulty of handling interlaced source material in advanced, video-oriented computers and workstations. The computer and workstation world was headed toward nearly universal reliance on progressively scanned video inputs and displays and would be handicapped if the input/output systems and video processors inside computers continued to have to be designed to handle both interlaced and progressively scanned source material, especially if the two types of sources continued to be in incompatible formats.

In addition, if HDTV signals were to be carried over the new information highways that were coming in the next decades, they should have the same sort of digital "headers" and "footers" that voice and data traffic have on existing telephone networks that permit new services like ISDN and caller ID. This would permit the manufacturers of television equipment to modify and upgrade their products and broadcasters or cable operators to offer new services to consumers without making existing equipment obsolete. In short, the computer types, represented here mainly by Mike Liebhold, but also by Robert Graves of AT&T and Jae Lim of MIT, were pushing for a sort of open architecture approach to

HDTV that was familiar to the microcomputer producers but inconsistent with the more closed architecture approach of the traditional TV manufacturers.

On the other side of this issue were the mass producers of television sets and the broadcasters (network and local) who argued that progressive scanning added to the cost of TV production equipment and receivers without producing better pictures. While it made sense to convert films in film libraries into progressively scanned video images, because one might be able to charge a premium for the higher quality of images, it made no sense to do this with video libraries. Live TV programming, like TV news and soap operas, would continue to be shot in interlaced video, or at least until inexpensive progressive-scan cameras were widely available.

The TV producers argued that televisions and computers were used differently by consumers and that the two industries were not merging as rapidly as the computer industry thought they were. Consumers, in their view, were not as demanding as computer users with respect to static picture resolution and were more likely to be confused than gratified by the extension of the open architecture approach to TVs. Also, they argued that since there were as yet no TV studio cameras to produce progressively scanned video, insisting upon an exclusive use of progressive scanning was a major flaw in the argument of the computer representatives.

The computer industry people countered with a variety of arguments. First, they pointed out that progressively scanned displays were not more expensive to produce than interlaced ones and that designing progressively scanned cameras was not a major difficulty, especially if the FCC created the financial incentives for doing so by opting for an all-progressive digital HDTV system. They conceded that some interlaced image sources would continue to be attractive to program producers, broadcasters, and consumers, but that eventually all would come to expect the higher quality of images that one could obtain with progressive scanning. Their strongest argument, in the end, was that the TV manufacturers and the broadcasters were trying to preserve a television infrastructure that was obsolescing or obsolete.

Most of the participants in this debate realized that an all-digital HDTV system would have important advantages over an analog system in permitting manufacturers to add computer-like features to television sets and set-top boxes, and that these features would require some agreement to limit the types of image formats and digital information that the digital HDTV signal could carry. Thus, a compromise was worked out prior to the 24 May 1993 announcement of the formation of the grand alliance. This compromise called for the US digital HDTV transmission standard

Table 7.2 *Six video formats in grand alliance*
system as of November 1994

Vertical pixels × horizontal lines	Frame rate in frames per second	Type of scanning
1280 × 720	24fps	progressive
"	30fps	"
"	60fps	"
1920 × 1080	24fps	"
"	30fps	"
"	60fps	interlaced

to be capable of encoding and decoding both interlaced and progressive source material. The interlaced material would have 960 scanning lines at 30 frames per second; the progressive would have 720 lines at 60 frames per second (see Table 7.2). Thanks to Kell's Law, which states that the resolution of interlaced displays is roughly seven-tenths of the resolution of progressive displays with the same number of lines, the two HDTV image formats proposed by the grand alliance would produce pictures of comparable resolution.

The original press release for the grand alliance announcement reported that all displays larger than 34 inches must be progressively scanned, but apparently that was an error. The grand alliance members felt that this would be an unnecessary handicap for them should non-members decide to offer (presumably cheaper) interlaced displays for large-screen TVs. Since they could not legally force all nonmembers to use progressive displays, they decided to abandon the requirement.

When the grand alliance took its compromise to ACATS, some members of ACATS objected particularly strenuously to the number of scanning lines in the interlaced format.[1] They claimed that it would be a major disadvantage for video producers wishing to sell into Europe to start with source material that had fewer than 1,000 scanning lines. They expressed a strong preference for the interlaced format to have 1,080 active lines. The members of ACATS (see Table 5.1 for the list of members) who were pushing for this change had some support outside the broadcasting and video production communities. Bell Labs, for example, also, expressed a preference for the 1,080 lines format, despite the fact that another part of AT&T, the part that had worked with Zenith on signal encoding and decoding, supported the 960 lines format. NHK said that

---

[1] One of them was Joseph Flaherty of CBS.

it would switch its MUSE Hi-Vision system from 1,035 scanning lines to 1,080 lines if the ACATS did so.[2] So, in response to pressure from ACATS, the grand alliance modified the two formats from 960/30/i and 720/60/p to 1,080/30/i and 720/60/p.

Initial reasoning behind Liebhold's position on interlace

For computer industry spokespersons like Apple Computer's Mike Liebhold, this change was further reason for abandoning interlacing altogether. In order to get the 1,080 active scanning lines in interlaced format, according to Liebhold, one had to reduce the horizontal resolution of the image and to accept nonsymmetrical pixels. The computer industry had been pushing for "square" or symmetrical pixels for HDTV as early as 1988. The proponents of the grand alliance system actually made the opposite point at the time that the move to 1,080 lines would make it easier not harder to get symmetrical pixels.

Because of Liebhold's strenuous complaints, and because of concerns about the additional expense of building equipment that could handle multiple formats, the HDTV community began to explore the possibility of moving eventually to a single progressive format of 1,080 lines at 60 frames per second. This became for a short time the explicit long-term goal of the grand alliance.[3] Doing progressive scanning of 1,080 lines at 60 frames per second represented a serious technological challenge, however, and was not possible within the grand alliance's self-imposed upper limit of a data rate of 19.3 megabits per second. The existing video compression methods and circuit technology were not capable of squeezing that much visual information into the required bandwidth without serious degradation of the image. Meeting that goal would require better compression algorithms and/or faster IC processing speeds.

Liebhold sent a letter to Richard Wiley on 8 June 1993 requesting that he be appointed to the Technical Subgroup of ACATS. Wiley told him that membership in that group had already been filled. Liebhold then wrote back protesting the exclusion of the "stakeholders in the National Information Infrastructure" from the ACATS process. Liebhold testified before the House Committee on Science, Space, and Technology in June 1993 that the grand alliance decision to support both interlaced and progressive-scan formats would result in a de facto interlaced standard.

---

[2] "HDTV Group Endorses Computer-Compatible 1,080-line HDTV Format," *Communications Daily*, 9 November 1993, p. 2 (accessed via Nexis-Lexis).
[3] Telephone interview by the author with Robert Graves.

This would be unfortunate because interlace did not permit flickerless rendering of text and graphics.[4]

Commentators at the time criticized Liebhold's position on a variety of grounds. First, they objected that some computer firms, notably IBM, Digital, and AT&T, had been represented in ACATS working groups. Second, they disagreed with Liebhold that interlace would become the de facto standard. They asserted that it was the intention of the equipment manufacturers to move to an all-progressive system as soon as possible. Finally, some claimed that what Liebhold and his friends in the computer industry were really trying to do was to force the television industry to adopt a system that would shift the costs of making television monitors compatible with computers on to the television industry, which these particular critics felt was a selfish and irresponsible position. The higher priced TV sets that would result would impose costs on both TV consumers and TV producers and would make it impossible to successfully introduce HDTV into the marketplace.

Wiley really hated dealing with Liebhold, but saw that the interest of the Clinton Administration in the National Information Infrastructure (the phrase that had replaced the "Information Superhighway" in official circles) had made it necessary to at least appear to try to accommodate the wishes of the computer manufacturers. So he suggested the appointment of an "interoperability subgroup" for ACATS, later to be called the Joint Experts Group on Interoperability. Wiley appointed Robert Sanderson of Kodak to be its chair. Sanderson, in turn, invited Mike Liebhold to be vice chairman. Wiley was not happy about this, nor were other members of ACATS like Robert Rast of General Instrument.

Liebhold was supported in his efforts by a newly formed group called the Program on Digital, Open High-Resolution Systems (DOHRS), which was headquarted at the MIT Media Lab and staffed by Media Lab employees like Russ Neuman, Suzanne Neil, and Lee McKnight. The director of the Media Lab, Nicholas Negroponte, was also openly critical about HDTV and the ACATS process. After a series of rather heated confrontations with Wiley and other ACATS members, Liebhold decided in late October 1993 to withdraw from the anti-interlace campaign, convinced that there was no possibility of achieving his aims from inside the system. Liebhold's campaign was revived in December 1995, however, by a considerably larger and more powerful coalition called CICATS (Computer Industry Coalition on Advanced Television Services).[5]

---

[4] Joel Brinkley, *Defining Vision: The Battle for the Future of Television* (New York: Harcourt Brace, 1997), p. 277.

[5] *Ibid.*, p. 283.

HDTV and the Information Superhighway

In the meantime, Reed Hundt had not yet been confirmed as chairman of the FCC and the Clinton Administration initially showed little interest in HDTV or the ACATS deliberations. Hundt himself was noncommittal. He was influenced in his views by his discussions with Negroponte and other computer industry notables. Hundt was looking for HDTV to play a role in the emergence of the National Information Infrastructure (NII). He wanted HDTV to be more like what George Gilder called a "teleputer" – a television/computer device that was seamlessly connected with computer networks. Wiley was worried that Hundt and the rest of the Clinton Administration would scrap the HDTV deals made by the Republicans in the Bush Administration. He felt that he no longer had the support of the chairman of the FCC as he did under Al Sikes. The National Association of Broadcasters chose this time of vulnerability to weigh in again against HDTV.

John Abel of the NAB began to focus on the opportunities presented by digital television as opposed to HDTV. Digital TV did not have to involve HDTV images. Instead, digital compression of standard definition signals would enable existing broadcasters to compress more than one program into a single channel, allowing them to provide a greater diversity of programming through a form of multiplexing. A digital broadcasting environment would permit broadcasters to offer all sorts of digital services such as data broadcasting, email, paging, telephony, software delivery, etc.

In February 1994, Michael Sherlock, Vice President of NBC, said that many broadcasters were interested in using the second channel that they would be given in the transition to HDTV for digital services. He knew that the only reason that the second channel was being given to broadcasters was so that they would be able to provide free over-the-air services for NTSC set owners until a large proportion of the viewing public could receive digital broadcasts. Nevertheless, he argued that the non-HDTV digital services might be more lucrative for the broadcasters than HDTV itself.[6]

Similarly, in March 1994, Rupert Murdoch began to talk about satellite and cable systems with large numbers of channels. In a March 1994 interview with *Forbes* magazine, Murdoch said: "The current proposal is that the FCC will give us that spectrum for high-definition television. But high definition is a luxury. Compared with a modern TV set it's not

[6] *Ibid.*, pp. 289–90.

that different. Why shouldn't that extra spectrum be given to me or you or anyone to put on that extra number of channels?"[7]

The NAB pursued this logic politically by proposing an amendment to the Telecommunications Act of 1995, called the "broadcast spectrum flexibility amendment." This amendment would broaden the range of services that broadcasters could provide on the second channel given to them in the transition to "advanced television." John Abel continued to argue that neither the broadcasters nor the consumers were demanding HDTV specifically, so broadcasters should not be forced to offer HDTV services.[8] The Telecommunications Act failed to pass in 1995, however, due to overwhelming Republican opposition to what they argued was an overly regulatory Democratic bill. The Republicans were strengthened in their opposition to the bill by their resounding victory in the 1994 Congressional elections.

Completion of the grand alliance system

Testing of the grand alliance system continued through the end of 1993 and into early 1995. The grand alliance's schedule called for completion of the system in 1995 and a demonstration of its capabilities at the 1996 Olympics in Atlanta. Technical evaluations were performed in 1994 at the Advanced Television Test Center in Alexandria, Virginia and at the Cable Television Laboratories (also called CableLabs) near Boulder, Colorado. Subjective viewer tests were performed at the Advanced Television Evaluation Laboratory in Ottawa, Canada. Field transmission tests were conducted by the Public Broadcasting Service, the Association for Maximum Service Television, Inc. (MSTV) and CableLabs in Charlotte, North Carolina. The transmission tests demonstrated some of the peculiar characteristics of digital broadcasting – the quick break-up of picture quality beyond the transmission range of the antenna – as opposed to the more gradual degradation of picture quality with analog transmission, but on the whole they were successful.

At the beginning of 1995, completion of the grand alliance system was delayed because of technical difficulties. The main problem was the encoder that turned baseband high-definition video into compressed digital high-definition video at the transmission end. The two grand alliance companies in charge of this effort were General Instrument and AT&T. Due to delays in getting the new combined system to work, the companies

---

[7] *Ibid.*, p. 304.
[8] *Ibid.*, pp. 308–9.

requested a postponement of the final testing date. This time, instead of readily accepting the delay, FCC Chairman Reed Hundt decided to speed things up. He pushed Richard Wiley, the head of ACATS, to put pressure on the grand alliance members to complete their system.

Hundt's perception of the value of HDTV had changed noticeably. Hundt was impressed with the emerging grand alliance system, particularly its usage of a packetized data structure similar to those used in telecommunications systems. A grand alliance HDTV receiver was a lot more like a computer, with its ability to process a variety of video signals and to display both interlaced and progressive-scan images, than earlier HDTV receivers. The successful introduction of digital NTSC satellite services in the form of the Thomson/Hughes DirecTV or DSS services, using a direct broadcast satellite to deliver digitized signals to homes with small satellite dishes, satellite tuners, and regular NTSC televisions, may also have influenced Hundt's change of perspective. The rapid consumer adoption of DBS services was eating into the audience share of both cable operators and terrestrial broadcasters thanks to the very high quality of the images and the large number of channels available on DBS services. Many of the successful satellite and cable channels in Europe and Asia also relied on digitized signals, especially for pay-TV channels where encryption was necessary to exclude nonsubscribers from receiving the signal.

The issue of auctions: round one

With the successful auction of spectrum for PCS (personnel communications systems) telephone services in 1994–5, the FCC became increasingly convinced of the desirability of auctioning spectrum rather than just giving it away to licensees, as had been done in the past. Selling spectrum had a number of advantages. The revenues raised could help to reduce the government's deficit. There would be no "wasting" of spectrum as had occurred in the past, for example, in the case of UHF channels. The highest bidder would have an incentive to utilize the spectrum in the most commercially viable way, within the parameters set by the terms of sale. And resale of spectrum would reallocate the spectrum purchased by auction winners who failed to achieve their financial objectives.

This shift in policy militated against the NAB's strategy of pushing for greater flexibility in the use of the "second channel." Now the NAB was threatened with a number of proposals for auctions instead of grants and other communications companies began to ask out loud whether it made sense to give spectrum to television broadcasters who were not going to use it for television broadcasting. Just as digitalization had introduced greater flexibility into the possible use of spectrum by broadcasters, so had it eroded their special status in the eyes of others.

Senator Joseph Lieberman (D.-Connecticut) wrote to the FCC in early September 1995 about the effect of auctioning TV spectrum on broadcasters and on the transition to digital television. The Commission wrote back to the Senator on 6 September 1995, telling him that "many broadcasters will compete for and likely win many digital licenses if Congress chooses to auction them." FCC Chairman Hundt apparently had raised the same issue in a meeting at the Office of Management and the Budget that week. The Association for Maximum Service Television (MSTV) wrote to Lieberman on 12 September, attacking the "incorrect assumption" in the FCC's letter that an auction would not harm the transition to digital television.[9]

On 12 September 1995, the chairman of the Senate Commerce Committee, Senator Larry Pressler (R.-South Dakota), unveiled a plan to auction off HDTV and other advanced TV spectrum in the largest twenty-five television markets. According to Pressler, the auction would raise more than $14 billion, which Pressler wanted to use to establish a trust fund for public broadcasting. Federal funding for NPR and PBS was under attack from the new Republican majority in Congress. The National Association of Broadcasters immediately criticized the plan and announced that they would oppose it.[10] Pressler dropped his proposal on 28 September.

Debates over the desirability of spectrum auctions continued, however (see section below on round two of the auctions debate). The FCC issued a request for comments on the issue. The due date for comments was 18 October 1995. FCC replies were due 1 December 1995. Larry Irving of the NTIA continued to favor an auction. So did the Benton Foundation, Americans for Tax Reform, and Thomas Hazlett, an economist and an expert on telecommunications policy.[11] In early December, the Clinton Administration floated a proposal for the auctioning of HDTV spectrum to create a fund for subsidizing consumer purchases of digital TV converters. The proposal called for a subsidy of around $50 per consumer.[12] The NAB and MSTV again objected to the idea of auctions and Irving's idea was strongly opposed by an FCC official on a televised debate. Nothing more of substance on auctions appeared until the middle of the 1996 election campaign.

---

[9] "Letters to Lieberman: Broadcasters Debate the Effect of Digital Auctions," *Communications Daily*, 18 September 1995, p. 1, via Nexis-Lexis.
[10] Dennis Wharton, "Spectrum Squabble: Plan to Fund PBS with HDTV Fees Raise Ire," *Daily Variety*, 12 September 1995, p. 6, via Nexis-Lexis.
[11] "Opposition Mounts to Fed's Billion Dollar Giveaway," *Washington Telecom News*, 16 October 1995, via Nexis-Lexis.
[12] *Television Digest*, 18 December 1995, p. 3, via Nexis-Lexis.

Table 7.3 *Eighteen video formats in the ATSC DTV Standard, May 1996*

Vertical pixels by horizontal lines	Aspect ratio	Frame rates
1920 × 1080	16:9	60i, 30p, 24p
1280 × 720	16:9	60p, 30p, 24p
704 × 480	16:9	60i, 60p, 30p, 24p
"	4:3	"
640 × 480	4:3	"

Note: In the frame rates column, "p" designates a progressively scanned and "i" an interlaced image format.
Source: "Fifth Further Notice of Proposed Rulemaking," FCC 96–207, Federal Communications Commission, MM Docket No. 87–268, adopted 9 May 1996, p. 4.

ACATS approves the grand alliance system

On 28 November 1995, ACATS made its final recommendations to the FCC on the HDTV standard, based on the laboratory and field testing of the digital grand alliance system. ACATS reported that each of the formats proposed for the HDTV system (see Table 7.3) exceeded targets established for static and dynamic luminance and chrominance resolution. ACATS ruled that the MPEG-2 compression system was superior to the four original ATV video compression systems and it selected the Dolby AC-3 audio system as superior to competing systems, including DTS (a digital sound system engineered by Lucasfilms with some Microsoft backing that was already in use in movie theatres). According to ACATS, the grand alliance's packetized data transport subsystem performed well, and appeared to be compatible with Asychronous Transport Mode (ATM) telecommunications technologies.[13] Finally, ACATS selected Zenith's VSB (vestigial sideband) transmission system rather than QAM (quadrature amplitude modulation) or COFDM (coded orthogonal frequency division multiplex) as the best method for assuring high-quality terrestrial over-the-air and cable transmission.[14]

The system recommended by ACATS to the FCC had been vetted earlier by the American Television Services Committee (ATSC). The ATSC was asked by ACATS to determine which aspects of the grand alliance system required action by the FCC in the form of mandatory

[13] "Bell South, Grand Alliance Transmit HDTV via ATM Network," PR Newswire, 8 November 1995, via Nexis-Lexis.
[14] Press release of ACATS dated 28 November 1995.

standards and which should be voluntary. The ATSC divided into five groups of specialists and proceeded to recommend mandatory standards in five areas: video, audio, transport, RF/transmission, and receiver characteristics. For this reason, the ACATS recommendations presented to the FCC in November 1995 were later referred to as the "ATSC DTV Standard."[15]

The National Association of Broadcasters announced that they would not oppose the adoption of the ACATS recommendations by the FCC, but were concerned about requirements to broadcast HDTV signals. As before, they worried out loud about the expense of equipping stations for HDTV broadcasting and their ability to obtain new revenues to offset these expenses. They continued to argue for the benefits of multiplexing NTSC signals instead of moving to HDTV. John Abel, recently retired from the NAB, said: "Consumers have always gone for more video choices rather than higher video quality." CBS lobbyist Marty Franks said that there was "no evidence that the public, if presented with one great picture or five pretty good ones, will pick just the one great one." Some local broadcasters disagreed, arguing that multiplexing would only further fragment audiences and thereby reduce advertising revenues. Phil Jones, President of Meredith Broadcasting in Des Moines, Iowa, said "People are smoking something funny if they think multiplexing is good for local broadcasters."[16]

On 12 December 1995 the FCC held en banc hearings on advanced TV systems. At those hearings, FCC Chairman Hundt said that Congress, not the FCC, would decide whether the spectrum needed for HDTV broadcasts would be auctioned, but that the FCC would still decide whether licensees were required to use their new spectrum for HDTV broadcasts. He also argued that broadcasters might be required to provide "public services" in exchange for the privilege of licensing the new spectrum. Hundt raised the question of the degree to which the regulatory structure already in use for NTSC broadcasting would translate into an appropriate structure for the new digital broadcasting system. He left this issue open for future discussion and deliberation.

At the 12 December hearings, Bruce M. Allan, Senior Vice President for Business Development at Thomson Consumer Electronics, urged the FCC to give prompt approval for the grand alliance digital system. Allan argued that "consumers are ready for the superior pictures and sound of digital TV." The Advanced Television (ATV) Task Force of the Electronic Industries Association (EIA), an organization that represented primarily

---

[15] Fifth Further Notice, paragraphs 6 and 7.
[16] Dennis Wharton, "Future Still Fuzzy for HDTV: FCC Mulls Merits of Multiplexing vs. Sharp Images," *Daily Variety*, 20 October 1995, p. 6, via Nexis-Lexis.

the manufacturers of consumer electronics equipment, agreed with Bruce Allan. The reader will recall from Chapter 5 that the EIA represented the mostly foreign-owned firms that produced these items for the US market.

Also at the 12 December hearings, a new organization called the Computer Industry Coalition on Advanced Television Services (CICATS), represented by Joseph Tasker of Compaq Corporation, argued for abandonment of the interlaced video format. Tasker warned that "Unless the deficits of the proposed standards are remedied, the potential of the technology revolution will be stifled at birth . . . Television will fail to live up to its potential, but will instead remain simply a vehicle for entertainment, news, documentaries, and advertisements."[17] The members of CICATS at this time were: Apple, Compaq, Hewlett-Packard, Intel, Microsoft, Oracle, Silicon Graphics, and Tandem Computers.[18]

CICATS was to lead the fight in 1996 to alter the grand alliance system prior to its acceptance by the FCC, focusing particularly on the question of requiring equipment manufacturers to support both progressive-scan and interlaced video formats in HDTV receivers. CICATS took up many of the arguments first articulated by Michael Liebhold, but added a few new ones. More importantly, a wider variety of industry notables stepped forward as advocates of the computer industry position, including Bill Gates of Microsoft and Andy Grove of Intel, leaders of the emerging Wintel (Windows and Intel) coalition that was already setting de facto microprocesor and operating system standards for desktop and laptop computers worldwide. They also managed to get the support of a number of Hollywood directors, producers, and actors for their views on HDTV. At the same time, the cost for broadcasters of converting to HDTV transmission, the idea of auctioning spectrum instead of loaning it to broadcasters, and the right of broadcasters to choose NTSC multiplexing instead of HDTV broadcasting for their "second channel" all remained contentious issues.

To these old disputes were added a few new ones. The two most important of these were whether the "must carry" rules for cable operators would be extended to ATV broadcasts and how to deal with the interests of low power television (LPTV) broadcasters who served small and remote communities mainly by repeating the broadcasts of larger stations. Cable operators were required to carry the signals of local broadcasters so that both over-the-air and cable customers would have access to the "free television" that terrestrial local broadcasters provided. Cable operators were, on the whole, happy to do this but wanted to exercise some

[17] *Electronic Buyers' News*, 18 December 1995, p. 1, via Nexis-Lexis.
[18] *Ibid.*

choice when it came to which local stations to carry. They were concerned that "must carry" in the ATV world would force them to allocate scarce channel space to ATV signals when it might make more sense for them to multiplex. The NCTA had challenged the "must carry" rules in the courts; the Supreme Court was to decide this issue in the summer of 1997.[19]

From this point on, most people began to speak about digital television (DTV) or advanced television (ATV) instead of HDTV. The grand alliance system (also called the ACATS or ATSC DTV system) was more than an HDTV system because of its adoption of a packetized digital transport system and internationally accepted compression standards like MPEG-2. Now it was possible to think about flexibly combining both high- and low-resolution video (and other kinds of digital information) on the same channels using "smart" television receivers. It was also possible to think of DTV as permitting both passive and interactive video applications.

Interlace vs. progressive: round two

On 11 April 1996 the Polaroid Corporation announced the introduction of a broadcast television camera capable of producing HDTV quality images using progressive scanning. The camera had been developed with funding from IBM, Philips, Broadcast Television Systems of Breda in the Netherlands, and the Advanced Research Projects Agency of the US Department of Defense. IBM helped to produce the charge-coupled devices (CCDs) that provided the imaging sensors for the camera. The first camera would be sold to MIT for experimental purposes and prices initially were around $500,000 per unit (about twice the price of a regular broadcast TV camera). This was clearly a shot across the bow by supporters of CICATS to counter the contention of broadcasters and consumer electronics firms that interlaced video would be necessary for TV programming because no progressive-scan cameras were available.

Commissioner Susan Ness began around this time to take the initiative within the FCC to reconcile the conflict between the computer industry and the other side. At the annual meeting of the National Association of Broadcasters on 15 April 1996, she argued that it was desirable to move quickly on the adoption of DTV standards: "The burden of proof on showing why we shouldn't adopt it is on the opponents... Let's not let the opportunity for world leadership slip away in the search for a perfect

[19] See "Grand Alliance Advanced TV System Gets Okay from Blue-Ribbon Group," *Public Broadcasting Report*, 1 December 1995, via Nexis-Lexis.

solution."[20] Ironically, at the same meeting, FCC Chairman Reed Hundt announced that there would be an FCC inquiry to determine whether the grand alliance DTV standard allowed for advances in video compression and other digital broadcast technologies.[21] Hundt and his deputy, Saul Shapiro, began to hint that they opposed mandating the grand alliance DTV standards, so that broadcasters and equipment manufacturers might continue to innovate new technologies and practices.

The FCC voted 4–0 at a meeting on 9 May 1996 to issue a notice of intent to issue a standard for digital television. At the 9 May meeting, Chairman Hundt mentioned that the computer industry had raised some concerns about the grand alliance DTV system and that the American Society of Cinematographers had objected to the inclusion of the 16:9 aspect ratio in the system. Hundt noted that "These concerns cannot be dismissed out of hand."[22] The split between Hundt and the other FCC commissioners broadened as Hundt tilted increasingly in the direction of the computer industry. The 9 May vote was the basis for the release of the Fifth Further Notice of Proposed Rule Making on 20 May. That document became the basis for a new round of submissions to the FCC concerning the desirability of setting a DTV standard and the possible implications of doing so.[23]

It turns out that Hundt had been consulting on the side with representatives of major computer hardware and software firms like Intel and Microsoft since 1993. Hundt was quoted in a news story published in July 1997 (after submitting his resignation from the Commission) that he was concerned about what he considered to be a "done deal" on HDTV.

When my team and I got here in late 1993, we were presented with a steamroller of a lobbying effort that was self-declared to be the Grand Alliance...Fundamentally, it was a political deal between the networks and TV manufacturers, spearheaded by executives from Zenith, the NAB, and CBS. Their fundamental view was that I ought to get out of the way or get rolled over [so] they get the spectrum.[24]

---

[20] "Kidvid Issues Raised: Ness Says at NAB That Opponents Must Show Why FCC Shouldn't OK HDTV," *Communications Daily*, 16 April 1996, p. 74, via Nexis-Lexis.

[21] George Leopold and Junko Yoshida, "NAB Meet Finds HDTV Pix Blurry," *Electronic Engineering Times*, 22 April 1996, accessed at http://www.techweb.com on 6 May 1997.

[22] Junko Yoshida, "Grand Alliance HDTV Gets FCC Green Light," *EETimes Interactive*, 13 May 1996, accessed via the World Wide Web on 30 May 1996.

[23] "Fifth Further Notice of Proposed Rulemaking, Before the Federal Communications Commission, In the Matter of Advanced Television Systems and Their Impact Upon the Existing Television Broadcast Service," MM Docket No. 87–268, FCC 96–207, adopted 9 May 1996, released 20 May 1996.

[24] George Leopold and Junko Yoshida, "When the Chairmen of the FCC and Microsoft Met, They Altered the Course of Advanced Television and Opened the Door to a New Force in Government," *Electronic Engineering Times*, 14 July 1997, Issue 962, accessed at http://www.techweb.com/on 18 July 1997.

Hundt approached Disney Corporation's Mickey Schulhof and Andrew Grove of Intel for advice on the grand alliance system. In early 1995, Hundt paid a visit to Microsoft headquarters in Redmond, Washington, to meet with Chairman Bill Gates and chief technical officer Nathan Myhrvold. One of Hundt's purposes was to get the management of Microsoft to weigh in on the major controversies surrounding DTV. Microsoft was a little nervous about this given that the Department of Justice had just concluded an antitrust investigation of their firm in July 1994, and had blocked the acquisition of Intuit Inc., makers of Quicken, a popular personal accounting package, in April 1995. But Gates was working on his soon-to-be-published book, *The Road Ahead*, and he quizzed Hundt on the DTV debate so that he could say something about it in the book.[25]

As a result of the meeting with Hundt, Gates asked Craig Mundie, head of Microsoft's Consumer Platforms Division, to study DTV and represent the firm in the national debates. Hundt quickly appointed Mundie to ACATS, but too late (in Hundt's view) to prevent the adoption of the grand alliance system. Mundie also began to represent Microsoft in CICATS and helped it to build bridges to Hollywood interests.

The Senate Commerce Committee held hearings on HDTV standards on 20 June 1996. The computer and film production industries testified in favor of a progressive-scan-only DTV system at these hearings. Mundie of Microsoft objected, as Mike Liebhold of Apple had done before, to the inclusion of interlaced formats in the system. Senator Larry Pressler (R.-South Dakota), the chairman of the committee, took up the cause of the computer and film production industries while the consumer electronics and broadcasting industry position was defended by Senators Ted Stevens (R.-Alaska) and Dan Coats (R.-Indiana). Coats was particularly concerned about the impact of another delay in setting HDTV/DTV standards on employment at Thomson Consumer Electronics, which had its headquarters in Indianapolis and a major assembly plant in Bloomington. Coats argued that a standard was necessary to assure a successful introduction of DTV – citing the failure of the introduction of stereo AM radio as an example of what can happen when the FCC neglects to set a standard.

On 11 July Larry Irving, Assistant Secretary of Commerce for Communications and Information and the administrator of the NTIA, wrote to Chairman Hundt to express his strong support for the grand alliance DTV system. He said that he supported the idea of revisiting the decision

---

[25] *Ibid.* At around the same time Apple Computer's representative in Washington, James Burger, was pressing his Microsoft counterpart, Jack Krumholtz, to get more involved in the DTV debate.

to include interlaced formats in the system at a later time, but encouraged the Commission to get on with setting the standard and launching the system. He recommended that, "The Commission should ensure that the industries involved develop a clearly-defined plan to ensure that the migration to an all-progressive scan system moves at an expeditious rate, including a target date for full transition, taking relevant factors such as the pace of technological development into consideration."[26]

On 11 July CICATS wrote to Chairman Hundt to warn the FCC that the broadcasters and the consumer electronics firms were foisting a very costly DTV solution on the public. CICATS argued that consumers were not really interested in HDTV, but under the grand alliance system they would get it and pay for it whether they wanted it or not. CICATS offered – for the first time – a counterproposal that would create a system that they claimed was technologically superior and would cost the taxpayers $44 billion less over the next seven years.

Gary Demos, an employee of Apple Computer and also ¹ᵣesident and CEO of a small firm called DemoGraFX which provided digital video services mostly to Hollywood film producers, drafted part of the counterproposal. Demos had been involved in the US debate on HDTV since 1988. He had been one of the early opponents of interlaced video formats in DOHRS and an early exponent of interoperable digital video systems – that is, video systems that bridged the TV and computer worlds. Demos's draft was incorporated into an umbrella document written by Alvy Ray Smith, one of the founders of Pixar (famous for producing the hit film *Toy Story* for Disney Studios), who was at that time a Microsoft employee. Smith's criticisms of the ACATS recommendation became part of a larger document submitted to the FCC for CICATS by Economics and Technology, Inc., an economic consulting firm run by Lee Selwyn and the law firm of Levine, Blaszak, Block, and Boothby.[27]

Demos's proposal called for a "layered" system in which the base layer would be standard definition television (SDTV). William Schreiber

---

[26] Letter from Larry Irving to Chairman Hundt dated 11 July 1986, concerning "Advanced Television Systems and Their Impact Upon the Existing Television Broadcast Service, Fifth Further Notice of Proposed Rule Making," MM Docket No. 87–268, accessed via the World Wide Web on 10 August 1996, at http://www.ntia.doc.gov.

[27] "Comments of the Computer Industry Coalition on Advanced Television Services," before the Federal Communications Commission in the matter of Advanced Television Systems and Their Impact Upon the Existing Television Broadcast Service, MM Docket No. 87–268, 11 July 1996; and "Reply Comments of the Computer Industry Coalition on Advanced Television Services," MM Docket No. 87–268, 12 August 1996. These documents were accessed on 25 August 1997, via the CICATS ftp server at ftp://ftp.research.microsoft.com/cicats/. See also the DemoGraFX site at http://home.earthlink.net/~demografx/.

explains this aspect of the proposal:

Since the cost of the MPEG decoder, which will be a significant part of the cost of a minimum receiver, depends primarily on its processing speed and the amount of memory, and because a standard-definition system requires only one fourth the speed and memory as an HDTV system, this difference is important. In the CICATS scheme, packets are available for enhancement since the SD base layer does not consume all the channel capacity. However, at least part of the base receiver circuitry must operate at the higher speed, and the total channel capacity available for enhanced receivers is just the 20–25 megabits per second provided in the GA [grand alliance] system.[28]

CICATS opposed the adoption of the ACATS recommendations and suggested that voluntary standards would be better than mandatory ones because of the rapidity of technological change in digital video and the likelihood that DTV receivers under the ACATS approach would be too expensive for most consumers, at least initially. In the absence of voluntary standards, CICATS recommend a "baseline" system which supported only three video formats (all progressively scanned): 480 × 640 with a 4:3 aspect ratio at three frame rates – 24, 36, and 72 frames per second. They presented a few other alternative "baseline" systems, but the basic point they tried to make was that the ATSC DTV standards mandated support for too many video formats and that by doing so they guaranteed that DTV receivers would be too expensive for most consumers. Their submission to the FCC argued that their alternative approach would result in lower cost receivers and a more successful introduction of digital television.

The main defect of the CICATS approach in the eyes of broadcasting and consumer electronics industry representatives was that it called for an initial emphasis on SDTV instead of HDTV, and therefore would not constitute a sufficiently large jump in image quality to entice consumers to buy new sets despite the possible lower costs. These interests reiterated their belief that it was unrealistic to eliminate interlaced video formats, especially the 1,080-line interlaced format, from the list of mandated formats, because of the ready availability of programming and video production equipment in that format and the need to broadcast HDTV programs as soon as DTV receivers were made commercially available. Representatives of companies like CBS, linked by long association with Sony Corporation, and Matsushita were particularly vehement on this matter. CICATS countered this argument with contentions that interlacing was obsolete and that the broadcasting and consumer electronics firms were "dinosaurs" unaware of the real dynamics of digital technologies.

---

[28] William Schreiber, "The FCC Digital Television Standards Decision: Executive Summary," unpublished manuscript, 28 January 1997, p. 7.

Table 7.4 *Supporters and opponents of the grand alliance system, July 1996*

Supporters	Opponents
Citizens for HDTV	Consumer Federation of America
CEMA	CICATS
NAB	NCTA
ALTV	Media Access Project
MSTV	Directors Guild
APTS	American Society of Cinematographers
ABC, NBC, CBS, Fox	Photographers Guild
PBS	
Tribune	
Chris-Craft	
MPAA	

Source: See text.

In a surprising development, the representatives of the cable industry in the National Cable Television Association (NCTA) also came out against the adoption of the ATSC DTV standard in their letter to the FCC of 12 July. Although they justified their position on the basis of the need to avoid freezing technologies during a period of rapid technological progress, their real basis for opposition at this time had more to do with the extension of "must carry" rules into the DTV era and the difficulty of adapting their QAM systems to the VSB transmission method favored in the grand alliance specs. Nevertheless, CICATS welcomed the NCTA into the anti-grand alliance fold.[29]

A segment of the film production industry also rallied to the side of CICATS, focusing on the aspect ratio problem. Many film makers liked working with widescreen images that would not fit in the 16:9 formats included in the grand alliance DTV system. The Directors Guild, the American Society of Cinematographers, and the Photographers Guild favored a 2:1 aspect ratio. It should be noted, however, that the Motion Picture Association of America (MPAA), representing the largest Hollywood movie studios, was a supporter of the grand alliance system. Table 7.4 above represents the two opposing coalitions at this time.

---

[29] "Cable Opposes HDTV Standards," *Television Digest*, 15 July 1996, p. 5, via Nexis-Lexis; Jon Van, "Digital TV Standards Go On Pause," *Chicago Tribune*, 12 July 1996, p. 2; and "Opposition Impact Unclear: Broadcasters and TV Set Makers Back Mandated HDTV Standard," *Communications Daily*, 15 July 1996, p. 4, via Nexis-Lexis.

Auctions: round two

On 2 January 1996 Senator Robert Dole (R.-Kansas) insisted that HDTV frequencies should be auctioned, and linked his support for the Telecom Reform Act to the adoption of this proposal.[30] Even though this linkage was severed prior to the passage of the Telecommunications Act of 1996, Dole held on to this issue as he made the transition from majority leader in the Senate to candidate for the presidency.

On 16 February 1996, the Consumer Electronics Manufacturers Association (CEMA) issued a lengthy defense of the FCC's decision to loan spectrum to broadcasters to ease the transition to DTV.

The temporary, cost-free loan of a second channel is essential if the broadcasters are to transition to a digital system. Broadcasters cannot offer both analog and digital transmissions over their current channel. Nor can broadcasters commence digital transmission over their current channel without instantly blacking out the more than 200 million existing analog television sets. To upgrade to digital, broadcasters will need to broadcast on two channels, one analog and one digital. This is not a "give away" of spectrum, nor does it allow the broadcasters to initiate an additional service. Instead, it is a one-for-one exchange of channels, with one channel to be returned to the government when the transition is complete.[31]

James Carnes, President of the David Sarnoff Research Center (a member of the grand alliance), announced the formation of the Citizens for HDTV Coalition on 8 March 1996. The members of the coalition are listed in Table 7.5. Funding for the Coalition came primarily from the CEMA. At the press conference, Carnes and Richard Wiley said that spectrum auctions would delay the rollout of DTV because broadcasters would have to budget expenditures both for auction payments and for equipment purchases. They also argued that auctions would result in more pay and subscription TV programming and less "free" (advertising-supported) TV.

Gigi Sohn, deputy director of the Media Access Project defended auctions as preferable to the "massive corporate welfare" she associated with the lending of spectrum for the DTV transition. Sohn also argued that if the broadcasters did not use the new spectrum for broadcasting HDTV programming, then it really did not make any sense to give them the spectrum for free. She also pointed out that the only consumer entity in the Citizens for HDTV Coalition was the National Consumers League and the only senior citizens' organization was the National Council of Senior

---

[30] "The Return of a Bid Idea," *Electronic Buyers' News*, 15 January 1996, p. 6.
[31] "HDTV: An American Technology Success," The Consumer Electronics Manufacturers Association, February 16, 1996, accessed at http://www.cdinet.com/Hy...et/Benton/forum/6/2.html on 30 May 1996.

Table 7.5 *Members of Citizens for HDTV Coalition*

CEMA of EIA
EIA ATV Committee
Home Record Rights Coalition
NARDA
PARA
Digital Multimedia Compression, Inc.
Digital HDTV Grand Alliance
National Consumers League
National Council of Senior Citizens
Communications Workers of America/NABET
Intl. Brotherhood of Electrical Workers
IUE

Source: Consumer Electronics, 11 March 1996, via
Nexis-Lexis.

Citizens, implying thereby that the Coalition was representing primarily the interests of the consumer electronics manufacturers and associated labor unions.[32]

In April 1986, Senator John McCain (R.-Arizona) and Representative Barney Frank (D.-Massachusetts) joined Senator Robert Dole (R.-Kansas) in his calls for ATV spectrum auctions. On 8 April 1986 Gigi Sohn was quoted as saying that "HDTV is dead . . . Broadcasters don't have a lot of interest in high-definition television." Sohn's arguments in favor of auctions had taken on a broadcaster-bashing element. The broadcasters responded by pointing out that winners of spectrum auctions in the past had quickly passed on the costs of auction bids to end-users but that this was unlikely in their case because advertisers would be unwilling to pay more for the same air time, even if the viewers were now receiving sharper images.[33]

Partly in response to these pressures from consumer advocates and Congress, the White House and the FCC began talking about an accelerated transition to DTV of seven years instead of the ten to fifteen years mentioned earlier. This would speed up the return of the analog channels to the FCC. The revenues obtained from auctioning that spectrum would then help to reduce the budgetary deficit a bit sooner than previously anticipated. FCC Commissioner James Quello objected to this policy shift

---

[32] "Coalition Calls Auctions 'Clear and Dire Threat' to HDTV," *Communications Daily*, 8 March 1996, p. 3, via Nexis-Lexis.

[33] Brian Santo, "Viva HDTV!" *Electronic Engineering Times*, 8 April 1996, p. 95, via Nexis-Lexis.

because he thought that people would hang on to their NTSC sets for considerably longer than seven years and that they would be angry if they had to scrap them prematurely.[34]

On 20 June 1996, at the Senate Commerce Committee Hearing on HDTV standards, Chairman Hundt again endorsed the idea of auctioning spectrum. Dr. Peter Bingham, president of Philips Research Laboratories, said that the spectrum auction hung "like a sword of Damocles over this digital revolution." He argued that the auction would only produce a marginal improvement in deficit reduction but that it would certainly undermine the economic incentives for broadcasters to introduce digital television expeditiously.[35]

During the week of 22 July 1996, the House of Representatives was scheduled to consider an amendment to the FY 1997 FCC appropriations bill proposed by Rep. Barney Frank that would prohibit the FCC from assigning licenses for ATV services. This amendment was designed to stymie efforts by the FCC to allocate ATV channels at a meeting on 25 July. Apparently the FCC was planning to free up channels 2 to 6 and 52 to 69 for nontelevision uses. The FCC promptly received a letter from ALTV, MSTV, NAB, the three major networks, Chris-Craft and Tribune opposing this. Senator McClain used the occasion to lecture Chairman Hundt in a letter to "keep government intrusion to a minimum" and avoid freezing innovation by setting inappropriate standards. Nevertheless, the FCC voted to announce its intention to allocate ATV channels at the 25 July meeting, although it left the decision about what channels to allocate and when to a later time.

NTSC multiplexing vs. HDTV

Cracks began to appear within the broadcasting community about the relative desirability of using the second channel for HDTV broadcasts or multiplexing digital NTSC signals. As stated above, cable and satellite operators like Ted Turner of Turner Broadcasting and Rupert Murdoch of News Corporation took an early position in support of multiplexing. Most other broadcasters were ambivalent. In the spring of 1996, however, some heavyweight players began to take the position that terrestrial broadcasters and the national network systems had to opt for HDTV as a way of countering the erosion in their audience share caused by

---

[34] John Van and Tim Jones, "Digital TV Promises an Unclear Revolution: Among the Questions: Better Images, or More?" *Chicago Tribune*, 7 April 1996, p. C1.
[35] "Philips Electronics Executive Declares FCC Standard Critical to Digital TV: Assails Computer Companies' Attack," *Business Wire*, 20 June 1996, via Nexis-Lexis.

competition from cable and direct broadcast satellite channels. Michael Jordan, Chairman of Westinghouse/CBS Broadcasting, said his network would almost certainly offer HDTV programming because "we can't afford to give our competitors a sustained technological advantage." Jordan was encouraged by information that the cost of equipping stations for DTV broadcasting was already declining and that there were indications that the government would not require spectrum auctions for DTV channels.[36]

Jordan's position was echoed shortly thereafter by Edward Horowitz, Senior Vice President of Viacom, who had always been a strong supporter of HDTV. Horowitz argued that interactive digital services would be particularly important for cable operators and that DTV standards would help to move the industry in that direction. Horowitz acknowledged that it would be necessary to upgrade many local cable systems to provide genuine interactive services, but looked to the growing popularity of the Internet and the heightened consumer demand for fast links to the Internet via cable modems to generate the necessary revenues to pay for this.

In contrast, Edward Grebow, President of Tele-TV, a firm that was pioneering the delivery of pay-TV programming over telephone company infrastructure, argued for the superiority of multiplexing over HDTV. In Grebow's view, the ability to obtain revenues by providing services tailored closely to the needs of individual customers was more likely to produce the desired increase in broadcasting revenues than was providing HDTV programming. In the pay-TV area, one way to do this would be to give customers "near video on demand" (NVOD) access to movies and other programming. To do this, one needed to multiplex. Grebow argued that terrestrial broadcasters and networks were likely to become more like cable operators in the future in providing programming for multiple channels.[37]

"Must carry" rules

Richard Wiley came down strongly on the side of those who favored the extension of "must carry" rules to ATV in a speech before the National Association of Broadcasters on 16 April 1996.[38] This position was strongly opposed by the cable operators and cable networks. The cable

---

[36] "Kidvid Issue Raised . . . " p. 74, via Nexis-Lexis.
[37] " 'Bright Future' for Networks: NAB is Told Cable Leads Telcos in Digital Transition," *Communications Daily*, 18 April 1996, p. 7, via Nexis-Lexis.
[38] "Station Freeze Likely: Broadcasters Press for Mandated Use of HDTV Standard," *Communications Daily*, 18 April 1996, p. 8.

industry wanted to clear their channels of certain TV stations in favor of more popular cable offerings. Their attorneys argued their case to the Supreme Court in November 1996.

On 31 March 1997, the US Supreme Court upheld a 1992 federal law requiring cable TV operators to carry local broadcast stations. This was a victory for the broadcasters and the networks. The vote was 5–4. Justice Anthony Kennedy wrote for the majority arguing that "must carry" was essential to assure "audience access and advertising revenue needed to support a multiplicity of stations." The cable industry had argued that "must carry" rules were a violation of its First Amendment rights. Kennedy countered this argument by saying that the Court had to defer to the wishes of Congress on this issue. Dissenting from the majority was Justice Sandra Day O'Connor. O'Connor's dissent stated that she thought that protecting the First Amendment rights of cable operators was more important than deferring to Congress.[39]

The Supreme Court's decision meant that "must carry" requirements would be extended to DTV signals of local terrestrial broadcasters for the same reason that they were applied to analog NTSC signals, to guarantee that all citizens would be exposed to a variety of broadcast opinions and that communications conduits could not be used by a small number of broadcasters to limit public discussion of important issues. The cable systems operators remained opposed to this, and vowed to fight on in other forums.

The negotiation of a compromise with the computer interests

CICATS continued to lobby for a change in the ATSC DTV standards throughout 1996, with heavyweights like Bill Gates and Andy Grove weighing in toward the end of the year and with letters, visits, and testimony from such film industry notables as Steven Spielberg, Clint Eastwood, Arthur Hiller, Martin Scorsese, Richard Dreyfuss, Dustin Hoffman, Sydney Pollack, and Robert Zemeckis. Many of the film industry representatives were more concerned about the 16:9 aspect ratio of the DTV standard than about interlacing. Martin Scorsese, for example, said that "This new technology will let us show movies at home as they are seen in the theaters... We will no longer have to tolerate the mutilation of films when they are shown on TV."

---

[39] "Where Things Stand," *Broadcasting & Cable*, accessed at http://www.broadcastingcable. com/wts.htm on 23 July 1997.

The computer industry representatives were more concerned about the effect of adopting the ATSC DTV standards on digital convergence. For example, in late October, Microsoft Chairman Bill Gates said:

We strongly support efforts to bring digital television to American homes... Unfortunately some critical parts of the "Grand Alliance" proposal would unnecessarily slow the convergence of PCs and televisions. Getting these standards right is vital to achieving the digital future where consumers will be able to watch television on their PCs or access the Internet from their TVs.[40]

Gates's position on DTV was undoubtedly influenced by his perception of the increased stake of Microsoft Corporation in helping customers use the World Wide Web. Microsoft purchased WebTV Neworks of Palo Alto, California, a small firm that made set-top boxes for TV sets to permit TV owners to cruise the Web inexpensively, for $425 million. This purchase was announced in April 1997 but probably was already in the works in late 1996. Microsoft bought 11.5 percent of the shares in Comcast Corporation, a cable television operator, in June 1997. These investments were part of a shift in Microsoft strategy toward a more Web-oriented approach to software. Gates began talking about supporting a "Web lifestyle" with Microsoft products, especially after the phenomenal early success of Netscape Communications, a start-up firm that battled Microsoft for control of the market for Web browsers and servers.[41]

CICATS members formed a new group called the Americans for Better Digital TV (see Table 7.6 below for membership). The combined lobbying efforts of the members of this group apparently convinced President Clinton to take a stand. On 23 September 1996, in an interview with a reporter from *Broadcasting and Cable* magazine, Clinton weighed in on the side of digital convergence:

The best standard would be one developed and supported by all the affected industries, which could then be endorsed by the FCC...We want to make sure that there are no roadblocks to future compatibility between televisions and computers.

Accordingly, on 24 October 1996, Commissioner Susan Ness sent a letter to the Broadcasters Caucus, the Consumer Electronics Manufacturers Association, and CICATS urging them to seek a consensus on DTV standards by 25 November. A series of intensive negotiations ensued resulting ultimately in a compromise to modify the ATSC DTV standard by removing the requirement that DTV receivers support the

---

[40] Elizabeth Corcoran, "A Bit of Bill in Every Box: Gates's Vision of Microsoft's Future Moves from PCs to TV, Phones," *Washington Post*, 10 August 1997, p. H1.
[41] *Ibid.*

Table 7.6 *Members of Americans for Better Digital TV*

CICATS
Directors Guild of America
Media Access Project
International Photographers Guild
American Society of Cinematographers
Digital Theater Systems (DTS)
Todd-AO Corporation
Artists Rights Foundation
Panavision International
American Homeowners Foundation
Computing Technology Industry Association
Business Software Alliance

Source: "Entertainment, High Tech, and Consumer Groups Call for Resolution of Digital Television Standard," *PR Newswire*, 28 October 1996.

eighteen video formats in Table 7.3 and leaving it instead to each equipment manufacturer to decide which formats to support. This compromise, in effect, recognized the split between computer and consumer electronics firms over interlaced formats and allowed them to pursue their own strategies. A letter documenting the compromise was signed on 27 November 1996, in Washington by Michael Sherlock of NBC, representing the Broadcasters Caucus, Gary Shapiro of the CEMA, and Paul Misener of Intel representing CICATS. This cleared the way for the FCC to issue its decisions on DTV without fear of further reprisals from the computer industry.

The FCC decisions of 26 December 1976 and 3 April 1997

On 27 December 1996 the FCC released its Fourth Order and Report accepting the recommendation of ACATS to adopt a modified version of the ATSC standard for digital television in the United States.[42] The decision was strongly praised by the broadcasting and consumer electronics firms and their representatives. The computer industry and particularly the members of CICATS also expressed satisfaction with the

---

[42] "Fourth Report and Order, Before the Federal Communications Commission, In the Matter of Advanced Television Systems and Their Impact Upon the Existing Television Broadcast Service," MM Docket No. 87–268, FCC Document 96–493, adopted 24 December 1996, released 27 December 1996. Accessed at http://www.fcc.gov/Bureaus/Mass_Media/Orders/1996/fcc96493.txt on 26 August 1997.

outcome. Media coverage of the DTV decision began to emphasize some of the problems that conversion to DTV broadcasting would create for the smaller terrestrial broadcasters, consumer electronics retailers, and owners of NTSC receivers. The FCC turned to the question of how to allocate the channels it would loan to broadcasters for the transition to DTV.

On 3 April 1997 the FCC issued its Fifth and Sixth Report and Order in the US advanced television proceedings, spelling out in great detail the plans for allocating loaner channels to terrestrial broadcasters. The problems they had to solve had to do mainly with assuring existing broadcasters that their new digital channels would permit them to cover approximately the same territory as their old analog channels. In addition, many low-powered television broadcasters in rural or mountainous regions were acting as repeaters for nearby terrestrial broadcasters. These stations were low-budget affairs with just enough revenues from advertising to generate a small profit. Such stations could not afford to quickly convert to digital broadcasting. Special provisions had to be made for them. A similar problem existed for public broadcasters, and they were granted more time to make the transition than commercial broadcasters.

An important part of the April 1997 decision was the plan to recover for non-television uses 138 MHz of spectrum – 60 MHz immediately and 78 MHz within ten years. The 60 MHz would come from the former television Channels 60 to 69 in the VHF band, which would no longer be reserved for television broadcasts (these channels were only infrequently used anyway, and then only in the most crowded urban areas). When the transition to DTV ended, in 2006, all the NTSC channels would be returned to the FCC, which would make an additional 78 MHz of spectrum available. The recovered spectrum would be auctioned or otherwise allocated to licensees for various purposes. The FCC committed itself in the Sixth Report to allocate 24 MHz of recovered spectrum in the VHF band for police and public safety purposes.

The idea of auctioning spectrum sooner rather than later was particularly appealing to the Clinton Administration, which at the time was looking for a way to guarantee further reductions in the deficit before 2002. Hence, one initiative undertaken by Chairman Hundt was to try to get the broadcasters in the largest urban media markets to accelerate their deployment of DTV. Instead of a transition period of ten years, he pushed the broadcasters to do it in two years. This generated great resistance on their part, but in the end the broadcasters committed themselves to a two-year transition in some major markets and a three-year transition in others.

Finally, an important aspect of the April 1997 decision was to reaffirm the earlier decision to allow broadcasters to choose between HDTV broadcasting and SDTV multiplexing, and between passive and interactive services, on their digital channels. Commissioner Hundt thought this proved that the FCC had embraced a "market orientation" that would give "broadcasters the flexibility to use the spectrum to respond to market opportunities."[43] Hundt's efforts to link the DTV spectrum allocation to new commitments on the part of broadcasters, for public service announcements and children's broadcasting, resulted in the appointment of a special commission to consider the matter.

Reactions to the April 1997 decisions

Now that both the standard and the channel allocation system had been decided, the major stakeholders in digital television began to play a new set of games. Whereas before the key question was whether the FCC would adopt any standard at all, now the game turned to optimizing one's chances for success under the new standard.

The most important reaction to the April 1997 FCC decisions on DTV came from the computer industry. On 7 April 1997 Compaq, Microsoft, and Intel announced the formation of the DTV Team composed initially of the three firms at the annual meeting of the National Association of Broadcasters in Las Vegas, Nevada. The DTV Team proposed to develop DTV for computers that supported a subset of the ATSC DTV video formats and pointedly excluded all but the simplest interlaced formats. They argued once again that doing this would make DTV receivers cheaper than those that supported all eighteen video formats of the ATSC DTV standard.

The DTV Team proposed that DTV receivers following their standard would support only nine of the eighteen video formats in the ATSC DTV standard. They are listed in Table 7.7.

Note that the only interlaced format included in the DTV Team's proposal permitted the DTV Team's receivers to display interlaced programming produced in NTSC formats and to down convert 1,080 × 1,920 interlaced HDTV images. Note also that the only true HDTV format in the DTV Team's list in Table 7.7 is the first one. This is the result of the DTV Team's belief that the processing capability of microprocessors and digital signal processors was not yet capable of handling

[43] Statement of Chairman Reed Hundt on the Adoption of Television Allotment and Service Rules Reports and Orders, 3 April 1997, p. 1. Accessed at http://www.fcc. gov/Speeches/Hundt/hundtv.html on 23 April 1997.

Table 7.7 *Video formats supported by the DTV Team*

Vertical pixels by horizontal lines	Aspect ratio	Frame rates
1,280 × 720	16:9	24p
704 × 480	16:9	24p, 30p, 60p, 60i
"	4:3	"

progressive-scan images of higher resolution using the MPEG-2 compression algorithm. They argued, as before, that Moore's Law, under which the memory and digital signal processing capability of integrated circuits doubles every eighteen months, would permit upgrading of DTV receivers later to process higher resolution video at acceptable performance levels. This is reminiscent of the "layered" or "baseline" approach of the CICATS DTV counterproposal of 11 July 1996, which indeed was the main inspiration for the DTV Team's approach.

A new emphasis in the DTV Team's rationale for its approach was the argument that interlaced programming was inherently passive, whereas progressive-scan programming permitted the easier integration of conventional video with digital multimedia content which was inherently interactive. Particularly interesting was the DTV Team's contention that their approach permitted broadcasters to diversify their programming content by combining video easily with World Wide Web content. The key problem with interlace, in their view, was the difficulty of displaying text (except in large formats with a limited number of fonts). They cited the increasing tendency of upper-income US households to cruise the World Wide Web rather than watching network televisions during prime time viewing hours as evidence of the compelling attraction of interactive digital multimedia content, even with inferior video quality. They pointed out that advertisers were switching to other media that offered better access to the "eyeballs" in these households, and would continue to do so especially if larger numbers of less affluent households started to cruise the Web.

Another important development was yet another flip-flop on the part of a major television network on the issue of HDTV vs. multiplexing of SDTV signals on the newly allocated digital channels. In early August 1997, Preston Padden, President of the ABC Television Network (and formerly a key employee in Rupert Murdoch's News Corporation), said that he saw no way to make money from broadcasting HDTV and so ABC and other Disney Corporation broadcasters would use their digital channels to broadcast multiplexed SDTV – possibly with some pay-TV channels included. NBC and CBS, in contrast, stuck with their earlier commitments to broadcast HDTV. Padden had only joined ABC in May 1997, and he justified his position by arguing that "Our share of the viewing audience will continue to erode as long as we remain a single channel in an expanding multi-channel universe."[44]

Thus, the split between future manufacturers of ATSC DTV receivers (mostly TV manufacturers) and DTV Team receivers (mostly computer firms) would be accompanied by a split between HDTV broadcasting networks and SDTV multiplexing networks, thus creating – at least initially – further confusion among consumers and other industry players about what to do next. These two splits were a consequence of the compromise between the computer industry and the TV and broadcasting industries embodied in the December 1996 decision of the FCC to allow the market to decide what kinds of digital television it wanted to consume. The compromise itself was a product of the desire of the computer industry to defend the possibility of digital convergence. Only time will tell if this was a wise strategy.

Conclusions

In 1993, the US debate on digital television focused on the feasibility of a unified grand alliance approach. By 1997, the debate had shifted away from a focus on television per se toward a consideration of the broader implications of digital television for the future of the American broadcasting and electronics manufacturing industries. The increased importance of the Internet and the World Wide Web, particularly for the Clinton Administration, but also for key players like Compaq, Intel, and Microsoft, had made a big difference in the level of attention given to HDTV and digital television by major political forces in the country. The grand alliance and ATSC approach had helped to focus the attention of these other players on the DTV issue by adopting digital packetization and transport schemes that were consistent with the idea of digital convergence but deviated from that ideal by forcing manufacturers to make more expensive DTV receivers and set-top boxes in order to satisfy the concerns of their coalition partners.

The Chairman of the FCC, Reed Hundt, and Commissioner Susan Ness played a crucial role in forcing the members of the grand alliance coalition to compromise with the "Johnnie-come-latelies" of the computer industry, but in doing so they were simply reflecting the ability

---

[44] Joel Brinkley, "Some Broadcasters Back Away from HDTV Programming Pledge," *New York Times*, 18 August 1997, accessed at http://www.nytimes.com/library/cyber/week/081897.html on 21 August 1997.

of the computer industry to generate support at high levels in a White House that had already tilted in their direction on a number of other occasions. Efforts on the part of members of Congress, even presidential candidates like Bob Dole, to force the FCC to auction DTV spectrum came to naught. Congress was split on this issue, with Senators Dole and McCain countered by Senators Coats and Stevens. Congress was also split on whether to support the TV broadcasters and manufacturers or the computer industry at various points in the debate. The FCC normally leans in the direction of TV interests because of the way in which commissioners are recruited and selected, but in this case that did not occur because the chairman confronted a divided Congress and a White House eager to placate the computer industry. The result, as discussed in the summary paragraphs of the previous section, was a compromise standard that reduced uncertainty about the future of digital television considerably but did not eliminate it.

8   Digital television in Europe and Japan

Introduction

The decision of the FCC in the United States to select an all-digital television system was a surprise to HDTV supporters in Europe and Japan. Both had adopted hybrid systems with both analog and digital features. Both had decided to use direct broadcast satellites as the primary means of delivering HDTV signals. Both had counted on their ability to market HDTV programming and equipment in North America, as well as in their home region. Now they were confronted with criticisms at home about the obsolescence of analog technologies and the need to keep up with the United States in digital technologies. To these criticisms the already existing complaints were added, mainly from private broadcasters and pay-TV operators, about the high expense and low benefit for both consumers and broadcasters of making the transition to HDTV. As a result, both regions reconsidered their earlier decisions.

Western Europe was somewhat quicker than Japan to move away from its previous arrangements. It dropped HD-MAC in June 1993 and moved on to create the Digital Video Broadcasting (DVB) group to support digital television. It also responded by increasing EU support for widescreen standard definition television programming and manufacturing. In Japan, NHK and its allies strongly resisted the idea of abandoning MUSE Hi-Vision but some of the major consumer electronics manufacturers and the Ministry of Posts and Telecommunications (MPT) wanted to speed up the transition to an all-digital HDTV system. NHK was able to delay serious discussion of all-digital HDTV until the last year or so. In the spring of 1997, all the top managers of NHK were replaced with individuals more inclined to go digital. In this chapter, we will consider these two stories separately, and then try to explain the differences in the reactions of the two regions.

The death of HD-MAC; the birth of DVB

On 22 July 1993, the EU Council of Ministers adopted an Action Plan for the Introduction of Advanced Television Services in Europe.[1] The Action Plan endorsed the idea of pursuing widescreen analog equipment in the near term and digital HDTV in the longer term. The Council agreed to provide 228 million ECUs to subsidize the production of programs in widescreen formats and the investment in broadcasting equipment for the transmission of wide-format analog images between mid-1993 and mid-1997. Whereas only twenty-two broadcasters in eight member states were transmitting widescreen signals in 16:9 format in 1994, thirty-nine broadcasters in thirteen member states were doing so in 1995. As a direct result of increased widescreen program availability, the sales of widescreen receivers increased from about 10,000 in 1993, to 135,000 in 1994, and to 220,000 in 1995.[2]

While the widescreen program continued, much of the debate over the future of television in Europe shifted to the question of how to take advantage of digital technologies. At the national level, private broadcasters continued to erode audience shares of the previously dominant public broadcasters and firms like BSkyB in Britain, Canal Plus in France, and Kirch and Bertelsmann in Germany were talking about moving into digital delivery of video signals.

In September 1993, a group of 120 organizations[3] – European broadcasters, satellite operators, manufacturers, and public agencies – signed a Memorandum of Understanding for the creation of a new organization called the Digital Video Broadcasting (DVB) Group.[4] The DVB Group focused on negotiating standards for digital video production, terrestrial, cable, and satellite broadcasting, and set-top boxes and encryption systems for pay-TV. They decided to tackle satellite and cable standards before working on terrestrial ones because the former were

---

[1] Decision 93/424/EEC. For a history of this document see the previous HDTV Report from Stanford Resources, Inc. See also the historical information provided by the EU at http://apollo.cordis.lu/.

[2] *Second Annual Report on Progress in Implementing the Action Plan for the Introduction of Advanced Television Services in Europe*, Report from the Commission to the Council, the European Parliament, and the Economic and Social Committee, COM (96) 346 Final, Brussels, 26 July 1996, p. 16.

[3] In mid-1997, the number of member organizations was 200.

[4] The DVB Group benefited from the earlier work of the European Launching Group for Digital Video Broadcasting, beginning in 1991, under the leadership of Peter Kahl of the German Ministry of Telecommunications. See Xiudan Dai, *Corporate Strategy, Public Policy and New Technologies: Philips and the European Consumer Electronics Industry* (London: Pergamon, 1996), pp. 248–9.

simpler and more immediate. One of the key goals of the Group was to avoid the proliferation of incompatible pay-TV decoders and set-top boxes.[5] The DVB itself was not empowered to set standards but instead passed along "technical specifications" to ETSI (the European Telecommunications Standards Institute) and CENELEC (the European Committee for Electrotechnical Standardization), both of which are recognized standards organizations in Europe. ETSI and CENELEC can ask international standards bodies like the International Telegraphic Union (ITU) to incorporate European standards into their lists of global standards.

According to one expert, the DVB

has speedily and painlessly produced specifications for digital satellite and cable TV transmission systems, which have sped rapidly through European standardization to achieve global acceptance as ITU Recommendations and seem set to achieve success in the global market. The terrestrial digital specification left the DVB earlier is year [1996] for formal standardization. Like all digital TV systems which ed the globally agreed MPEG-2 compression system, the DVB systems work n either 4:3 or 16:9 formats.[6]

The DVB fastened upon MPEG-2 for video compression at a time when most computer firms were doing the same thing. It also adopted the idea of putting digital video information in packets with headers containing information about the type of content contained in the packet using the model successfully pursued in international telecommunications standards negotiations. But the most important secret of DVB's success, according to one observer, "lies in first defining broadcasters' user requirements and then matching technologies to those requirements, rather than the other way round, which has been more usual in Europe in the past."[7] This is a roundabout way of saying that the DVB, unlike the grand alliance in the United States, steered clear of insisting on the inclusion of high-definition video formats in its proposed standards, on the

[5] The group had been meeting on an ad hoc basis for over a year prior to the signing of the Memorandum of Understanding. A smaller pan-European group began to discuss digital television in 1991 soon after the announcement by General Instrument in the United States that it had succeeded in building an all-digital HDTV system. D. Wood, "The DVB Project: Philosophy and Core System," *Electronics and Communication Engineering Journal*, 9: 1 (February 1997), p. 5; Suzanne Perry, "European Group to Announce Digital HDTV Strategy," *The Reuter Business Report*, 26 May 1993; and Andrew Hill, "Europe Switches Over to Digital TV," *Financial Times*, 17 December 1993, p. 16.
[6] Ivo Addams, *Reshaping TV for the Information Society, Background Brief for the European Commission's Conference on Wide-Screen Television* (Brussels: 1996). Ivo Addams is a pseudonym for Adam Watson-Brown.
[7] *Ibid.*

presumption that it was too early to do so. According to one participant in the process:

High-definition television (HDTV) has been considered but so far no European program service provider has been able to devise a satisfactory business plan to use it. Domestic HDTV receivers, and HDTV studio equipment are likely to be expensive. The viability of HDTV broadcasting, at least for Europe, in today's highly competitive broadcasting environment, seems years away. Nevertheless, if there is a demand for HDTV, the DVB systems will all have the capacity to transport the signals.[8]

This argument was quite similar to that made by the DTV Team in the United States. The DVB project focused particularly on finding a standard interface for enhancements to digital set-top boxes that would permit pay-TV operators to use proprietary encryption systems without requiring consumers to buy a separate box for each system. This was a serious problem because not all pay-TV operators in Europe could agree on encryption methods and other aspects of set-top boxes. The DVB's proposed solution to this problem involved the use of plug-in cards, identical to those used in laptop computers (PCMCIA cards), which contained the proprietary encryption algorithms. A "smart card" had to be inserted into the encryption card to show that the individual using the encryption card was a paid subscriber to the service.

The DVB cable standard called for the use of a QAM (quadrature amplitude modulation) transmission system, which was preferred by most cable operators in the United States over the VSB (vestigial sideband) system selected by the grand alliance and endorsed by the FCC. The DVB terrestrial system used channel-coded orthogonal frequency division multiplexing (COFDM) instead of VSB. The DVB selected COFDM because it wanted the terrestrial system to have as much commonality as possible with the cable and satellite systems, and because digital audio broadcasting in Europe had already been introduced successfully with COFDM technology.[9]

On 29 May 1997, the DVB project announced that it would promote the formation of patent pool for all DVB standards with the exception of MPEG-2. Theo Peek, Chairman of the Steering Board of the DVB project said:

Now that much of the technical work of the DVB Project has been completed, we can turn to ensuring that the IPRs [intellectual property rights] associated with

---

[8] Wood, "The DVB Project," p. 7.
[9] Ulrich Reimers, "DVB-T: The COFDM-Based System for Terrestrial Television," *Electronics and Communication Engineering Journal*, 9: 1 (February 1997), pp. 28–32.

our standards are available efficiently and on terms which are fair, reasonable, and non-discriminatory.[10]

This was a notable difference between the DVB Group and the grand alliance: the latter failed to agree on a patent pooling arrangement. After the DVB proposed and won acceptance in Europe for its recommended standards, European electronics manufacturers were criticized by US broadcasters for their failure to adequately support HDTV broadcasting within the DVB framework. Joseph Flaherty, Senior Vice President of CBS, in a speech at ITU Telecom '97 on 10 June 1997, said:

Only the European consumer equipment industry is still ignoring HDTV in its digital receiver plans and this in my opinion is a grievous mistake. European broadcasters with the ability to broadcast HDTV through the DVB system, will be prevented from doing so by the inability of European digital receivers to decode the HDTV signal.[11]

In order to understand the achievements of the DVB Group, one needs to view the efforts of the Group from the perspective of the accelerating interest in digital television broadcasting in the individual member states of the European Union.

Digital television in Europe

In the member states of the European Union, a few influential private broadcasters were converting to digital standard definition television (SDTV) systems in order to protect their investments in programming and infrastructure for pay-TV and cable TV systems in Europe. They needed to use encrypted signals to make sure that only paid subscribers could receive the signals; and digitization of the signals was a natural adjunct to encryption. Digitization would make multiplexing possible, which was desirable because of the obvious appeal of greater programming choice for consumers. The first to digitize its satellite broadcasts in Europe was Canal Plus in France, but it was followed in short order by the Kirch Group in Germany.

The British government, frustrated with the slow growth of cable TV services in Britain, and concerned about the lack of competition to BSkyB's direct broadcast satellite TV services (Rupert Murdoch's News

[10] DVB Press Release dated 29 May 1997.
[11] Joseph Flaherty, "2000 and Beyond . . . The Digital Millennium," *HDTV Newsletter*, 11 (June–July 1997), pp. 29–32; and "Flaherty Says TV Set-Makers Are Stalling European HDTV," *Communications Daily*, 11 June 1997, via Nexis-Lexis. See also Joel Brinkley, "US and Europe in Battle Over Digital TV," *New York Times*, 25 August 1997, via the World Wide Web at http://www.nytimes.com.

Corporation owned 40 percent of the equity of BSkyB) coming from either terrestrial broadcasters like the BBC or British cable operators, adopted the policy of promoting a rapid transition to digital terrestrial broadcasting.

The impetus behind all of this was the pressure from European consumers for more choice in television programming. The reason for that pressure was the slowness with which the public broadcasters, who still dominated television broadcasting throughout Europe, recognized the consumers' desire for greater variety in programming and therefore failed to see the attraction that the new private pay-TV satellite services would hold for them.

Digital broadcasting in Britain

As early as 1993, Rupert Murdoch's News International was funding research on the development of a digital system for satellite services in Britian. The BBC began its own program of research into digital signal delivery.

On 9 August 1995, the British government published a White Paper announcing plans to create eighteen new digital terrestrial TV channels.[12] An industry-wide forum called the Digital TV Group was formed to discuss this proposal just after the publication of the White Paper. Members of the Group included the BBC, British Telecom, and the ITV companies (Carlton, Pearson, and Granada). A new broadcasting bill was introduced to Parliament by the Major government on 15 December 1995. The Broadcasting Act of 1996 empowered the ITC to establish digital terrestrial television in Britain. On 21 May 1996, the Independent Television Commission (ITC) began public consultations on digital terrestrial TV.

Rupert Murdoch responded to this government initiative by announcing his plans to deploy 120 channels of digital television via direct broadcast satellite. Granada Television, one of the members of the ITV group, formed a joint venture with BSkyB in December 1995 called GSkyB. All of the programming that Granada provided to British audiences via terrestrial analog broadcasting would now be available to satellite subscribers. Granada had recognized the growing market appeal of BSkyB's pay-TV services, which had over 5 million British subscribers at the time. In December 1995, the Office of Fair Trading initiated a review of BSkyB's "dominant position." This review was later dropped, much

---

[12] *Digital Terrestrial Broadcasting: The Government's Proposals* (London: Her Majesty's Stationery Office, August 1995), Cm. 2946.

to the displeasure of public broadcasters like the BBC, but it reflected a growing concern over the seemingly unstoppable momentum of Murdoch and BSkyB.

In May 1996, the BBC launched a new program called "Extending Choice in the Digital Age."[13] The basic idea was to digitize the signals of the two BBC terrestrial channels (BBC1 and BBC2) and 24-hour news services in widescreen format and offer them to subscribers on digital satellite, cable, and terrestrial systems. This was the BBC's first move in an attempt to match the boldness of Murdoch's strategy.

On 31 October 1996, the Independent Television Commission invited applicants to apply for licenses to run twenty-four new terrestrial digital television channels. Six "multiplexes" or packages of new channels would be available. The first three were reserved for the BBC, the ITV group, Channel 4, Channel 5, and the new Welsh channel S4C with the proviso that these broadcasters would use some of the spectrum to simulcast their existing services digitally. The other three multiplexes would be open to newcomers. Applications were due on or before 31 January 1997.

Two rival groups bid for the licenses: British Digital Broadcasting (BDB) and the Digital Television Network (DTN). BDB was initially made up of BSkyB with Carlton Communications PLC and Granada Group PLC (the latter two were both members of the ITV group). The three partners committed $490 million to the venture. BSkyB had almost 6 million subscribers to its analog satellite services at the time and wanted to add subscribers via terrestrial broadcasting. DTN's members included US-owned CableTel, Britain's third largest cable company and owner of NTL (National Transcommunications Limited), a TV transmission company that had formed after the decommissioning of the Independent Broadcasting Authority, and United News and Media, owner of the Express newspapers and two ITV companies. The DTN group was financially smaller and weaker than the BDB group, and to compensate for this it promised to add telephony and interactive services to its digital terrestrial services. It also promised that its set-top decoders would be compatible with decoders for other services (terrestrial, satellite, or cable) so that consumers would need only one box if they decided to subscribe to multiple services. The DTN argued in its application that "the BDB bid will effectively prevent DTT [digital terrestrial television] from developing as a major platform for pay-TV in competition with BSkyB's services."[14]

---

[13] See the BBC website at http://www.bbc.co.uk/info/digital.
[14] "Digital Television Network: Evidence to the Inquiry into the Future of the BBC and British Broadcasting," *M2 Presswire*, 21 February 1997, via Nexis-Lexis.

British Telecom began negotiations with Matsushita and BDB at the end of February 1997 to furnish subsidized set-top decoders for BDB's digital terrestrial services if it received a license from the Independent Television Commission (ITC). On 7 May 1997, BSkyB announced the formation of British Interactive Broadcasting (BIB), a joint venture of British Telecom, Matsushita, and Midlank Bank which would be responsible for the design, manufacturing, and financing of the subsidized set-top boxes for digital terrestrial television. BIB intended to offer home banking and shopping services over the BDB multiplex, if BDB won its bid for a licence.[15] On the same date, BSkyB announced that it had awarded a contract to Grundig and Hyundai to provide digital DVB/MPEG-2 and SCTE compliant set-top decoders, and other types of transmission and reception equipment. Hyundai's TV/COM subsidiary, based in the United States, would handle Hyundai's part of the contract.[16]

When the Labour Party won the elections in early May, it was thought that DTN's chances of winning its bid for a digital terrestrial TV license were improved because Lord Clive Hollick, chief executive to United News and Media, was a Labour peer and a prospective adviser to the new government of Tony Blair. On 9 May 1997, Hollick announced that he would purchase a large stake in DTN if it won its bid for a license. However, this was not sufficient to reduce the ITC's worries about the financial soundness of the DTN group, especially relative to the BDB group. The ITC did not like the participation of BSkyB in the BDB, however, and insisted in early June 1997 that BSkyB withdraw from the partnership. The group was duly restructured and the ITC announced its decision on 24 June to award a license to the restructured BDB. BSkyB was directly compensated for withdrawing from the group (£75 million) and was permitted to supply programs to BDB, a right potentially worth £1 billion over five years if the services were successful.[17]

The BDB deal was not quite complete, however, because on 27 August 1997, the Commission of the European Union announced that it would open a probe focusing particularly on the cooperative arrangements between British Telecom and BSkyB in the BDB bid. EU Competition Commissioner Karel van Miert said on 4 June 1997: "There is a problem

---

[15] Raymond Snoddy, "BIB Plans Shopping Lines on Terrestrial Television," *Financial Times*, 6 May 1997, p. 22, via Nexis-Lexis.

[16] "Hyundai-TV/COM and Grundig Alliance Awarded Digital Satellite Receiver Contract by British Sky Broadcasting," *Business Wire*, 7 May 1997, via Nexis-Lexis.

[17] Raymond Snoddy, "ITC: Challenge Over Award of Digital Licenses," *Financial Times*, 25 June 1997, via the World Wide Web at http://www.ft.com/hippocampus/723c6.html.

as far as the pay-TV business is concerned because there could be an enhancement of an already dominant position."[18]

The Commission was also concerned that BIB would hold a monopoly
of digital interactive services in Britain. It decided to put pressure on the
BDB and the BIB (jointly with British regulators) to make their digital
program guides and set-top boxes open to other competitors in the future.
Still, unless the Commission or some other EU body decided to intervene,
the parameters for the introduction of digital terrestrial television services
in Britain were set.

Digital broadcasting in Germany

On 22 December 1995, the German government unveiled a proposal for
legislation to foster the growth of multimedia industries by the building
of an Information Superhighway – the so-called "Infobahn." The main
purpose of the legislation was to do away with the red tape that was
limiting the growth of information industries in Germany. The intention
was to open up telecommunications markets completely by 1 January
1998 by privatizing Deutsche Telekom and permitting private companies
to bid for licenses to operate competitive telecommunications services
businesses in Germany.[19]

In broadcasting as in telecommunications, the German market was
dominated by public firms. The two largest television broadcasters
in Germany were ARD and ZDF, the national public broadcasters.
ARD and ZDF controlled terrestrial broadcasting in Germany indirectly
through their links with the regional public broadcasters who owned the
enormous broadcasting towers that could be found in most major urban
areas, while Deutsche Telekom controlled directly or indirectly most cable television operations in the country. Because of this, the main vehicle
for the delivery of private broadcasts was via direct broadcast satellites.
Attempts by the public broadcasters to control satellite transmission of
TV signals failed when SES-Astra (a company based in Luxembourg)
succeeded in delivering analog TV beginning in 1988 to German audiences via lower-powered communications satellites.

By the mid-1990s, the eroding audience shares of the public broadcasters, increasing costs of production, and stable license fee revenues
made ARD and ZDF particularly anxious to find new ways of competing in the broadcasting marketplace. They played a significant role in the

---

[18] "EU's Van Miert Voices Concern Over BDB Digital TV License Bid," *AFX New*, 5 June
1997, via Nexis-Lexis.
[19] "Germany's Ground Breaking Multimedia Legislation," *Newsbytes*, 22 December 1995,
via Nexis-Lexis.

formation of the European Launching Group for Digital Video Broadcasting and its successor, the DVB Group. Yet it was the private broadcasters who were most aggressive in pushing Germany toward digital television broadcasting.

The main players in the private broadcasting side in Germany were: (1) the Kirch Group, (2) Bertelsmann, and (3) the Compagnie Luxembourgeoise de Télévision (CLT). The Kirch Group was run by the reclusive Leo Kirch, a Bavarian media mogul who made his fortune by licensing and distributing films and TV programs from Hollywood producers. Kirch controlled two commercial TV channels in Germany: Sat.1 and DSF (a sports channel), both of which were delivered to German households primarily through satellite and cable systems. The Kirch Group owned 25 percent of a pay-TV service called Premiere (the other owners were Bertelsmann with 37.5 percent and Canal Plus with 37.5 percent). Kirch also owned 35 percent of the Axel Springer publishing group.[20]

In 1994, a proposed joint venture called Media Service GmbH, combining the resources of Bertelsmann, Canal Plus, and the Kirch Group (co-owners of the Premiere analog pay-TV service) to launch a digital pay-TV service, was blocked by the Commission of the European Union on the grounds that it would negatively affect competition in broadcasting. In the summer of 1995, Bertelsmann negotiated a deal with ARD, ZDF, and Canal Plus to create a common standard for decoders. Apparently these negotiations were not successful, but in February 1996, a joint venture of Deutsche Telekom (26.8 percent), Vebacom (23.9 percent), Bertelsmann (9 percent), CLT (8.8 percent), ARD (4.5 percent) and ZDF (4.5 percent) called the Multimedia Betriebsgesellschaft (MMBG) was announced. The MMBG would offer digital pay-TV services via satellite and cable using a decoder called the "Mediabox" developed by Seca, a French-based firm jointly owned by Bertelsmann and Canal Plus. MMBG said that it had already ordered between 100,000 and 150,000 Seca decoders to prepare for the launch of the service.

In early March 1996, an alliance was announced involving Rupert Murdoch's News Corporation, Bertelsmann, Canal Plus, and CLT. Murdoch apparently had his eye on winning a stake in Premiere and using it as a platform for launching his digital services on the European continent. Premiere had 1.2 million subscribers to its analog services as of the summer of 1996, but it was still not profitable. Nevertheless,

---

[20] "Mediaset Agreement Reached with Strategic Partners: A First Step Towards a Public Offering of the Company," *PR Newswire*, 20 July 1995, via Nexis-Lexis.

Premiere was headed toward digitization and increasing the number of channels to 100 and Murdoch must have figured that it was his best bet to get a piece of the lucrative German media market. Kirch was intent on blocking this. Murdoch eventually opted out of the deal on 7 March 1997.[21]

The Kirch Group was excluded from the MMBG and the Murdoch deal because Kirch thought that the Seca encryption system was not strong enough to prevent the sale of inexpensive decoder clones. Because of this, other pay-TV services would not use Seca decoders and customers would have to buy or rent more than one kind of decoder box if they wanted to subscribe to more than one pay-TV service. On 12 March 1996, Vebacom, the telecommunications subsidiary of Veba AG, said that it had abandoned MMBG to set up a new joint venture with Metro Group (one of Germany's largest retailers and operator of the Kaufhof department stores) and the Kirch Group to launch a digital pay-TV service called DF1 in Germany. Murdoch announced that BSkyB would also participate in DF1 on 8 July 1996. The digital signals would be delivered by twenty Astra transponders (ten each for Kirch and BSkyB) and decoded by set-top boxes developed by a subsidiary of the Kirch Group, BetaTechnik. Kirch's DF1 channels included a lot of movie channels (Kirch owned the rights to a number of major film libraries) and two digital sports channels: DSF Plus and DSF Golf. BSkyB's channels would be quite similar to those it already offered in Britain. The Kirch decoder was called the "D-box" and the company claimed that it was capable of being reconfigured to provide decoding of signals from more than one pay-TV system.[22]

Kirch intended DF1 to be a "body blow" to MMBG. According to one analyst, the root of the problem was the intense rivalry between Kirch and Bertelsmann:

Everything is up for grabs . . . Kirch and Bertelsmnan will fight it out to the end to win market share, to control Premiere and to be the best in providing content. It will be a bitter contest. The market may not allow both to survive. It may force them to unite.[23]

---

[21] "Euro Pay TV Alliance Appears to Hit Snag," *The Reuter European Community Report*, 5 June 1996, accessed via Nexis-Lexis.

[22] Ashley Seager, "Germany's Vebacom, Metro Set Up Digital TV Firm," *The Reuter European Business Report*, 5 March 1996, via Nexis-Lexis; Judy Dempsey, "Fight to the Finish in German Digital Television: Kirch's Lead Over Bertelsmann in the Race to the Marketplace May Be Shortlived," *Financial Times*, 12 March 1996, p. 31, via Nexis-Lexis. The remaining MMBG partners criticized the D-box for precisely the same reasons that Kirch had objected to the Seca decoder: that it would require consumers to purchase a separate decoder for each new pay-TV service.

[23] Dempsey, "Fight to the Finish."

DF1 was launched formally at a Formula One grand prix race in Hockenheim on 28 July 1996, but unfortunately no one was watching because the decoders had not been manufactured in time to be distributed to retail outlets. The initial price was DM1,100 (over $600); and there would also be a monthly charge of DM30 per month for the basic package of channels. Until May 1997, the boxes had to be purchased; after that date, they could be leased for DM20 per month.

DF1 was not successful. Only 11,000 subscribers signed up as of November 1996. The high price of the decoders was a major deterrent for consumers. Even though Astra's analog satellite signal was available to over 10 million German households, consumers still needed to buy or rent a new digital decoder, a D-box, to enjoy the new digital services. Kirch's efforts to negotiate access to the high-quality cable services delivered by Deutsche Telekom were unsuccessful, thus excluding DF1 channels from the 16 million German households who had cable but no satellite connection. Deutsche Telekom rejected Kirch's demands for exclusive control over the digital program guide that came along with DF1 services.[24]

Bertelsmann AG was a multinational company headquartered in Gütersloh with annual revenues of $14.7 billion in 1996, that had started out as a book and magazine publisher and later became a diversified media company. Bertelsmann had four main divisions: BMG Entertainment, Books, Gruner+Jahr (newspaper and magazine publishing), and the Industry Group. BMG Entertainment was in charge of a wide variety of businesses, including several recording studios, a record club, videotape distribution services, and a television channel called RTL, which it operated in partnership with CLT. BMG Entertainment also owned a stake (along with Kirch) in two pay-TV operations: Premiere and Vox.

In July 1996, Bertelsmann purchased CLT and merged it with its Ufa film and television division to form CLT-Ufa. The new company had ownership interests in seventeen European television channels: RTL, RTL2, Super RTL, Premiere, and VOX in Germany; M6, Serie Club, Multivision, TMC, and RTL9 in France; RTL4, RTL5, and Veronica in the Netherlands; RTL TV 1 and Club RTL in Belgium; RTL Tele Leutzberg in Luxembourg; and Channel 5 in Britain.[25] The European Commission approved the merger on 8 October 1996, because it recognized that CLT-Ufa would have to compete with the Kirch Group in

---

[24] "Kirch's DF1 Channels Energy Toward Christmas Shoppers," *Variety*, 28 October 1996 to 3 November 1996, p. 37, via Nexis-Lexis; "Kirch's Digital TV Hits Launch Snag," *The Reuter European Business Report*, 4 July 1996, via Nexis-Lexis.

[25] See the Bertelsmann website at http://www.bertelsmann.de/bag/gesch_ber96/bmg/index.html.

Germany and media enterprises in other countries and therefore would not have a dominant market position.[26] The German Cartel Office approved it in January 1997.[27]

In December 1996, ARD and ZDF announced that they would offer a "free" (unencrypted) digital TV service on the Astra satellite. In order to receive the signals, all one needed was a satellite dish (with Universal LNF) and a DVB – compatible television receiver. According to SES estimates, 1.4 million German households were already equipped with the right kind of satellite dish, but it remained to be seen whether those households would run out and purchase a new receiver, especially since the receivers were still quite expensive and the new services were basically just simulcasts of the existing ARD and ZDF programs.

ARD and ZDF also tried to make their Electronic Program Guide (EPG) a standard in Germany for digital television services. Such a guide had proved important to the success of the DirecTV services in the United States, because it made possible "point and click" access to programs and to easier taping of broadcasts on connected VCRs.[28] But obviously there might be problems for consumers if the ARD and ZDF program guide were not compatible with the one offered by Kirch and his partners on DF1.

On 21 May 1996, the chief executive of ARD, Albert Scharf, predicted that low-income households would become "isolated" if pay-TV were allowed to purchase the rights to broadcast sporting events and recently released movies.

Events that people will be talking about cannot be reserved for a small group of wealthy people – the free TV viewer must continue to have open access in the future to top films and sporting events.[29]

Scharf was criticized immediately by private broadcasters for proposing restrictions on the activities of pay-TV operators. A spokesperson for Sat.1, Kristina Fassler, said:

He's not living in the real world . . . The public broadcasters are obligated to provide basic television. There is no way that top sporting events and top Hollywood films can be included in that basic package. People are willing to pay for these things. They have market value.[30]

---

[26] Peter Klanowski, "Ufa/CLT Deal Cleared," *Tele-satellit News*, 8 October 1996, via the World Wide Web at http://www.tele-satellit.com.
[27] "CLT-Ufa to Pay DM850M in Kirch TV Pact," *Dow Jones Newswires*, 17 July 1997, via the World Wide Web at http://www.wsj.com.
[28] See Astra's website at http://www.astra.lu/company/poress/97/970828.html.
[29] Erik Kirschbaum, "ARD Attacks Pay TV: German Pubcaster Calls Feevee Unfair," *Daily Variety*, 21 May 1996, p. 10, accessed via Nexis-Lexis.
[30] *Ibid.*

Fassler went on to point out that the German public broa casters were being squeezed financially as advertising revenues were de ining in the face of increase competition from private broadcasters ar.. that Scharf was simply making an argument for "more money."[31]

On 23 June 1997, the Kirch Group and CLT-Ufa announced a compromise deal to develop digital pay-TV around Premiere using the D-box decoder. Canal Plus agreed to sell its share of Premiere so that Kirch and CLT-Ufa would both own 50 percent of the joint venture. In return, Canal Plus would be allowed to purchase Kirch's interest in the Italian pay-TV venture, Telepiu. Kirch was forced to make this deal with Bertelsmann because DF1 still only had 30,000 subscribers and Deutsche Telekom continued to refuse to permit DF1 to access the Telekom-controlled cable networks.[32] If German and European authorities approved the new deal, the way was cleared for the launch of a successful digital pay-TV service in Germany. There would be only one of them, however.

Digital broadcasting in France

Canal Plus was the first company to offer digital pay-TV services in Europe with the launching of its Canalsatellite Numerique service with twenty channels in April 1996. By the end of June 1997, it had 400,000 subscribers. By fall 1997, the service would have forty-six channels. Canal Plus had over 4 million subscribers for its analog pay-TV services. Canal Plus acquired Nethold BV, the main pay-TV company of the Netherlands, for $2 billion in September 1996. Nethold had 8.5 million subscribers in Europe, Africa, and the Middle East. Nethold had already launched digital services in Italy, Benelux, and Scandinavia.[33] So Canal Plus would now have a major presence in those countries as well as in Spain (see the next section for details).

The main competition to Canalsatellite in the digital category was TPS, a joint venture of TF1 (the privatized public broadcaster that was now the top broadcaster in France), France Télévision (the non-privatized public broadcaster), M6-Metropole Télévision (owned by Bertelsmann and CLT), and Compagnie Générale des Eaux. TPS began broadcasting

---

[31] *Ibid.*

[32] Frederick Studemann, "Pay-TV: German Rivals Agree Joint Venture," *Financial Times*, 24 June 1997, at http://www.ft.com.

[33] "Hyundai to Incorporate OpenTV Technology in Set-Top Boxes for Nethold Networks," *Business Wire*, 20 November 1996, via Nexis-Lexis.

in January 1997 and had more than 175,000 subscribers by September 1997.[34]

Another potential competitor for Canal Plus and TPS in France was Multicable, a 60/40 joint venture between Lyonnaise Communications and France Télécom that operated a cable pay-per-view system in Paris. The service, which included cable modems that permitted high-speed Internet access, was launched in October 1995.[35]

To summarize, digital television had been introduced earlier in France than in the other large Western European countries. French consumers were particularly eager to subscribe to both the analog and digital services provided by Canal Plus because they were dissatisfied with the restricted choices of programming available to them via terrestrial broadcasts (dominated until recently by public broadcasters). Cable services were just beginning to be offered and they still had a very limited share of French households. It helped somewhat, also, that the managers of Canal Plus were strong supporters of François Mitterrand and the Socialist Party.

Digital broadcasting in the rest of Europe

In the rest of Europe, the basic story was of partnering of local interests with one of the European media giants for analog and digital pay-TV services. Deal-making accelerated as the 1998 EU deadline for deregulating telecommunications approached. The main pay-TV service in Italy as of summer 1997 was Telepiu. Prior to the Kirch–Bertelsmann détente in Germany, it was jointly owned by Kirch (45 percent), Canal Plus (45 percent), and Mediaset (10 percent) – an arm of Silvio Berlusconi's holding company, Fininvest. After the détente, Canal Plus held 90 percent of the venture. In Spain, there was a joint venture between Canal Plus and Prisa, Spain's largest media group and publisher of *El País* (a national newspaper), called Sogecable that owned the first digital pay-TV service, CanalSatelite Digital (CSD). Its main rival was Distribuidora de Television Digital (DTD) which was owned by Spanish telecommunications company Telefónica and a variety of other shareholders. The two Spanish rivals fought over the decoder issue, as in Germany.

---

[34] Amy Barrett, "Canal Satellite Anticipates Passing Its Subscriber Goal," *Wall Street Journal Interactive Edition*, 25 August 1997, accessed via the World Wide Web at http://www.wsj.com; and Melissa Pozsgay, "Canal Plus, TPS Back-to-School TV Battle," *Bloomberg News*, 18 August 1997, via the World Wide Web at http://nytsyn.com/live/News/230_081897_110001_25750.html.

[35] "Interactive Multimedia Trial for Paris Cable," *New Media Markets*, 29 June 1995, via Nexis-Lexis; and "Cable Modem Trial Takes Off in French Riviera: French Cable Operators Increasingly Are Looking to the Internet as a Revenue Source," *European Media Business and Finance*, 29 July 1996, via Nexis-Lexis.

Summary of the digital scene in Europe

By the summer of 1997, digital TV services had been successfully launched in France, the Benelux countries, and Scandinavia and were in the process of being launched in Britain, France, Italy, and possibly also Spain. All of these services used equipment compatible with the DVB transmission and reception standards, but there remained some disagreement over standards for "controlled access" – the way in which encryption was incorporated into set-top boxes and receivers to guarantee that only paid subscribers could receive broadcasts. The two basic encryption systems were controlled by Canal Plus and Kirch (although Kirch relinquished some control over the D-box to Deutsche Telekom in July 1997 to secure access to the German cable network). Digital television in Europe was limited to standard definition television with 4:3 or 16:9 aspect ratios. Europe was not implementing HDTV versions of DVB yet.

NHK sticks with MUSE

As the FCC process unfolded in the United States, NHK made efforts to accomodate the FCC's preferences for an HDTV system that was compatible with the US system of local terrestrial broadcasting. When the FCC called for a simulcast approach to the transition from NTSC to HDTV broadcasting, NHK put forward its "narrow MUSE" system which allowed the broadcasting of a lower-quality MUSE signal over existing 6 megahertz channels. NHK engineers were well aware that narrow MUSE was not likely to fare well against rival American and European systems because the latter did not have to be compatible with the original MUSE/Hi-Vision approach. They believed that their experience in creating and operating working HDTV broadcasting systems would help to make up for their disadvantages elsewhere. Nevertheless, the spirit of the effort was one of grudging acceptance of the new rules and gloom about the expected outcome.[36]

Things got worse for Hi-Vision when the FCC decided in late 1990 to favor an all-digital HDTV system. There was no way to erase the analog parts of the MUSE/Hi-Vision systems without giving up on the idea of exclusive DBS delivery of HDTV and reengineering the MUSE circuitry designs, the two cornerstones of NHK's HDTV technology strategy. Still, there were those in Japan who argued for just such a development – particularly the private broadcasters and some of the manufacturers, especially

---

[36] For details, see Joel Brinkley, *Defining Vision: The Battle for the Future of Television* (New York: Harcourt Brace, 1997).

those who were behind in building the analog systems. NHK and its chief allies stuck with MUSE Hi-Vision, however.

As the future for international acceptance of MUSE/Hi-Vision grew dimmer, there were a number of minor rebellions within Japan. The first rebellion was connected with the formation of the Broadcasting Technology Association (BTA) in 1983 for investigating the possibility of deploying an improved definition television (IDTV) system in Japan. While this group included nineteen manufacturers and a number of private broadcasters, and it had the somewhat unenthusiastic blessing of the Ministry of Posts and Telecommunications (MPT), it was opposed by NHK and MITI as being antithetical to the notion of fast deployment of HDTV systems.

The BTA favored the deployment of what they called an enhanced definition TV (EDTV) approach for private broadcasters, which would provide sharper pictures first without the wider aspect ratio (EDTV-I or "Clear-vision") and then with wider screens (EDTV-II or Wide-aspect Clear-vision) but would not require satellite delivery or major upgrading of terrestrial facilities. EDTV-I experimental broadcasts began in 1989; EDTV-II broadcasts were scheduled to begin in 1995. In February 1989, the BTA invited Faroudja Laboratories of the United States to demonstrate its Super NTSC system, an IDTV system that was considerably better than their EDTV-I. The manufacturers supported these efforts as a hedge on their investments in HDTV technologies, but they still put most of their money into the development of Hi-Vision products.[37]

The early days of the Japanese HDTV market

Japanese manufacturers began to offer HDTV equipment on the consumer market in very small quantities and at very high prices as early as 1990. Sony's HDTV receiver, for example, was priced at around $33,000 when introduced in December 1990. Subsequent products marketed by Matsushita, Hitachi, Mitsubishi, and JVC were all priced at over $30,000 per unit. In March 1992, Sharp introduced a product that it called "Home Hi-Vision" with much lower picture resolution than the earlier products, but with all the other attributes (widescreen, CD-quality stereo sound, and the ability to decode MUSE-encoded signals) at a price of $7,500. Some of the other manufacturers claimed that this product should not be marketed under the Hi-Vision label because of its lower resolution, but others moved quickly to develop and market similar products. They

---

[37] John Sie, "HDTV and Japan, Inc.," unpublished manuscript, Tele-Communications, Inc., Denver, CO, revised draft, 28 April 1989.

soon put their own "dumbed-down" versions of Hi-Vision receivers on the market in the $5,000 to $7,000 per unit range.

NHK and the larger manufacturers remained committed to a full implementation of Hi-Vision for receivers and tried to make the best of a bad situation by marketing the early products primarily to industrial and business users. They were helped considerably during this period by the initiation of two public programs funded respectively by MITI and MPT: the "Hi-Vision Communities Concept" and the "Hi-Vision Cities Concept." The MPT program was a bit grander than the MITI one, but neither was very specific about its goals and focused primarily on subsidizing local purchases of HDTV equipment for community purposes.

A successful example was the establishment of a "Hi-Vision Gallery" in Gifu, a small town between Tokyo and Osaka. The Gifu Museum digitized a number of works in its collection and displayed them, along with a linked database, in a special gallery devoted to this purpose. As a result of the success of the Gifu Gallery, NHK worked hard to try to get other museums in Japan and abroad to use Hi-Vision technologies in exhibitions. The Metropolitan Museum of Art in New York did so in 1991 for an exhibition on the works of Frederick Remington. Unfortunately for NHK, the Metropolitan's program was badly executed and did very little good for the global Hi-Vision cause.

There was also talk of reviving the neighborhood movie houses of small-town Japan with these programs, an issue of considerable importance to the Japanese elite. But the total financial support for these efforts was extremely limited and therefore not much came of them. Indeed, one can argue that both MPT and MITI were somewhat relieved that the NHK-led efforts failed because they did not relish the idea of further decentralizing governmental control over high technology industrial promotion efforts.

In the meantime, prices for genuine HDTV receivers had declined considerably. In June 1993, Sony introduced a 32-inch set priced at 1.3 milllion yen ($13,000) and Matsushita marketed a 36-inch set in November 1993 at 1.5 million yen ($15,000). The lowest priced (non-dumbed-down) sets cost 980,000 yen ($9,800) in 1992–3.[38] Only 15,000 units were sold in 1993, however.[39] A consortium of Japanese and American semiconductor firms was established in January 1992 to

---

[38] *Japan Economic Newswire*, 5 April 1993, story 11, p. 1; "NHK Develops Converter for Japanese, European HDTV Sets," *Agence France Presse*, 13 October 1992, via Nexis-Lexis.

[39] "Is Widescreen Killing Japanese HDTV?" *Consumer Electronics*, 34: 9 (28 February 1994), via Nexis-Lexis.

develop less expensive Hi-Vision chip sets. Its members were: Fujitsu, Hitachi, Texas Instruments Japan, and Sony. On 6 December 1993, the consortium announced the marketing of a new Hi-Vision chip set at 70 percent of the price of previous sets. However, even at the lower price, the set still cost over $900.[40]

NHK responded by developing inexpensive "down converters" which enabled homes with satellite dishes and tuners and regular NTSC or PAL/SECAM TVs to watch Hi-Vision broadcasts. These down converters sold well. So did widescreen EDTV televisions (without HDTV circuitry). About 1.5 million widescreen sets were sold in 1994 and about 3 million in 1995.[41] If you combined the number of HDTV sets, with the number of regular and widescreen sets that could display HDTV broadcasts thanks to a down converter, the number of households that could view "HDTV" began to look pretty respectable (see Table 8.1). In 1994, NHK upped the number of hours of Hi-Vision broadcasting per week from eight to nine. The plan was to go to a full day of HDTV broadcasts by 1996.

The MPT pushes for all-digital HDTV: the Egawa incident

On 18 February 1994, Akimasa Egawa, Director General of the Broadcasting Bureau of the Ministry of Posts and Telecommunications (MPT), discussed NHK's annual budget proposal at a closed meeting with the Social Capital Committee of the Shinseito (Renaissance) party, a newly formed offshoot of the Liberal Democratic Party that allied itself with the Komeito (Clean Government Party) and the Minshato (Democratic Socialist Party). At the meeting, Egawa argued that Hi-Vision was becoming obsolete because the trend in television globally was toward digitalization. He said that he thought that Japan needed to make a rapid transition from Hi-Vision to an all-digital system. Egawa did not receive any support from the politicians at this meeting, and his proposals were leaked to the press.

On 22 February 1994, Egawa held a press conference in which he repeated his arguments of 18 February. Loud and immediate protests came from NHK, the Electronic Industries Association of Japan (EIAJ), and a number of consumer electronics manufacturers, retailers, and

---

[40] "Fujitsu Develops Low-Cost HDTV Image Processing Chip Set," *Comline*, 8 December 1993, via Nexis-Lexis.
[41] "Japan Widescreen Broadcasting," *Consumer Electronics*, 17 June 1995, p. 15, via Nexis-Lexis.

Table 8.1 *Cumulative sales of Hi-Vision receivers, MUSE-NTSC converters, and wide NTSC receivers in Japan, April 1996 to June 2000*

Month	Hi-Vision receivers	Receivers with MUSE-NTSC converter	Wide NTSC receivers
Apr 96	158	260	5187
May 96	169	274	5363
Jun 96	191	303	5590
Jul 96	212	339	5866
Aug 96	217	354	6050
Sep 96	233	373	6266
Oct 96	249	392	6481
Nov 96	278	416	6768
Dec 96	314	451	7173
Jan 97	321	462	7307
Feb 97	336	477	7492
Mar 97	359	504	7803
Apr 97	371	530	8010
May 97	382	547	8157
Jun 97	398	572	8335
Jul 97	413	598	8521
Apr 98	595	1473	9971
May 98	610	1505	10088
Jun 98	630	1545	10251
Jul 98	641	1572	10401
Aug 98	649	1591	10512
Oct 98	691	1681	10801
Nov 98	712	1725	10955
Dec 98	739	1790	11161
Jan 99	746	1805	11221
Aug 99	811	1941	
Jan 00	820	1985	12172
Mar 00	829	2018	12347
May 00	837	2049	
Jun 00	839	2058	

Sources: NHK and the Electronic Industries Association of Japan via the World Wide Web at http://www.nhk.or.jp and http://j-entertain.co.jp/hpa-data/.

consumer groups who considered this move to be precipitous. Tadahiro Sekimoto, President of NEC Corporation and Chairman of the EIAJ said: "The . . . Hi-Vision system is the only HDTV system in practical use in the world today. We believe that this system will be used long . . . into the next century, and we will firmly support the system."

The official position of NHK was that Japan should continue to use the MUSE/Hi-Vision approach until it is clearly demonstrated that an all-digital system is both of higher quality and of comparable or lower price. The large investment in new satellites, picture tubes, and chipsets as well as the relatively early rollout of the system made it very difficult for Japan to put MUSE Hi-Vision on hold while waiting for all-digital HDTV. For the most part, the consumer electronics manufacturers agreed with NHK.

The EIAJ asked Egawa to withdraw his proposal and the latter complied immediately.[42] However, there were many favorable comments in the Japanese press about his stand, and even a few manufacturers admitted that the MUSE Hi-Vision system might become obsolete in an age of all-digital systems. Other manufacturers argued that Hi-Vision was already mostly digital, so they did not see going to an all-digital system as a radical improvement. But they were obviously concerned about the slow growth in sales of HDTV receivers. A spokesman for Matsushita Electric Industrial Company said "As a manufacturer, we will offer what the consumer wants."[43] Seichiro Ujiie, President of Nippon Television Network (NTN), a private broadcasting network that had been critical of MUSE Hi-Vision from the start, said that he thought Egawa's remarks constituted "a good start" toward an all-digital system in Japan. The National Association of Commercial Broadcasters (NABC) proposed adopting a digital TV system with the launch of the BS-4 broadcast satellites, scheduled to begin in 1997. NHK was opposed to this because they wanted to protect their investment in MUSE Hi-Vision technologies.

NHK's counterstrategy was to talk about its own vision for the future of broadcasting: integrated services digital broadcasting (ISDB). Digital HDTV would be one of the new services provided via ISDB. NHK proposed the goal of offering ISDB by the year 2007 (or perhaps as early as 2005). Until that time, MUSE Hi-Vision would remain the system of choice for HDTV. ISDB would permit enhancements to existing services in two main areas: (a) interactive video and (b) 3-D and virtual reality video. An experimental broadcasting satellite in the 21 GHz band called COMETS was scheduled for launch in 1996. NHK engineers would use COMETS to do experiments related to ISDB. In addition, they would test new digital transmission technologies like orthogonal frequency division multiplexing (OFDM) in the next few years. The President of NHK, Mikio Kawaguchi, defended the continued reliance of Japan on

---

[42] Eiji Kawabata, "The Politics of HDTV in the US and Japan," paper prepared for delivery at the Annual Meeting of the American Political Science Association, San Francisco, 29 August–1 September 1996, p. 10.

[43] *The Reuter Asia-Pacific Business Report*, 28 April 1994, via Nexis-Lexis.

satellite broadcasting by arguing that satellite systems were very reliable and that cable and optical fiber systems were vulnerable to disruption by earthquakes.[44]

On 27 April 1994, the MPT released the report of an advisory panel to Mr. Egawa that argued that the Japanese government should establish digital broadcasting standards by 1996 in order to "keep pace with global trends in communications."[45] The report stated that one of the key advantages of digital broadcasting was that it would permit a rapid increase in the number of television channels via multiplexing. It pointed to the rapid development of digital systems in the United States and Europe and to the need for Japan to maintain consistency in its terrestrial, cable, and satellite broadcasting systems.

On 29 March 1995, the MPT released a report of the Study Group on Broadcasting System[s] in the Multimedia Age.[46] This report was much like the one released the year before, but contained updated information about the deployment of digital television systems in Europe and the United States and announced the intention of the Telecommunications Technology Council of MPT to formulate standards for digital broadcasting in Japan by 1996. Apparently, the same Council had already devised a temporary standard for digitizing television services for communication satellites (CS), distinguished from the broadcast satellites (BS) by having somewhat lower-powered signals and therefore requiring slightly larger dishes for reception.

Toshiba introduced a 32-inch Hi-Vision receiver in June 1995 at a price of 530,000 yen (around $5,300).[47] On 31 July 1995, Shigeru Yamazaki, director of the Digital Broadcasting System Research Division of NHK's Science and Technical Research Laboratories, warned that there were still "a number of unresolved technical issues" standing in the way of making a transition to digital satellite and terrestrial broadcasting. He called for more work on COFDM and on multiplexing of SDTV signals. Japanese government officials and business representatives began to debate the

---

[44] Keiji Urakami, "HDTV Format Switch Not to Change Makers' Basic Strategy," *Japan Economic Newswire*, 23 February 1994, via Nexis-Lexis; Yoshiko Hara, "Japan Still Riding Digital Fence," *Electronic Enginering Times Interactive*, 7 March 1994, p. 40, via the World Wide Web at http://tech.web; and "NHK Plans 50" Plasma Tube," *Consumer Electronics* 34: 24 (13 June 1994), via Nexis-Lexis. See also Junji Matsuzaki, "The Scenario for Hi-Vision Broadcasting in Japan," unpublished manuscript, NHK, Tokyo, June 1993.

[45] "Panel Urges Digital Broadcasting Standard by 1996," *Japan Economic Newswire* (*Kyodo*), 27 April 1994; and *The Reuter Asia-Pacific Business Report*, 28 April 1994, both via Nexis-Lexis.

[46] English translation accessed at http://www.mpt.go.jp/policyreports/english/Broadcasting-system/press/release.html.

[47] *COMLINE Daily News Electronics*, 20 July 1995, via Nexis-Lexis.

question of whether it was desirable to digitize the MUSE Hi-Vision system or to start from scratch.[48]

The MPT changed its strategy after the failure of its direct attack on MUSE Hi-Vision in February 1994. In May 1994, the MPT's Telecommunications Council made public its report on Japan's advanced information network. The report was a response to the initiative of the Clinton Administration to create a National Information Infrastructure (NII) on the model of the Internet and the feeling of many Japanese that Japan had fallen behind in this area. The Ministry of Education and the MPT had fought over the building of Japan's Internet, thus causing a serious delay. As a result, Japan had not benefited from the rapid growth in demand for Internet services that accompanied the invention of the World Wide Web and Web browser software like Netscape Navigator and Microsoft's Internet Explorer.

The MPT began to hit on the theme of promoting multimedia business and making Japanese businesses more Web-savvy by upgrading the national telecommunications infrastructure. The MPT had been trying for years to find a convincing rationale for spending trillions of yen on adding optical fiber to the infrastructure. There was also a bit of bureaucratic competition in all of this. The idea of promoting multimedia businesses by building a new information infrastructure was a way for the MPT to wrest some control over high technology programs from the Ministry of International Trade and Industry (MITI).[49]

Digital multiplexing in Japan

The MPT was responding to the rise in interest in digital multiplexing as a way to quickly provide Japanese households with a greater range of choice in television programming. Cable TV penetration was limited (20 percent in 1993) in Japan thanks to a combination of high costs and regulatory barriers. In the late 1980s, JCSAT, a joint venture of Hughes Aerospace and a collection of Japanese firms, began to offer a bouquet of channels to subscribers with special satellite dishes to receive CS signals. In April 1991, Japan Satellite Broadcasting (JSAT or JSB) began broadcasting encrypted "conditional access" (pay-TV) television signals via the BS-3

[48] Junko Yoshida, "Japan's Broadcast Entity Drags Feet," *Electronic Engineering Times Interactive* 589 (31 July 1995).

[49] See Chalmers Johnson, "MITI, MPT, and the Telecom Wars: How Japan Makes Policy for High Technology," in Chalmers Johnson, Laura D'Andrea Tyson, and John Zysman (eds.), *Politics and Productivity: How Japan's Development Strategy Works* (New York: HarperBusiness, 1989).

broadcast satellite. JSAT was owned by Itochu Corporation, Mitsui and Company, Ltd., Sumitomo Corporation, and Nissho Iwai Corporation (all four are *sogo sosha* or trading companies). The satellite service of JSAT was called WOWOW and competed directly with the NHK NTSC and HDTV satellite services. Unlike NHK, JSAT decided to speed adoption of its services by subsidizing the costs to consumers of acquiring decoders. It also began to market its services aggressively in department stores and consumer electronics outlets. The number of subscribers grew rapidly to around 2 million in late 1996.[50]

In the fall of 1996, three new firms were created with the intention of providing digital TV via direct broadcast satellites: PerfecTV, JSkyB, and DirecTV Japan, Inc.

PerfecTV was a joint venture of the same firms that owned JSAT. It launched a seventy-channel service in October 1996 and was able to sign up 100,000 subscribers by January 1997. PerfecTV planned to increase its channel offerings to 100 by the fall of 1997.

JSkyB was a joint venture between Rupert Murdoch's News Corporation Ltd. and Japan's Softbank Corporation. It planned to offer initially a twelve-channel service (to increase later to 150 channels) in alliance with Nippon Television (NTV) beginning in April 1997. News Corporation and Softbank each purchased 21.4 percent of the equity of Asahi TV, hoping that they might also provide terrestrial broadcasts of their services using Asahi's terrestrial antennas. Asahi was unwilling to do this, however, so in March 1997 News and Softbank invited Sony and Fuji Television to become equal partners in JSkyB. The addition of these two new partners gave a considerable boost to the venture's future prospects.[51]

DirecTV Japan (DTVJ) was a joint venture of Hughes Electronics (35 percent), Culture Convenience Club (35 percent), Matsushita (10 percent), Mitsubishi Corporation (5 percent), Mitsubishi Electric Corporation (5 percent) and Dai-Nippon Printing Company (5 percent). It planned to offer a 100-channel service beginning in the fall of 1997.

Sony was awarded a multimillion dollar contract to build satellite broadcasting facilities for DTVJ in March 1997.[52] It received a contract to build similar facilities for JSky B. All of the digital broadcasters planned

---

[50] *Japan Electronics Almanac 95/96* (Tokyo: Dempa, 1995), p. 202.

[51] "Murdoch's Japanese TV Venture Unveils New Partners," *Reuter European Business Report*, 14 May 1997, via Nexis-Lexis.

[52] "JSkyB to Lauch 150 Digital TV Channels in Japan," *Financial Times*, 18 December 1996, p. 30; "JSkyB to Employ NTV's Digital High-Quality System," *Japan Economic Newswire* (*Kyodo*), 14 December 1996, via Nexis-Lexis; and "Sony Awarded Multi-Million-Dollar Contract to Build Direct Broadcast Satellite Facility for DIRECTV JAPAN," *Business Wire*, 5 March 1997, via Nexis-Lexis.

to use MPEG-2 video compression, consistent with the DVB's effort to foster global standards for digital television broadcasting.

JSkyB and PerfecTV agreed to offer each other's programs, to share the same JCSAT-4 communications satellite, and to use the same satellite decoders for their services.[53] DTVJ would also use the JCSAT-4 satellite (since Hughes was already a major shareholder in JCSAT), but reserved the right to use a different type of decoder. On 17 June 1997, however, all three digital satellite broadcasters announced their agreement to adopt a common standard for decoders so as to avoid consumer confusion. Apparently, DTVJ was responding to pressure from the MPT to adopt a common decoder.

The Radio Regulatory Council had to decide whether to permit digital broadcasting on the new BS-4 broadcast satellites, and if so whether it should encourage digital HDTV or multiplexed SDTV broadcasts. On 11 March 1997, Shuji Jusuda, the new Director General of the Broadcasting Bureau of the MPT, said that the start of digital broadcasting in Japan would be moved up to begin before the year 2000. Jusuda said the MPT intended to conduct experiments using the BS3-b satellite to test a variety of digital broadcasting systems. The MPT was pushing, in particular, for the Radio Regulatory Council to authorize the use of the BS-4 satellites for digital broadcasting instead of waiting for another five to ten years for the launching of the next generation of satellites operating at 21GHz (as NHK preferred). NHK said that it was willing to conduct research on this question, but added: "There will be many issues to be solved for the realization [of the digital broadcasting] to take place because it will have a big impact on television viewers as well as broadcast stations. Consensus must be built among concerned people."[54]

There was a major shake-up in the top management of NHK in the spring and summer of 1997. A new Executive Director General of Broadcasting, Naoyuki Kohno, was appointed on 21 May 1997. A new President of NHK, Katsuji Ebisawa, was appointed on 31 July 1997. Early statements by both new executives pointed to a change in attitude in the NHK management toward the acceleration of digital broadcasting in Japan.[55] Many additional questions will remain, of course, but it appears that the long campaign of NHK to delay digitization was over and that the various commercial interests desiring a rapid transition to all-digital

[53] "JSkyB, PerfecTV Agree to Offer Each Other's Channels," *Japan Consumer Electronics Scan (Kyodo)*, 11 November 1996, via Nexis-Lexis; "JSkyB to Share Operations with PerfecTV," *Japan Economic Newswire (Kyodo)*, 18 October 1996, via Nexis-Lexis.
[54] "Ministry Announces Plan to Go Digital in Land TV Broadcasting," *Daily Yomiuri*, 11 March 1997, p. 20.
[55] See "Comments from the Top" at the NHK website at http://www.nhk.or.jp.

systems had carried the day. What remained unclear, however, just as in Europe and the United States, was the future of digital HDTV as opposed to digital standard definition television.

Conclusions

In Japan and Western Europe, the response to the US decision to pursue an all-digital HDTV system was to reexamine their earlier decisions to adopt hybrid (partly digital, partly analog) standards. The Europeans dropped HD-MAC quickly, whereas in Japan resistance from NHK and allied consumer electronics manufacturers to abandoning MUSE/Hi-Vision delayed the decision to move to digital broadcasting. By mid-1997, both Europe and Japan were committed to a rapid transition to digital broadcasting via direct broadcast satellite. Neither was likely to move quickly to digital HDTV broadcasting, however, for the same reasons that computer companies in the United States were reluctant to support the grand alliance/ATSC HDTV standard. They worried that the HDTV consumer equipment would be too expensive and that there would not be adequate sources of new revenues to justify the purchasing of transmission equipment by broadcasters. They eventually responded positively to the evident desire of consumers for greater programming choice and widescreen, but not high-resolution, images.

Both Europe and Japan were moving, therefore, toward the digital delivery of widescreen and regular standard definition signals with MPEG-2 compression, QAM modulation for satellite and cable, and COFDM for terrestrial. The United States, in contrast, had chosen to pursue both HDTV and multiplexed standard definition broadcasting with MPEG-2 compression, and VSB transmission for satellite, cable, and terrestrial services. As before, Europe and Japan chose greater certainty in television standards than the United States, but this time they listened to the objections of their private broadcasters and consumers and did not permit the consumer electronics manufacturers and public broadcasters to control the standards-setting process.

9   Examples of global standards

The debates over HDTV and DTV standards did not result in the selection of uniform global standards or in uniformity of standards even at
the regional or national levels. Within Western Europe, for example, the
various pay-TV operators implemented digital television in distinct and
somewhat incompatible ways. In the United States, the final compromise on DTV standards created a variety of DTV production and delivery standards. The major television networks and cable companies could
not agree initially on which ones to deploy. Only in Japan were uniform
HDTV standards adopted and deployed, but even there consumer acceptance was limited. Contrast this with the nearly global acceptance of such
computer and telecommunications standards as the IBM-PC platform
(combining Intel microprocessors with Microsoft operating systems), the
TCP/IP protocols of the Internet, HTML (the scripting language of the
World Wide Web), and the Linux[1] operating system. Why did uniformity
arise in these areas but not in advanced television?

The IBM-PC-platform

The broad acceptance of the IBM-PC-platform for personal computers
resulted primarily from the ability of Intel and Microsoft to market a
family of products and services that appealed to consumers. The main
competitor to PC-platform was first the Apple II and later the Apple
Macintosh platform. While Macintosh survived the general trend toward IBM-PC dominance, the platform of choice for the overwhelming
majority of users by the late 1990s was the PC-platform.[2] The global

---

[1] Some people prefer "GNU/Linux" to Linux to recognize the importance of the GNU
software developed previous to Linux for the success of the latter. I agree with this point
but will still use Linux as a shorter name for the GNU/Linux operating system. See
Eric Kidd, "A History of 'Open Source,'" 19 August 2000, at http://static.userland.
com/userLandDiscussArchive/msg019844.html.
[2] According to IDC, Apple/Macintosh computers constituted less than 3 percent of the
world market for desktop PCs in 2002. See http://www.idc.com.

acceptance of uniform PC platform standards arose primarily from the fact that consumers wanted to have access to a wide variety of packaged computer software and computer peripherals at low average prices. Since the average price of packaged software depended on the number of users, because of low costs of reproducing software, this gave a major incentive for software companies to create products for the platform with the most users.[3]

In Japan, the IBM-PC-platform was not accepted as rapidly as elsewhere. A major Japanese computer firm, NEC, had a line of personal computers and an operating system that were successful initially in the Japanese market because they supported word-processing and other applications using Japanese katakana characters. It was only after IBM developed a method for representing both Chinese and Japanese characters in a way that was consistent with the handling of fonts in Microsoft Windows that Japanese consumers began to purchase IBM-PCs in large numbers. NEC was not able to match the variety and low cost of Windows-compatible software suddenly available to IBM-PC users in Japan and so lost its first-place position in the Japanese market to its IBM-PC-compatible competitors.[4]

The TCP-IP protocols

A different logic was behind the widespread adoption of TCP/IP standards.[5] Here a major factor was the early support of the US government for the inclusion of a TCP/IP kernel in the Unix operating system, an operating system that would come first to dominate the minicomputer and then the computer workstation market.[6] TCP/IP quickly spread from Unix-based workstations and minicomputers to mainframes using a variety of operating systems, and later to personal computers. The spread to mainframes was surprising because of the many rival proprietary mainframe network standards. Email software was an important early driver of the spread of Unix, but just as important was software for remote access (telnet), email and rapid file-transfer protocols (FTP). But the main value of TCP/IP was that it allowed people using machines with very different architectures and performance characteristics to communicate with

---

[3] Jeffrey Hart and Sangbae Kim, "Explaining the Resurgence of US Competitiveness: The Rise of Wintelism," *The Information Society*, 18 (February 2002), pp. 1–12.

[4] Sangbae Kim, "Wintelism vs. Japan: Standards Competition and Institutional Adjustment in the Global Computer Industry," Ph.D. dissertation, Indiana University, September 2000.

[5] TCP/IP stands for Transmission Control Protocol/Interconnection Protocol.

[6] James Wilson, *Berkeley UNIX: A Simple and Comprehensive Guide* (New York: Wiley, 1991), p. 2.

one another. It could connect the largest possible number of computer users without using up scarce computing resources and without burdening users with clumsy proprietary interfaces.

Thanks to work of thousands of computer scientists around the world, the definition and implementation of TCP/IP standards resulted in networks that were robust, reliable, less expensive, and less requiring of maintenance and support than the network systems created by large computer firms like IBM, Digital Equipment, Siemens, and NEC. In addition, the international collaborative work on TCP/IP protocols helped to create support for other "open systems" approaches to building computer hardware and software.[7]

Traffic measured in terms of bits per second on the Internet doubled every year in the 1990s.[8] The rapid growth in Internet content and traffic was a major surprise to the computer and telecommunications industries. Because it helped them to sell faster computers, improved software and internet access services, it was a very pleasant surprise.

HTML

Hypertext Markup Language (HTML) was invented in 1989 by Tim Berners-Lee and Robert Caillau at CERN, an international center for research in high-energy physics near Geneva, Switzerland. Berners-Lee and Caillau were inspired by the ideas of Ted Nelson, a scientist who initially proposed a method for linking documents on networks and who coined the term "hypertext" in 1965.[9] They conceived HTML as a better alternative to the preexisting systems for sharing documents over the Internet. Those systems – such as FTP and Gopher – were primarily text-based and provided only limited information about the content of linked sites.

In 1991, CERN launched the World Wide Web (WWW) featuring HTML pages that contained beautiful graphics along with extensive textual information about linked sites and were accessible using "browsers" such as Cello, Viola, and MidasWWW. The WWW was a success right from the start. The combination of Web pages in HTML and browsers

---

[7] Jeffrey A. Hart, Robert K. Reed, and Francois Bar, "The Building of the Internet: Implications for the Future of Broadband Networks," *Telecommunications Policy* (November 1992), p. 671.

[8] Andrew Odlyzko, "Internet Growth: Myth and Reality, Use and Abuse," *Information Impacts* (November 2000), http://www.cisp.org/imp/november_2000/odlyzko/11_00odlyzko.htm. Odlyzko's estimates are more conservative than those of others, such as Larry Roberts.

[9] Ted Nelson coined the term "hypertext" in *A File Structure for the Complex, the Changing, and the Indeterminate*. 20th National Conference, New York, Association for Computing Machinery, 1965. For his curriculum vitae see http://ted.hyperland.com/bio.txt.

more flexible and easier to use than previous navigation software made it possible for millions of users to find more quickly what they wanted on the Internet.[10]

In mid-1993, Marc Andreessen and Eric Bina at the National Center for Supercomputing Applications (NCSA) at the University of Illinois developed a browser called Mosaic that added graphics to text displays and quickly became the standard for WWW browsing. At first Mosaic was "freeware" – it could be downloaded for free by anyone on the Internet. Andreessen left NCSA in December 1993 to co-found, with James Clark, a firm that was at first called Mosaic Communications and later Netscape Communications.[11] Their browser, Netscape Navigator, was made available to the public at the end of 1994. It was an instant success.

Clark and Andreessen began giving Netscape Navigator away for free over the Internet in a marketing tactic that has since been called "viral marketing." The strategy was based on the assumption that if enough users adopted Netscape Navigator as their browser of choice, then companies wishing to make information available over the WWW would pay Netscape Communications for related technologies such as server hardware and software that would give them access to these users.[12]

The Linux operating system

In 1991, a Helsinki University student named Linus Torvalds began developing a free Unix kernel for IBM-PCs using a toolkit made available by the Free Software Foundation.[13] His initial success with this project along with help from a large number of volunteer programmers led to the development of Linux, a full-featured Unix with entirely free and redistributable sources. Linux had its competitors, including a version of

---

[10] Tim Berners-Lee and Michael Fischetti, *Weaving the Web: The Original Design and Ultimate Destiny of the World Wide Web by its Inventor* (San Francisco: Harper, 1999); Katie Hafner and Matthew Lyon, *When Wizards Stay Up Late: The Origins of the Internet* (New York: Simon and Schuster, 1996).

[11] The name was changed after NCSA sued Mosaic Communications over the use of software developed at NCSA in the newer versions of the browser. The settlement of the suit involved both the name change to Netscape Communications and payments to NCSA.

[12] Michael A. Cusumano and David B. Yoffie, *Competing on Internet Time: Lessons from Netscape and Its Battle with Microsoft* (New York: Free Press, 1998); and Nathan Newman, "Storming the Gates," *The American Prospect*, 5: 11 (27 March 2000).

[13] The Free Software Foundation (FSF) was the principal organizational sponsor of the GNU Project. The GNU Project was launched in 1984 to develop a complete Unix-like operating system which was free software: the GNU system. (GNU is an acronym for "GNU's Not Unix"; it is pronounced "guh-NEW".) For further information, see http://www.fsf.org.

BSD Unix ported to PCs by William and Lynne Jolitz called 386BSD. According to Eric Raymond:

The most important feature of Linux, however, was not technical but sociological. Until the Linux development, everyone believed that any software as complex as an operating system had to be developed in a carefully coordinated way by a relatively small, tightly-knit group of people.[14]

By late 1993, Linux was as stable and reliable as many commercial Unixes and compatible with a large library of Unix software that was in the public domain.

Although Linux was initially distributed as freeware on the Internet, it was later distributed for a small fee as a CD-ROM under a GNU General Public License (GPL)[15] by small companies like Red Hat, SuSE, Caldera, MandrakeSoft, and others. Ten years later, large computer companies like Sun Microsystems, Silicon Graphics, Compaq, Hewlett-Packard, IBM, and Dell began to offer Linux as one of several options for operating systems on their server hardware.[16] High-end database vendors like Oracle and SAP rewrote their applications so they could run on Linux.[17]

Red Hat currently controls around 50 percent of the world market for Linux software.[18] Linux currently is competing neck and neck with Microsoft Windows NT for first place on servers[19] but is still very much behind both Windows and Apple's OS/X operating systems for desktop users. This may change as new Linux-based desktop applications are added. In 2002, for example, a line of inexpensive desktops was marketed with a Windows-like operating system called Lindows.[20]

The success of Linux was partly a result of the fact that it had the reliability and stability of Unix and the low cost associated with open source software. Another attractive feature of Linux was that it was not Microsoft Windows. In the late 1990s and early 2000s, as companies like Microsoft, SAP, and PeopleSoft began to increase their fees for licenses

[14] Eric S. Raymond, "A Brief History of Hackerdom," in *Open Sources: Voices from the Open Source Revolution* (New York: O'Reilly, 1999), http://www.oreilly.com/catalog/opensources/book/raymond.html.

[15] Everyone is permitted to copy and distribute verbatim copies of a GNU GPL license document, but changing it is not allowed.

[16] Newman, "Storming the Gates," p. 8.

[17] "Going Hybrid," *The Economist*, 25 July 2002.

[18] Marsha Zager, "The State of Linux in 2002," *NewsFactor Network*, 26 September 2002, http://www.newsfactor.com/perl/story/19512.html.

[19] David Wheeler, "Why Open Source Software/Free Software (OSS/FS)? Look at the Numbers!," revised as of 13 July 2002, http://www.dwheeler.com/oss_fs_why.html.

[20] See http://www.lindows.com for more information.

and network services, business users looked to Linux as a cheaper and stabler alternative to Windows for building enterprise systems.[21]

Open source code tended to be more transparent and generally less buggy than other kinds of code. In addition, the community of creative computer programmers had moved slowly toward a consensus that programming in C++, the programming language that underpins Unix and Linux, was the best way to achieve greatness. A general philosophy of open systems was developed by people like Richard Stallman and Eric Raymond that was very attractive to these individuals.

The ideas of Richard Stallman

Stallman was the founder of the GNU project and the Free Software Foundation and author of the GNU Compiler Collection. He was also the developer of two important software tools, Emacs (a programming editor) and NeWS. Stallman was an advocate of "free software" – not in the sense that the software cost nothing but that it conduced to freedom.

Free software is a matter of the users' freedom to run, copy, distribute, study, change and improve the software. More precisely, it refers to four kinds of freedom, for the users of the software:
- The freedom to run the program, for any purpose (freedom 0).
- The freedom to study how the program works, and adapt it to your needs (freedom 1). Access to the source code is a precondition for this.
- The freedom to redistribute copies so you can help your neighbor (freedom 2).
- The freedom to improve the program, and release your improvements to the public, so that the whole community benefits (freedom 3). Access to the source code is a precondition for this.

A program is free software if users have all of these freedoms. Thus, you should be free to redistribute copies, either with or without modifications, either gratis or charging a fee for distribution, to anyone anywhere. Being free to do these things means (among other things) that you do not have to ask or pay for permission.[22]

His main enemy was "proprietary software" because he wanted to be able to share software with his friends and collaborators without having to do so illegally. According to Stallman:

You deserve to be able to cooperate openly and freely with other people who use software. You deserve to be able to learn how the software works, and to teach

---

[21] An example is IBM. In 2001, IBM spent approximately $1 billion to help increase corporate use of open source software. See Spencer E. Ante, "Big Blue's Big Bet on Free Software," *Business Week*, 10 December 2001, p. 78.

[22] Richard Stallman, "The Free Software Definition," http://www.gnu.org/philosophy/free-sw.html.

your students with it. You deserve to be able to hire your favorite programmer to fix it when it breaks.[23]

While many programmers agreed with Stallman's ideas, others (including Linus Torvalds and Eric Raymond) found them too radical. They favored "open source software" over Stallman's "free software." In their opinion, the phrase "free software" frightened away the large corporations whose support was needed to win broader social acceptance for Linux and its communities of programmers. The essence of the idea of free software was "open source" anyway, they argued.[24]

The current compromise between these two positions is OSS/FS (Open Source Software/Free Software) which is defined by David Wheeler as "programs whose licenses give users the freedom to run the program for any purpose, to study and modify the program, and to redistribute copies of either the original or modified program (without having to pay royalties to previous developers)."[25]

The cathedral and the bazaar

Eric Raymond first published his essay, "The Cathedral and the Bazaar," on the Internet in 1996. In this essay, he contrasted "two fundamentally different development styles, the 'cathedral' model of most of the commercial world versus the 'bazaar' model of the Linux world."[26] Both models refer to software development. In the cathedral model, small collections of software tools are built by software craftsmen using large tools like the Emacs programming editor. These tools are closely held until they are bug-free. Then they are released to the public. In the bazaar model, tools are released early, before they are completely debugged, in hopes that the others in the programming community will fix whatever errors still exist. In effect, the bazaar programmer delegates to others many important tasks that the cathedral programmer arrogates to herself. Raymond found the evident success of the bazaar model as evidenced particularly in the development and promulgation of Linux by Linus Torvalds to be surprising and requiring an explanation.

---

[23] Richard Stallman, "Why Software Should Not Have Owners," http://www.gnu.org/philosophy/why-free.html. Also available in essay form in Richard Stallman, *Free Software, Free Society: Selected Essays of Richard M. Stallman* (Boston: GNU Press, 2002).

[24] For a less diplomatic version of this story see Eric Kid, "A History of 'Open Source,'" posted 19 August 2000, http://static.userland.com/userLandDiscussArchive/msg019844.html.

[25] Wheeler, "Why Open Source Software?"

[26] Eric S. Raymond, "The Cathedral and the Bazaar," Version 3, http://www.tuxedo.org/~esr/writings/cathedral-bazaar/cathedral-bazaar/index.html#catbmain, abstract.

The answer to Raymond's question came from his own efforts to find a solution to an email problem that he was trying to solve. In a nutshell, the answer comes in the form of Linus's Law:

In Linus's Law, I think, lies the core difference underlying the cathedral-builder and bazaar styles. In the cathedral-builder view of programming, bugs and development problems are tricky, insidious, deep phenomena. It takes months of scrutiny by a dedicated few to develop confidence that you've winkled them all out. Thus the long release intervals, and the inevitable disappointment when long-awaited releases are not perfect.

In the bazaar view, on the other hand, you assume that bugs are generally shallow phenomena – or, at least, that they turn shallow pretty quickly when exposed to a thousand eager co-developers pounding on every single new release. Accordingly you release often in order to get more corrections, and as a beneficial side effect you have less to lose if an occasional botch gets out the door.[27]

On 22 January 1998, Netscape Communications decided to give away the source code for Netscape Communicator, the successor to Netscape Navigator software. According to Netscape, CEO James Barksdale:

By giving away the source code for future versions, we can ignite the creative energies of the entire Net community and fuel unprecedented levels of innovation in the browser market. Our customers can benefit from world-class technology advancements; the development community gains access to a whole new market opportunity; and Netscape's core businesses benefit from the proliferation of the market-leading client software.[28]

This unprecedented gift of a formerly valuable piece of intellectual property shocked the commercial software world, but Raymond saw it as vindication for his cathedral/bazaar theory. It was at this point that he approached other Linux programmers about using the phrase "open source software" instead of "free software."

The open source initiative

The "open source" label itself came out of a strategy session held on 3 February 1998 in Palo Alto, California. Those present included Todd Anderson, Chris Peterson (of the Foresight Institute), John "maddog" Hall and Larry Augustin (both of Linux International), Sam Ockman (of the Silicon Valley Linux User's Group), and Eric Raymond. These individuals came up with a way of defining open source software[29] and

[27] *Ibid.*, http://www.tuxedo.org/~esr/writings/cathedral-bazaar/cathedral-bazaar/ar01s04. html. There is a working definition of open source software also at http://www. opensource.org/docs/definition.php.

[28] http://wp.netscape.com/newsref/pr/newsrelease558.html.

[29] http://www.opensource.org/docs/definition.php.

institutionalized the movement in the form of the Open Source Initiative[30] with a board of directors[31] and a method for certifying software compliance with OSI standards.[32]

As of January 2003, the OSI website listed around thirty different types of licenses that the OSI deemed consistent with the open source definition.[33] The diversity of licenses reflected disagreements about what was to be made available freely and what was proprietary. The procedures for submitting proposals for new licenses was given in detail on the OSI website as was information about what criteria would be used to make decisions. Once a license was judged consistent with the OSI definition of "open source software," the manufacturer could use the OSI logo in any promotional materials for software distributed under the license.

Government policies toward open source software

In the late 1990s and early 2000s, a number of major governments and the European Union actively supported the development of open source software.

In February 1999, the US President's Information Technology Advisory Committee (PITAC) issued an overview analysis of information technology research arguing that federal government support for IT was inadequate. The report was followed by the convening of a series of panels on various topics. In October 2000, PITAC published a report on the development of open source software for advanced high-end computing.[34] PITAC made three specific recommendations:

- the government should support the development of open source software for high-end computing;
- it should allow open source software to compete on a level playing field with proprietary software in government procurement; and
- it should analyze existing open source licensing agreements and distribute the results to agencies that fund high-end computing.

The PITAC report was an attempt to deal with major changes in advanced computing. Networked computers rather than supercomputers had become the focus of most advanced computing research and a lot of the work in that area required open source approaches.

---

[30] http://www.opensource.org/index.php.
[31] http://www.opensource.org/docs/board.html.
[32] http://www.opensource.org/docs/certification_mark.php#approval.
[33] http://www.opensource.org/licenses/index.html.
[34] President's Information Technology Advisory Committee, Panel on Open Source Software for High End Computing, *Report to the President: Developing Open Source Software to Advance High End Computing* (Washington, DC: PITAC, October 2000), http://www.ccic.gov/pubs/pitac/pres-oss-11sep00.pdf.

A report by the Mitre Corporation to the Department of Defense (DoD) in May 2002 concluded that open source software development in DoD often resulted in more secure and less expensive applications and that banning OSS/FS from the Department would be highly undesirable.[35] The report identified 249 existing uses of OSS/FS applications, including a Web portal for the Defense Intelligence Agency. While the Agency depended primarily on proprietary software applications, the importance of OSS/FS systems was growing.

The European Commission's initiative *eEurope – An Information Society for All* issued an Action Plan dated June 2000. This Action Plan sets as one of its targets for 2001 that "the European Commission and Member States will promote the use of open source software in the public sector and e-government best practice through exchange of experiences across the Union."[36] A European branch of the Free Software Foundation was established in the late 1990s along with an organization supporting open source software called OpenForum Europe.[37] Several member states of the EU developed their own programs for supporting open source software development, including the UK,[38] Germany,[39] and France.[40]

In Asia, there was growing support for OSS/FS software development. Japan adopted a policy of using open source for its e-government projects; India's Department of Information Technology in New Delhi disclosed details of a move called the Linux India Initiative just weeks before an upcoming visit of Microsoft chairman Bill Gates to the country; and China was becoming a stronghold of open systems in Asia.[41]

[35] Mitre Corporation, *Use of Free and Open Source Software (FOSS) in the Department of Defense*, Version 1.2.04, January 2003, http://www.egovos.org/pdf/dodfoss.pdf.

[36] e-Europe Initiative, "Action Plan: Government Online – Electronic Access to Public Services," Targets for 2001–2002, http://europa.eu.int/information/society/eeurope/action_plan/stimulate/egov/eu/targets_2001_2002/index_en.htm.

[37] http://www.fsfeurope.org/index.html; http://www.openforumeurope.org/index.php.

[38] Office of the e-Envoy, "Open Source Software Use in UK Government," Version 1, 15 July 2002, http://www.e-envoy.gov.uk/oee/oee.nsf/sections/frameworks-oss-policy/$file-oss-policy.htm.

[39] The German support for open source software is called BerliOS and is funded by the Bundesministerium für Wirtschaft und Technologie. See http://sourcelines.berlios.de/solutions.php?solu_id=1&SourceLines_Session=bf388fdcd5ce88523f3fcb18c09d67c1.

[40] The French support for public open source software creation and sharing is the responsibility of the Agence pour les Technologies de l'Information et de la Communication dans l'Administration (ATICA). For an example of an ATICA document, see *Guide de choix et d'usage des licences de logiciels libres pour les administrations* (Paris: ATICA, December 2002).

[41] Winston Chai, "Japan Mulls Windows Replacement," *CNet Asia*, 21 November 2002, http://zdnet.com.com/2100-1104-966700.html; "Japan May Drop Windows to Boost Security," *Reuters*, 16 November 2002, http://www.ciol.com/content/news/repts/102111608.asp.

Microsoft fights back

All of this talk about government support for open source software brought about a concerted effort on the part of executives of Microsoft Corporation to try to counter moves toward increased use of open source systems. On 26 July 2001, Microsoft Senior Vice President Craig Mundie addressed the open source community during the morning keynote at O'Reilly's Open Source Convention in San Diego, California. In his address, Mundie argued that Microsoft was not threatened by OSS/FS per se, but that widespread support for the open source approach was bound eventually to damage the "software ecosystem."

At the end of the day, the biggest concern that Microsoft has is about the long-term preservation of what we think of as the software ecosystem. This ecosystem, like those in the physical world, evolved over quite a long period of time, and they reach usually some state of equilibrium where people are happy with the results for a long time. But as we've learned in the physical world, certain actions that people can take on or certain things that they do can have some long-term effects on that ecosystem.[42]

Mundie went on to argue that the software industry was a strategic industry for the United States, generating jobs, revenues, and exports that the country badly needed. These jobs and revenues depended on the willingness of people to pay for software and Microsoft was concerned that extremists, particularly those associated with the free software movement, did not understand this and that if the views of those individuals prevailed, customers would not have access to the broad spectrum of software products and services that were currently available.

In May 2002, the Computer Technology Industry Association (CompTIA) launched a new program called the Initiative for Software Choice. CompTIA was funded mainly by Microsoft and Intel as an answer to the Computer and Communications Industry Association (CCIA),[43] a coalition of firms that were competitors of Microsoft and supporters of the antitrust case brought against that firm. According to the CompTIA website:

The Initiative for Software Choice is a growing global coalition of large and small companies committed to advancing the concept that multiple competing software markets should be allowed to develop and flourish unimpeded by government preference or mandate. The Initiative actively educates policymakers and

---

[42] http://linux.oreillynet.com/pub/a/linux/2001/08/09/oscon_debate.html?page=2.
[43] http://www.ccianet.org/index.php3.

regulators worldwide about the benefits of this approach and its value to future innovations.[44]

One aspect of this new campaign was an effort in the summer of 2002 to oppose a proposal by a Peruvian congressman, Edgar Villanueva Nuñez, that all public software be required to be free software in order to protect the right of the public to get access to information acquired by public funds (in this case the source code for software used by government agencies). Such a law, according to Microsoft, would prevent the sale of proprietary software to the Peruvian government.[45] Similar campaigns were mounted against new laws and regulations in the state of California, India, and Denmark.

Microsoft representatives paid numerous visits in the spring and summer of 2002 to Secretary of Defense Donald Rumsfeld to protest the Mitre Report mentioned above. They argued that "some free-licensing regimes are antithetical to the government's stated policy that money-making application should develop from government-funded research and that intellectual property should be protected."[46]

Summary

The computer programming community took a position of supporting Internet-based collaboration with respect to the development of both hardware and software in the 1990s that became impossible even for the largest firms and governments to ignore. The development of the Internet itself was driven initially by the US military's desire to be able to connect up incompatible electronic systems via highly robust and survivable electronic networks. So the Internet's designers started with an "open systems" perspective on interconnection. This idea was also embodied progressively in the initial versions of the UNIX operating system, which was seen from the beginning as an alternative to the proprietary operating systems of large mainframe computer firms like IBM. When UNIX itself became a proprietary system, the programming community responded by building the public-domain version that is now called Linux.

The strong interest in Linux in recent years was a function of the increasingly wide acceptance of Microsoft Windows and Intel

---

[44] http://softwarechoice.org/.

[45] "Ley de uso de software libre en la administración pública," Bill No. 1609, http://pimientolinux.com/peru2ms/law_project4.html. See also, Agustin d'Empaire, "Microsoft's Big Stick in Peru," *Wired News*, 27 July 2002, http://www.wired.com/news/business/0,1367,54141,00.html.

[46] Jonathan Krim, "Open-Source Fight Flares at Pentagon," *Washington Post*, 23 May 2002, p. E01.

microprocessors as the basis for the IBM-PC-compatible microcomputer platform. The market power this gave to Microsoft, in particular, made people dependent on such systems much more eager than they might otherwise have been to support the development of Linux and Linux-compatible application software. The antitrust case brought against Microsoft during the Clinton Administration also helped the cause of Linux and open source software considerably.

More fundamentally, however, the global acceptance of the IBM-PC, TCP/IP, HTML, and Linux was a result of a sea-change in attitudes among engineers about how best to design complex electronic systems. Between the 1980s and the present, they witnessed a series of problems caused by too much concentration of market and engineering power in too small a number of large firms and a series of engineering triumphs resulting from the decentralization and distribution of design efforts (including, but not limited to, TCP/IP, HTML, and Linux).

The global engineering community took unusual steps during this period to prevent the politicization of competition in key infrastructural technologies by bringing as many people from as many different societies as possible into the inner sanctum of design. Doing this early in the design cycle ensured that governments would discover only too late that global standards had evolved. Later governmental intervention would generally serve only to speed this development by providing governmental subsidies to ongoing engineering efforts.

Why was HDTV and digital television different?

Why did this not occur in the realm of advanced television technology? The global acceptance of many of the standards discussed in this chapter had a lot to do with: (1) the emergence of consensus in scientific and engineering circles about what constituted the best approach to solving problems, and (2) the ability of standards-making bodies to minimize the extent of political involvement until after most important technical problems had been solved. In addition, the global standards that emerged in the cases discussed above were often seen as answers to problems posed by imposition of standards by private firms like IBM and Microsoft. Each of the standards in this chapter was consistent with an "open systems" approach that allowed for considerable variation in both hardware and software because it focused on methods of allowing different systems to communicate and interoperate with one another and thus did not assume that all innovation would occur in one or a small number of innovating companies.

Readers of previous chapters of this book will recognize various points in the narrative in which the "open system" approach influenced the various standards debates. In the United States, for example, the effort to get agreement on formats for the packetizing of digital television signals was a direct descendant of similar efforts in getting standardized formats for the exchanges of files on the Internet and the World Wide Web. In Europe, the Digital Video Broadcasting (DVB) approach was basically an open systems approach.

Overall, however, the standards debates for HDTV and DTV suffered much more than the standards discussed in this chapter from the injection of politics, particularly national and nationalistic politics, into the debates. This is not to argue that politics was entirely absent in standards debates over the IBM-PC-platform, TCP/IP, HTML, and Linux. It would be more correct to say that politics entered the debates later in the development of attendant technologies and mostly after the most important technical problems had been solved. When national and international politics entered the discussion, they tended to simply endorse or support the technical solutions that the scientific and engineering communities had already agreed upon. That was decidedly not the case in HDTV and DTV.

10   Conclusions

Summary of previous chapters

There were two clear turning points in the history of the debates over high definition and digital TV (HDTV and DTV). In 1988, the US government chose not to adopt the Japanese standard and instead looked for an all-digital standard to succeed the existing standard for color TV (NTSC). The second turning point was the adoption of a US digital television standard in 1993 and subsequent reactions to that in Western Europe and Japan. Thus, we are left trying to explain outcomes in three periods:

- *Period 1*: beginning with the development of an HDTV standard in Japan in the early 1980s and ending with the US rejection of that standard in 1988;
- *Period 2*: beginning with the rejection of the Japanese standard in 1988 and ending with the adoption of a digital television (DTV) standard in 1993 in the US;
- *Period 3*: from 1993 to the present.

I will try to summarize below what happened during the three periods for each industrialized region: the United States, Japan, and Western Europe.

There was a distinctly game-like quality to these standards debates. Business players were seeking advantage both in domestic markets and in international competition; national governments were lobbied by a combination of domestic and international interests and were maneuvering for advantage with other governments. Because of the increasing globalization of the world economy, it was possible for both domestic and foreign firms to try to influence the outcomes of both domestic decision processes and international negotiations.[1]

---

[1] The classic work on this subject is Robert O. Keohane and Joseph S. Nye, Jr. (eds.), *Transnational Relations and World Politics* (Madison, WI: University of Wisconsin Press, 1972).

The United States

The first period was a period of strong concern on the part of many people in the United States that they could no longer compete with Japan in high technology industries. Some firms took advantage of this concern to plead for standards that benefited local firms at the expense of foreign firms. Key decisions about HDTV and DTV were strongly influenced by the desire to restore the US economy to international competitiveness.

Normally the combination of consumer electronics firms, national television networks, and TV/film production firms, who initially preferred adoption of the Japanese HDTV system, would have prevailed. However, the information technology industry had a different view and was successful in having its view heard at the highest levels of the US government. It was able to convince key officials that the nation's welfare depended upon the continued competitiveness of the digital electronics industry. If Japan had not done so well in advanced electronics during the 1980s, the US electronics companies would have had a much harder time making their case.

During the second period, these concerns were replaced by a sense of greater optimism, especially after the end of the Cold War in the late 1980s, and a feeling that the US economy was strong and that US firms could compete on equal terms with Japanese and European firms. Part of this renewed optimism was the rise of the personal computing and Internet, the bursting of the Japanese economic bubble, and a widespread feeling that television per se did not matter so much as preserving the US lead in digital technology and particularly in computers and telecommunications.

Japan

From the Japanese perspective, the first period was an unsuccessful experiment in getting Japanese firms to replace US firms as leaders in the setting of global broadcasting standards, appropriately (in the view of key Japanese decision-makers) reflecting Japanese preeminence in the production of consumer electronics. The Japanese public broadcaster, NHK, led the Japanese electronics companies in the creation of a family of new technologies for HDTV production, transmission, and reception. The major Japanese electronics firms contributed manpower and investment capital to the creation of HDTV systems under the guidance of NHK. When both the Europeans and the Americans rejected the Japanese approach to HDTV, NHK was surprised and was never able to recover its momentum in leading the electronics industry.

The Japanese electronics firms supported NHK generally because they were concerned about loss of market shares in consumer electronics to their competitors in East Asia, particularly South Korea and Taiwan. They hoped that HDTV would help them to raise the overall level of sophistication of Japanese electronics and give them a better base from which to challenge the US computer industry. As these hopes diminished, the Japanese electronics firms put less emphasis on HDTV and more on other technologies.

The second period in Japan was characterized by a determination on the part of both NHK and the electronics companies to push ahead with HDTV (MUSE Hi-Vision). This strategy was not successful, however, because the high price of equipment combined with the scarcity of high quality programming made the uptake of HDTV in Japan very slow. Widescreen sets sold fairly well, but only a limited number of HDTV sets were purchased.

The third period saw the Japanese Minister of Communications taking the initiative to go beyond Hi-Vision, a hybrid of both digital and analog technologies, to some form of digital video broadcasting. Even NHK began to see the writing on the wall by the late 1990s, proposing something called Integrated Systems Digital Broadcasting (ISDB) as its answer to digital television in the United States and Western Europe. Nevertheless, NHK continued to support Hi-Vision technologies by continuing its satellite HDTV broadcasts and conducting further research on HDTV at NHK Labs.

Western Europe

The first period in Europe was dominated by discussions about the need to do something to prevent the proliferation of satellite TV standards. The public broadcasters were trying to maintain their domestic dominance (as in Japan) by using preferential access to satellite broadcasting. However, the earliest attempts to do this via the MAC standards resulted in many different and incompatible versions of MAC.

To avoid a recurrence of this, European officials tried to get European public broadcasters and electronics firms to adopt a single standard for HDTV. They were successful with a high-definition version of MAC called HD-MAC. HD-MAC was to be a regional and not a global standard. Although the Europeans were pleased when previous European standards like PAL and SECAM were adopted outside of Europe, they had no illusions that HD-MAC would be attractive outside of Europe. European firms like Thomson and Philips did not even try to get HD-MAC adopted as an HDTV standard in the United States. However, the

HD-MAC coalition had not reckoned on the growing power of private broadcasters in Europe who were able first to undermine the HD-MAC coalition politically and then to convince European officials that Europe, like the United States, needed to adopt a digital broadcasting system. This became a much easier job after the US government adopted its own DTV standards in 1993.

After 1993, the Europeans quietly pursued a set of DTV standards under the rubric of Digital Video Broadcasting (DVB). DVB standards, unlike the previous HD-MAC standards, were consciously designed to incorporate the best ideas of engineers from around the world rather than just in Europe – somewhat on the model of standards creation for the Internet. Foreign firms were allowed to participate in the various DVB committees. There would be DVB standards for terrestrial, cable, and satellite broadcasting. Open architecture and interoperability of systems were principles adopted as a response to the success of the PC industry in the 1990s. One could also argue that the Europeans had learned from their success in establishing GSM as a global standard in the cell phone industry. Europe again moved toward its own variety of DTV, but this time with a greater possibility of having its solutions adopted outside the region.

Theoretical implications

The debates over HDTV and DTV during the last two decades are important for what they tell us about the politics of standards as digitalization proceeds. I suggested in chapter 1 that this particular set of standards debates can tell us a lot about the competition among advanced industrial nations in high technology industries and particularly about the role of *institutions* (like the broadcasting institutions discussed in chapter 2), *interests* (like the consumer electronics interests discussed in chapter 3), and *ideas* (like the idea of "digital convergence" also discussed in chapter 3). At the level of the international system of nation-states, there is also something to be learned about how the familiar old games of power politics have been transformed in the age of digitalization.

The role of institutions

Institutions played a central role in influencing both the rules of the game and the outcomes of bargaining over standards for advanced television. In particular, the divergent manner in which the major industrial nations structured their television broadcasting institutions – particularly the split between dominant public broadcasting systems in Europe and

Japan and dominant private broadcasters in the United States – had a major impact on the way the three regions defined their interests in international standards forums. These differences contributed tangibly to the level of conflict within and across regions in both domestic and international debates about advanced television standards, with both Japanese and European public broadcasters attempting to use satellite HDTV standards to maintain their national dominance.

Institutional differences did not remain constant, however. The Europeans clearly moved more in the direction of the US approach to broadcasting, especially after private satellite operators in Europe were able to capture audience share away from public broadcasters. The European audiences voted strongly in favor of increased diversity of programming by signing up in large numbers for pay-TV services of various kinds. In Japan, there was some movement in this direction, but much less than in Europe. As a result, by the third period discussed above, the Europeans had moved faster to embrace the idea of digital television (albeit with a standard that differed significantly from the one adopted in the United States) than the Japanese.

The role of interests

The activities of organized interests played a key role in determining outcomes in advanced television standards debates. Organized interests are always to some degree a function of preexisting institutions. Interests are organized around institutions and their institutional environment influences their interactions. Still there are certain aspects of interest politics that are relatively independent from national institutional environments because of a convergence of interests that springs from subnational or supranational phenomena. For example, if world markets are in a state of excess supply, then firms that depend on world markets will experience pressures for downsizing independently of whatever national institutions they depend on for political and economic support. Similarly, in markets that are undergoing "globalization" – that is, where value chains are becoming more and more geographically dispersed so that firms must distribute research, production, and distribution across many national jurisdictions to be competitive[2] – industry-specific, or even firm-specific, factors can play an important independent role in determining outcomes.

[2] Aseem Prakash and Jeffrey A. Hart, "Globalization and Governance: An Introduction," in Aseem Prakash and Jeffrey A. Hart (eds.), *Globalization and Governance* (London: Routledge, 1999).

The consumer electronics industry was undergoing a substantial transition to globalization. But so was the film production and distribution industry and even, although to a lesser extent, the television broadcasting industry (with giants like Sony, Bertelsmann, Microsoft, News Corporation, and others becoming globally oriented media concerns). Even public broadcasters, like the BBC and NHK, were undergoing some transition to globalization.

In addition, the Japanese consumer electronics industry was coming under increasing competitive pressure from other East Asian producers: most notably, South Korea and Taiwan. In the late 1980s, Japan was globally dominant in the consumer electronics industry; by the end of the 1990s, it no longer held that position. Similarly, the international structure of key stakeholders like the computer and telecommunications industries underwent major changes as networked personal computers took over the role of mainframes and minicomputers in businesses and began to supplement the television as an entertainment device in homes.

The vertically integrated Japanese electronics firms were not as strong in computers globally as they were in consumer electronics. Japan suffered from a combination of US dominance of microprocessor and software industries and an insufficiency of antitrust enforcement and intellectual property protection at home.[3] As a result, by the end of the 1990s, the Japanese were beginning to discuss institutional changes that would permit them to participate more fully in the new electronic markets made possible by the Internet.[4]

It is not surprising, therefore, that concern over Japanese dominance in consumer electronics, which was running very high in both Europe and the United States in the 1980s, began to diminish in the 1990s. This concern was replaced in Europe by worrying about how not to miss getting on the Internet train before it left the station. When the United States adopted a DTV standard in 1993, the European electronics interests were willing, albeit reluctantly, to give up HD-MAC in favor of an all-digital approach. They were pushed strongly to do this by European politicians like Martin Bangemann and John Major.

One surprise in the analysis of US debates over advanced television was the ability of the computer and electronics firms to win the day in their quest for a digital television standard that would work well with the existing computing and communications infrastructures over the opposition

---

[3] Jeffrey A. Hart and Sangbae Kim, "Explaining the Resurgence of US Competitiveness: The Rise of Wintelism," *The Information Society*, 18 (February 2002), pp. 1–12.

[4] Sangbae Kim, "Hardware Institutions for Software Technologies: The Limits of Institutional Adjustment Strategies in the Japanese Computer Industry," unpublished manuscript, 10 December 2000.

of a coalition of interests that included the broadcasting networks, the television station owners, and the TV programming interests. Most political analysts in the late 1980s expected that the latter would remain the dominant players in public debates over advanced television.

One reason this did not happen was institutional. The main forum for debates after the late 1980s was the FCC. The FCC had a clear legal mandate to consider the interests of consumers as well as those of producers. That legal mandate made it possible for the FCC, and particularly Reed Hundt, to go against the wishes of the usually dominant players and to tilt the Commission's decisions in the direction desired by the US electronics industry. Still, the compromise that emerged, with its eighteen formats, was not a good solution to the problem of creating producer and consumer confidence, thus delaying the rollout of DTV considerably. Further uncertainty was created by the inability of broadcasters to agree on which DTV formats to transmit and when to begin transmissions.

There are some defenders of the FCC who argue that the time was not ripe for a standards decision. The technology was still changing rapidly. The major firms involved were not willing to freeze the technology by adopting a fixed standard. There is some truth to these arguments. Nevertheless, the selection of a confusing, complex, and possibly unworkable standard was the result of FCC deliberations. It is hard to argue that this was an optimal outcome.

The role of ideas

The key ideas that influenced the outcomes of advanced television debates were "digital convergence" and what I will call "digitalism." Digital convergence was the notion that digitalization of audio and video signals (as part of the larger project of digitalizing all signals that could be transmitted or received over existing and future telecommunications infrastructures) would produce a convergence across separate (and separately regulated) industries, a blurring of the lines of distinction that would eventually result in a new constellation of industries not recognizably like the old one. The old ways of regulating these industries would also, obviously, have to change. This was supposed to be good news for consumers because digitalization would mean more competition and lower prices.

I am coining the word "digitalism" to stand for an ideological belief in the superiority of digital technology over analog technology. Digital technology was potentially cheaper and more flexible than analog technology, according to digitalists. Transmission of digital signals required lower power outlays than analog signals. Digital error correction could ensure error-free reception of data that did not have to be instantaneously delivered. As transmission and processing speeds increased, and as compression algorithms became more sophisticated, real-time digital video data could be delivered on demand with little or no loss of quality at a very reasonable price.

More importantly, digital technologies benefited from the economies created by "Moore's Law" – the rapid decline in costs for storing and processing bits of information (and somewhat less rapid declines in transmission costs). Digital technology was also more flexible because "a bit is a bit" and one could do whatever one wanted with a given amount of "bandwidth." Consumers would no longer be the passive recipients of high bandwidth information (TV broadcasts) but instead would be able to actively seek out information that they considered to be most important. There was even the possibility that each individual would be able to "program" his/her own daily menu of media content: what Eli Noam called "MeTV."[5]

These alleged benefits of the transition to digital technology were in the minds of many participants in the debates over advanced television. They were particularly in the minds of policy-makers who participated in the debates. What was difficult for them was to figure out how fast the process of digitalization was proceeding, how blurred the boundaries were becoming, and most importantly how to alter the regulatory systems to take digital convergence into account. Digitalists generally exaggerated the speed of the transition, the extent of the blurring, and the need for altered regulation. Antidigitalists successfully exploited the uncertainties and doubts that continued to exist about timing, the extent of the blurring, and the need for reregulation. But antidigitalists were generally unsuccessful when they argued that the transition would never take place at all. This gave the digitalists an important advantage in regional and international standards debates. In the next section, I will try to demonstrate how digitalism worked together with nationalism to influence the outcomes of standards debates.

The role of power politics

The United States emerged as a hegemonic power once again after the end of the Cold War. In the late 1980s prior to the end of the Cold War, it looked like the United States would continue to share power with

---

[5] Eli Noam, "The Stages of Television: From Multi-Channel Television to the Me-Channel," in Claude Contamine and Monique van Dusseldorp (eds.), *European Institute for the Media*, 10–12 November 1994, pp. 49–58.

its allies in most important decisions regarding the world economy. US international competitiveness was declining relative to that of Western Europe and Japan. Its major trading partners were challenging the US for leadership in a variety of international forums. But when the Soviet Union fell apart in the early 1990s, there was suddenly a new rationale for US global leadership.

US leadership was needed to contain the negative consequences of the end of the Cold War: e.g., chaos in the Balkans, economic difficulties in the transition from communism to capitalism, and the temptation to export sophisticated weaponry and weapons expertise. Although great powers like Britain, France, Germany, and Japan played a larger role during this period than they had after 1945, none of them could take on the larger tasks without the support of the United States.

The resurgence of US international competitiveness in the 1990s implied a continued role for the United States in managing the global economic system.[6] In the PC industry, for example, US firms led the industry overall and dominated many related segments including microprocessors, operating systems, and packaged applications where control over standards was critical. Throughout the PC era, US firms held the greatest share of world shipments for PC systems. Among the top ten PC makers, "US firms held a 59% share of the world market in 1985 and still held 40% in 1995."[7] In microprocessors, most of the highest value-added design, engineering, and wafer fabrication activities took place in the United States. And, "US companies still control about 75% of the software industry overall, and they have virtually 100% of the operating system market. The vast majority of that software is still developed in the United States."[8]

A revived optimism in the United States combined with the rise of the industries dependent on digital technologies resulted in a marriage of convenience between old-fashioned nationalists and new-fangled digitalists. Nationalists began arguing for the need to support the digital industries and digitalists in the United States jumped on the nationalist bandwagon whenever they thought doing so advanced their interests. A prime example of this was the 1993 decision of the FCC.

Digitalists outside the United States, particularly in Europe, perceived a window of opportunity for changing what appeared to be a done deal on HDTV. Thus, the HD-MAC coalition crumbled rapidly as it came under attack from European digitalists. Digitalists in Japan were less successful.

[6] Hart and Kim, "Explaining the Resurgence of US Competitiveness."
[7] Jason Dedrick and Kenneth L. Kraemer, *Asia's Computer Challenge: Threat or Opportunity for the United States and the World?* (New York: Oxford University Press, 1998), p. 58.
[8] *Ibid.*, pp. 63–4.

NHK and the Japanese electronics firms had already sunk considerable investment into MUSE Hi-Vision and could not simply write off that investment. Antidigitalists in Japan were more successful than those in other regions in arguing that all-digital technologies were untried and untested and that it was better to continue with the hybrid analog-digital system they had adopted. However, the slow uptake of MUSE Hi-Vision equipment by consumers eventually tilted the balance in the direction of the digitalists.

Conclusions

The purpose of this chapter was to summarize the outcomes of regional and international debates over HDTV and DTV and to provide some theoretical explanations for these outcomes. The complexity of bargaining and negotiation in an environment characterized by increasing globalization of markets and digitalization of technologies makes it difficult to provide a simple explanation for these outcomes. Nevertheless, a key common feature to the debates across the three regions was the eventual victory of digitalists and the idea of "digital convergence" in public debates over standards. Nationalism – or regionalism in the case of Western Europe – combined with digitalism to produce three different DTV standards in the three regions.

Nevertheless, there were certain elements of convergence within the digital divergence that characterized the outcomes of standards debates. First, all three regions ended up developing systems that could deliver digital signals both over the air (via terrestrial and satellite antennas) and using wired systems (cable TV and telephone networks). All three regions ended up looking for ways to benefit from the enormously successful experiments with Internet-like systems of delivering digital data – including adoption of global standards for digital compression of video signals like the MPEG family of video compression standards and the use of packets or cells of video data that were compatible with asynchronous transfer mode (ATM) switching on telecommunications networks. Even though the United States and Western Europe rejected the Japanese HDTV standard, still the US DTV and the European DVB standards left room for MUSE Hi-Vision signals to be transmitted and received on US and European standard receivers and Japanese electronics companies remained well positioned to be major players in the DTV markets of both Europe and the US.

The "pretty picture" that had motivated the initial investment in HDTV research and development in Japan was no longer the issue in television standards debates. While the parties were debating HDTV, ideas, interests, and institutions had changed as a result of the rise of the Internet and associated digital industries. Indeed, one could even argue that the global distribution of power was influenced by the rise of the networked PC.

Some commentators asserted that the United States was the big winner of the advanced television standards debates because US institutions better represented the interests of consumers and producers outside the broadcasting industry. I would argue, in contrast, that the US strategy after 1993 was faulty in many important ways. The uptake of DTV in the United States was just as slow as the uptake of HDTV in Japan. In Europe, digital broadcasters did not even attempt to provide high definition images. Of the three regional approaches, the European one seemed to hold the best promise for commercial success. Digital delivery of NTSC or PAL quality images on widescreen receivers was a winner in all three regions, not HDTV. The rapid market success of digital satellite pay TV services and DVD players was clear evidence for consumer acceptance of digital video. HDTV products, in contrast, were still too expensive and complicated for most consumers. Consumers were not yet willing to pay the required premium for sharper pictures in HDTVs, even though many were willing to pay higher prices for wider screens and digital signal delivery.

From a policy standpoint, the lessons to be learned from the debates over advanced television standards were not simple but they were nevertheless important. First, while digital convergence was not happening as fast as some digitalists argued it would, there was plenty of evidence that it was happening. The difficulties of negotiating DTV standards in all three regions were at least partially the result of institutional inertia and errors in the re-regulation of the digitally converging media industries. The interests that attempted to influence the outcomes of standards debates included very powerful actors: the broadcasting industry, the TV and film production firms, and the consumer electronics industry. These actors were all experiencing considerable pressures to change because of digitalization and the resulting shifts in consumer demand toward digital products and services. They were also undergoing pressures to change because of globalization of production in consumer electronics and related industries.

Public policy-makers had a very difficult task. They could not simply negotiate bargains among existing stakeholders if they expected bargains to persist. They had to anticipate how the interests of stakeholders would change in the light of changing technology. They had to anticipate how new stakeholders would arise and how they would alter the balance of power among existing stakeholders. Defining the public interest in such a fluid policy environment certainly was not easy. The tendency of some governments (including the US government) to simply identify the public interest with the interests of the digital industries was understandable. In the long run, however, this would not hold. A new way of defining the public interest in television broadcasting would have to be found.

So, the debates over advanced television are not over. Even though the HDTV and DTV standards debates have ended, the question of how to regulate digital television in the public interest remains an active issue in all three regions. The globalization of culture that has been made easier with the rise of the Internet and digital delivery of video images will be accepted by some and resisted by others. Debates over how to redefine and harmonize laws governing free speech, intellectual property protection, antitrust enforcement, pornography, and taxation, just to mention a few important areas of contention, will continue.

Index